AMERICAN
GIANT

OTHER WORKS BY FRANCES WINWAR

Novels

THE ARDENT FLAME

THE GOLDEN ROUND

PAGAN INTERVAL

GALLOWS HILL

Translations

THE DECAMERON OF GIOVANNI BOCCACCIO

History

PURITAN CITY: THE STORY OF SALEM

Biographies

FAREWELL THE BANNER
   (Coleridge and the Wordsworths)

THE ROMANTIC REBELS
   (Byron, Shelley and Keats)

POOR SPLENDID WINGS
   (The Rossettis and Their Circle)

OSCAR WILDE AND THE YELLOW NINETIES

WALT WHITMAN, THE WOUND DRESSER
From a photograph by Brady

"They were the eyes of a man who had seen hell but who had visions of the spiritual good accruing from that pain."

AMERICAN GIANT
WALT WHITMAN
and His Times
By Frances Winwar

ILLUSTRATED

HARPER *&* BROTHERS PUBLISHERS
NEW YORK AND LONDON

AMERICAN GIANT

WALT WHITMAN AND HIS TIMES

Copyright, 1941, by Frances Winwar Grebanier
Printed in the United States of America
All rights in this book are reserved.
No part of the book may be reproduced in any
manner whatsoever without written permission
except in the case of brief quotations embodied
in critical articles and reviews. For information
address Harper & Brothers

10-1

FIRST EDITION

I-Q

I DEDICATE THIS BOOK TO ALL

AND THEREFORE TO YOU

CONTENTS

ILLUSTRATIONS

When the true poet comes, how shall we know him—
    By what clear token,—manners, language, dress? . . .

Thus shall ye know him—this shall be his token:
    Manners like other men, an unstrange gear;
His speech not musical, but harsh and broken
    Shall sound at first, each line a driven spear:
For he shall sing as in the centuries olden,
    Before mankind its earliest fire forgot;
Yet whoso listens long hears music golden.
    How shall ye know him? ye shall know him not
        Till ended hate and scorn,
        To the grave he's borne.

RICHARD WATSON GILDER
From *The Century Magazine*
November, 1881

Foreword

I GIVE you back Walt Whitman, the virile author of *Leaves of Grass*, the giant "free, fresh, savage, fluent, luxuriant, self-content," the poet of democracy in whose first utterance Thoreau heard a trumpet note singing through the American camp. I give you back to lover of humanity, the large tolerant spirit who embraced the universe and who could say to the lowest outcast, "Not till the sun excludes you do I exclude you." I give you back the brave dreamer who saw his vision in young manhood and had the courage to pursue it to the end against reviling and misunderstanding. I give you the man of generous life, the comrade of the open road, the free companion of men and women, the peaceloving Quaker and the mighty fighter for principle. I give you the wound dresser of the battlefield, the Answerer in the conflict of life. I give you the symbol of America, Walt Whitman.

My book is a refutation of the cliché "the good gray poet," first used to defend Whitman against charges of immorality. From the many contradictions wilfully perpetrated by the poet and persisted in by his disciples I have endeavored to arrive at the truth of his life, drawing for the purpose upon the history of the America with which he identified himself, upon *Leaves of Grass*, his spiritual autobiography, upon his notebooks and letters, his writings in newspapers and periodicals, upon his recorded conversations and the reminiscences *(cum grano salis)* of those who knew him. If what I offer on many disputed points seems startling, it is because the facts themselves are so. I have only correlated internal evidence with known biographical material, and drawn objective inferences. From first to last it has been my aim to present him as he was,

FOREWORD

without apology or equivocation. If his faults were great, his virtues were greater still. "I am large, I contain multitudes."

No book would be complete without mention of the many who contribute their encouragement and inspiration. To Mrs. Martha Lippincott Davis of the Whitman Foundation, my gratitude for countless favors. My thanks also to Mr. and Mrs. I. A. Stern and their son Edward for joining me on Whitman pilgrimages, to Prof. H. R. Ede, Alan Branigan, Mr. and Mrs. David Davidson, to Miss Rosamond Gilder and Miss Bertha Johnston, and to many others who have taken a personal interest in the progress of the book.

For the title, I have to thank Mr. Cass Canfield. Dr. Asa Don Dickinson has, as usual, put me in his debt by his indefatigable assistance in obtaining me a working library. A tribute, too, must inevitably be paid the Whitman scholars who have unearthed writings buried in collections, newspapers and periodicals. To Prof. Emory Holloway and to those associated with him in research, as well as to Doubleday, Doran, my thanks for their permission to quote from the inclusive edition of *Leaves of Grass* and from *The Uncollected Poetry and Prose of Walt Whitman*. To Cleveland Rodgers and John Black and to G. P. Putnam's Sons, my gratitude for their allowing me such generous use of Whitman material in *The Gathering of the Forces*; also to Clifton Joseph Furness and the Harvard University Press for permission to quote from *Walt Whitman's Workshop*.

F. W.

Greenshade,
Wilmington, Vermont

AMERICAN
GIANT

Chapter I: Beginnings

WHEN Walter Whitman and Louisa Van Velsor married in 1816, they were content to remain in the old Whitman farm in West Hills, Long Island, instead of joining the movement westward like many young people of their class. Throughout that year and many more following the inauguration of President Monroe, the whole East was in constant flux. Prairie wagons in nondescript processions filed through New York and Pennsylvania toward the land of promise which, in the euphoria of the "era of good feeling" the government was selling in lots on the installment plan. From western New York to Indiana and Illinois settlements sprang up almost overnight. The log cabin with its window of greased paper and plank floor, the primitive smithy and the mill dotted the prairie. Corn patches and fields of wheat gave new color to the land, and comradeship grew closer at the threshing and husking bees. The West was being called to life.

A period of prosperity had come. With the re-chartering of the National Bank in Philadelphia at the beginning of Monroe's term, the whole country gained heart. Business flourished in a burst of enterprise. Commerce expanded. To bring the great harbor of New York closer to the inland lakes, the ground was broken for the Erie Canal as an adequate celebration of Independence Day, 1817. That year too New York and Liverpool diminished the distance of the Atlantic with a line of fast packets. In St. Louis the first steamboat was launched.

Europe was slowly recovering from the long struggle with the Eagle, chained now at St. Helena. But it was a wary and suspicious Europe, ready with brute force to discourage the ideas that had brought about the French Revolution. As reforms managed to make their way into the legislature, restrictive measures kept pace and often outstripped them. When, in England, industrial repression fomented riots against the government, they were ruthlessly put down by the suspension of the *habeas corpus* act and frequent executions. The Manchester Blanketers, protesting workingmen who marched to London carrying their blanket rolls on their backs, met the bayonet points of the military. Members of the Luddites died at the end of the rope for breaking labor-saving machines. Conditions were made no easier to bear by the scandals of the Regent and his wife Caroline.

Meanwhile Metternich, the watchdog of Europe, kept his eyes open for any flicker of revolution. When in 1819 a hot-headed young liberal, Sand, assassinated Kotzebue for quenching academic freedom, Metternich saw in the deed the spark of the dangerous flame. "By the help of God," he threatened, "I hope to defeat the German revolution, just as I defeated the conqueror of the world."

It was the signal for widespread persecution. No man was safe who thought of freedom. But the worst off were the university men, for Sand had been a leader in the liberal student movement. Under Metternich's direction a committee of investigation was formed in Mainz, with the power to arrest any subject of the German states. Homes were broken into and hundreds of innocent persons dragged to the prisons. In every university sat a special police commission to keep strict watch over professors and scholars. All student organizations were suppressed; it was treason for anyone to wear the black and yellow ribbons, the symbols of German freedom.

A reign of terror followed. Out of two hundred students arrested for wearing the ribbons, ninety-four were condemned to death. Noted professors lost their chairs and with them all chance of employment in any other German state. For daring to send a letter of sympathy to the mother of Sand on his execution, Professor De Wette had to flee to Switzerland. Fries was expelled from Jena, the poet Arndt from Bonn. It was either tyranny or exile, if not death. Then it was that a new kind of emigrant fled to America, the intellectual refugee, as group after group of professors, accompanied by their disciples, sought freedom of thought in the New World. They were a few years too early to profit from the provision of Napoleon who left a sum of money in his will "to be distributed among such proscribed persons as wander in foreign countries, whether they be French, Italians, Belgians, Dutch, Spanish, or inhabitants of the departments of the Rhine."

Probably Walter Whitman and his wife knew nothing of the German refugees, or of the sensational details of the royal divorce trial in England. But they followed important events at home closely enough to form their own estimates of deeds and men. It was no mere infatuation with high-sounding names that made them call three of their sons George Washington, Thomas Jefferson and Andrew Jackson. Washington as the father of his country had always held first place in the esteem of the "powerful uneducated" class to which the Whitmans belonged. But the bond was closer with Jefferson, an old man now, yet still the most conspicuous apostle of democracy in America. For Jefferson had known Tom Paine, that stormy petrel of liberty, and Paine, who died in 1809, had been a friend of Jesse Whitman, Walter's father.

A tradition of democracy had been almost a religion with the Whitmans and as strong an influence in their lives as their spiritual leaning toward the Quakers. Truth had in a sense come down to them direct—the secular from Paine, the religious from Elias Hicks, the thundering Quaker preacher whose meetings Walter and Louisa faithfully attended.

As for Andrew Jackson, he was the hero of the day, the fearless soldier who knew when to fight for his country's advantage. True, there had been criticism of him in Congress for acting so highhandedly in the Florida affair and almost precipitating a

3

war with Spain. But had not Spain failed to restrain the Florida Indians in their hostilities against the States? "The cause of the United States must be carried to any point within the limits of Florida where an enemy is permitted to be protected." So General Jackson declared and so he did. The result—a vast slice of territory ceded by a weakened Spain to the rapidly growing United States. Imperialism? The word was unheard of. Swelling with patriotism, the powerful uneducated rejoiced in the nation's gain and named their children after the conqueror. The year of Jackson's conquest a foresighted Congress approved a bill changing the design of the American flag. Until then it had borne eighteen stripes, red and white. Now they were reduced to thirteen, the number of the original states. On the field of blue, however, room was provided for expansion: henceforth it was to hold as many stars as there were states in the Union.

However adventurous the large life of the nation, it was peaceful enough in West Hills near Huntington where the Whitman family had been living for more than a hundred years. The homestead itself had been up since 1705. Old Jesse Whitman had been born in it, and his children; and now his son's children were coming into the world. A plain, story-and-a-half house of shingles, weathered a soft gray by the years, it commanded a barn and the brood of outhouses and sheds that cluster about the traditional American farm. A fine old place it was, solid and unpretentious, set in its five hundred acres of lovely Long Island landscape. A short walk from the house, along infrequent roads edged with scrub oak, locust and hickory, their branches linked by a thick undergrowth of climbing vines, stretched a chestnut forest, primeval in its denseness. Grand old trees, oaks of indefinite age, fronded locusts and walnut patriarchs made familiar landmarks in that unspoiled country. Toward the west low hills, wooded on every inch of their slopes, marked the season of the year in the changing foliage. Here and there the houses, shingled like the Whitman farm, with the usual fruit orchard in the back and its flower garden in an enclosure of white palings, huddled in small groups just close enough for neighborliness.

The region about Huntington had been settled toward the middle of the seventeenth century. The land, purchased from the Long Island Indians, had been colonized by two different waves of immigration, one from New Amsterdam, the other from England, by way, however, of Connecticut. In 1635, according to the records, Rev. Zechariah Whitman, then forty years of age, had come to America and established himself in Milford, Connecticut. But the family was destined to spread its roots when in 1660, Zechariah's son Joseph crossed Long Island Sound, and finding the region about Huntington to his liking, decided to settle. It is not certain whether he bought the property at West Hills. At any rate, by the next generation, it held the rooftree of the Long Island Whitmans.

Louisa's people, the Van Velsors, were of Holland Dutch descent with, later, an admixture of Welsh on the female side. At Cold Spring, not far from West Hills, the Van Velsors kept a stock farm, raising blooded horses for the market. Louisa herself as a girl had been known as a daring rider.

With the years both families had been reduced in circumstances. The Whitman farm, once of vast extent, had shrunk considerably since the days Sarah Whitman, Walter's grandmother, had watched over her slaves and her acres with the energy of a man. On the intellectual side, too, the stock had weakened. Although the original New England Whitmans distinguished themselves as ministers and professional men, the Whitmans of Long Island followed the manual trades. They were good farmers and skilled carpenters, however, and loyal soldiers whenever their country needed them. During the Revolution they had fought as staunch patriots under Washington. One of them, Nehemiah Whitman, a lieutenant, gave his life in the Battle of Brooklyn. Another ancestor died in the English

5

prisons. All of them, whether in a foreign grave or in the family burial plot in West Hills, earned the final commendation of good and faithful servant.

The present Walter Whitman a large, shambling, slow spoken man not much given to laughter, practiced the family trade of carpenter and was known as an excellent framer. Some of the houses he built are still standing after a century. His neighbors, humble folk like himself, respected him. He lived at peace with the world, a good citizen and a solid member of that modest community. On the 31st of May, 1819, his family was increased by the birth of his second son, named after him, Walter.

It was an eventful year abroad and at home. In Europe the usual crop of revolutions broke out, only to be quickly quelled. Tyrants met their doom and liberals fled to exile. At Kensington Palace a girl child was born to Edward Duke of Kent and Maria Louisa Victoria of Saxe-Coburg. They named her Alexandrina Victoria, but the nineteenth century and the years to come were to know her simply as Victoria.

In the United States the year seethed with political agitation, with feuds, quarrels and dissensions, the fiercest of them kindled over the admission of Missouri into the Union. The nation now contained twenty-two states, eleven free and eleven slave. Missouri threatened the balance.

Early in the year James Tallmadge, Jr., of New York, introduced a bill to prohibit slavery in the new state except in the case of men and women already in bondage; but they too, the bill provided, were to be freed within a certain period of time. Proposals and counter proposals rained down upon Congress, heatedly argued on both sides. The South would not yield an inch in its defense of the slavery issue and found its ablest spokesman in Caleb of Georgia who prophesied that such interference with tradition would destroy the peace and harmony of the Union. Those who advocated it, he declared, were "kindling a fire which all the waters of the ocean could not extinguish. It can be extinguished only in blood."

At that session the amendment was defeated. The question of Missouri, however, came up again in subsequent meetings. New bills were introduced, compromises offered, with each side holding doggedly to its point of view and feelings rising to hostility on the perilous issue. At last a modified form of the original amendment passed by a majority of eight. But the two Houses remained firmly opposed, the Representatives holding for the prohibition of slavery in Missouri, the Senate more than ever determined to admit it only as a slave state. The compromise measure which finally passed, though a triumph for the North, gave it only the moral victory of a vague promise that slavery would be prohibited in future states admitted to the Union. The South, on the other hand, rejoiced over the material gain of another slave state. Peace was restored, and the fire that had been kindled was temporarily under control. But Caleb's words were to be recalled many years later when they proved too tragically prophetic. "It can be extinguished only in blood."

Chapter II: Paumanok

BROOKLYN in the 1820's, a thriving town of some ten thousand inhabitants, drew to itself people from the neighboring counties who, not yet ready for the sophisticated bustle of the still more thriving Manhattan, tried the stepping stone before venturing farther. Among these migrants from the outlying sections came Walter Whitman with his family in 1822 or '23.

What prompted him to leave the comfortable West Hills farm? Perhaps he had exhausted the possibilities of livelihood in the little rural community. Perhaps Louisa, seeing her rapidly growing brood, had spurred her husband on to improve his fortune in the competitiveness of the prosperous town. However it was, the Whitman family like hundreds of others attracted to the metropolitan centers, took a house in Brooklyn and lived under a strange roof until Walter had the means to build them a home of their own.

It was a fascinating change for little Walter Whitman, or Walt as they called him to distinguish him from the head of the family. A sturdy, apple-cheeked youngster of five, he trudged the city streets as he had tramped the hills and meadows of Long Island, mingling with the crowds, noticing everything, remembering everything.

As the Front Street house was not far from the water, Walt haunted the harbor. He knew every ferry, but best of all the one at the foot of Catherine Street which had recently been opened and still went under the name of the New Ferry. Even more constant than the throngs of workingmen and women who crossed to the factories in Manhattan early in the morning and back again at nightfall, was the plump little boy whom the bluff

8

gatekeepers petted and the deckhands "deadheaded." Sometimes they would let him up into the ferryboats where he would pry into every nook and cranny. But it was the team of horses in the central houses that he loved to watch as they plodded round and round making the power that set the boat in motion.

Louisa at home had no worries about the safety of her infant gadabout. Ever since he could walk, Walt had gone off wandering by himself much as he pleased, early asserting an independence that Louisa, and later the other members of the family, learned to respect. As it was, Louisa had enough to do, what with childbirths coming with clockwork regularity and household tasks requiring constant re-doing, without her wasting time brooding on possible accidents. There existed an attachment, however, between her and her independent little boy that was not the less close for being undemonstrative. The daughter of a Quaker mother, Louisa believed in deeds more than in words. Her household ran with the smoothness of an oiled machine, and if there was never any luxury, there was always plenty of plain, honest comfort, centering round the warm hearth in winter and the kitchen table, redolent of pies and traditional dishes on bake days and holidays.

From Front Street the family moved to Cranberry and then to Johnston Street where Walter built a house. They lived in it for a time but it was mortgaged and they lost it. He built another soon afterward on Tillary Street to which they moved as soon as the roof was weatherproofed and the latch was on the door. Young Walt began going to school, but he did not let it interfere with his peregrinations. The New Ferry now gave way to the picturesqueness of the Old, as Fulton Ferry was then called. Besides the primitive horse-boats, the Old Ferry had a new wonder, a boat that went by itself, so far as one could see, though people explained that steam did the work which the horses had done before.

Wonderful it was to watch the crowds of people coming to

shore during the busy hours—first the boat, steadily approaching the wharf, the water parting at its breast and trailing off in a white froth at the stern, then the passengers dashing forward and standing eagerly in front as if in a race to reach the landing. There it is! Only three feet of water between the deck and the shore. Wildly the men spring across, looking back as they jump to see how much better they've done than the rest. What shrieks from the women! What excitement! In vain the watchmen shout to keep the young fellows from the dangerous game. They will have their sport, even knowing that several men had been crushed to death between the boat and the landing for that very pastime.

Here it was, at the Old Ferry, that a famous person was received by the high functionaries of Brooklyn one day in 1825—none other than Lafayette come to revisit the Republic whose independence he had helped to win. He was now a white-haired man, far different from the twenty-four-year-old major-general who had fought and been wounded at the Battle of Brandywine nearly half a century earlier. He had arrived as the nation's guest in 1824. From city to city his proud hosts escorted him that he might see the progress of the American Republic. Years ago he had left thirteen poor, struggling states, exhausted from the war that had drained their manpower and their resources. He now found a powerful nation of twenty-four independent commonwealths stretching from the Atlantic border a thousand miles to the west.

Everywhere in his triumphal progress Lafayette had been received by enthusiastic crowds. Cavalcades of citizens in uniform paraded in advance of his carriage, the bells pealed, while amid the salvos of artillery and the discharge of rockets, the people cheered as from one mighty throat. He was entertained in the governors' mansions; he laid cornerstones; he held babies in his arms. And in Boston a commemorative arch was erected for the occasion, with the inscription by Charles Sprague:

WELCOME LAFAYETTE!

The fathers in glory shall sleep,
That gathered with thee to the fight;
But the sons will eternally keep
The tablet of gratitude bright.
We bow not the neck; we bend not the knee:
But our hearts, Lafayette, we surrender to thee.

Brooklyn, like the rest of the country, would not be outdone in that generous surrender. Here, too, the bells pealed, the rockets flared and a cornerstone was provided for him to lay— the cornerstone of the Apprentices' Library. School was let off so that the future citizens might have something to tell their grandchildren, and thus a whole bank of well-scrubbed young faces beamed upon the great man as he descended from his barouche at the corner of Cranberry and Henry Streets. The foundation had been dug, the ceremonial implements lay ready for Lafayette's hand, when someone discovered that the children who stood too near the foundations were in danger of being pushed into the ditch. Several men, therefore, took them one by one and handed them over to safety. Lafayette, by this time past master in the art, stooped down, lifted up a particularly sturdy lad, gave him a hug and then, tempted perhaps by the plump, shining, rosy cheeks, kissed him before setting him down. Walt Whitman never forgot this unexpected accolade. To the child of five it must have been like a moment in the arms of legend.

Although the Whitmans were now city folk, they never lost touch with the family homesteads and not a week passed throughout Walt's childhood without a visit either to West Hills or Cold Spring. He knew every winding of the brooks in the Van Velsor meadows, every knot on the trunk of the two-hundred-year-old oak that shaded one of the newer houses on the property at West Hills, every heart-shaped leaf of the lilacs in the dooryards. Those fresh, green bushes became part of the

11

boy's life; their fragrant sprays of blossoms whispered to him of the returning spring, and life renewed, and simple earthy beauty. The grove of black walnuts sheltering squirrel and bird was a favorite playground, so too the apple orchard of over twenty acres on the other side of the road. With every May the gnarled old trees put on incongruous pink blossoms that turned each autumn to ruddy, heavy fruit. The ground under the branches would be covered with apples, and there in the sun they would send up a warm sweetness like the earth breathing.

Sometimes the boy would climb up the burial hill where generations of Whitmans rested within view of the houses they had built with their own hands, of the soil they had turned and made fertile. Some of the graves were so old that the mounds could hardly be discerned in the leveling of time. The stones lay broken amidst the sparse grass of the sterile gray earth, the names themselves obliterated by the moss. With a strange, precocious interest in death the boy would brood, not too unhappily, on the vanished Whitmans, and then lie listening to the wind through the branches of the chestnut clump nearby.

At the Van Velsors he loved to sit in the vast kitchen of the farmhouse where Grandmother Amy presided, her sweet face framed in its Quaker cap, as she went about her duties without bustle, always gently smiling. She was a deeply spiritual woman, sensitive and intuitive, yet not too good for the common tasks of life. Her daughter Louisa resembled her in her serenity, but had also, doubtless from her father, a reserve of strength and energy. A contrast to Grandmother Amy, Major Cornelius Van Velsor was a hearty, red-faced, corpulent old fellow who talked loud and loved his comfort. For over forty years he had driven a stage and market wagon from the farm to the Brooklyn ferries. Sometimes, as a special treat, Walt was taken to ride with him. The Major no longer bred horses as his father had done, but still kept a few on the farm.

Grandmother Hannah Whitman, who had been a schoolteacher, was already a widow when Walt came into the world. She had a great deal to tell him, in the timbered, low-ceilinged rooms of the ancient house whenever he called on her, the only woman amidst her large family of sons. She told him stories of the Revolutionary War that had been fought when she was a girl, and of the part his great-great-kin on both sides of the family had played in it. She told him about the great man Paine whom Grandfather Jesse had known, of how he had lived in the service of freedom and of how he died, neglected and reviled, an undesirable alien in the nation he had helped to make.

In the rude simplicity of the old house with no carpets or pictures and with furniture of the homeliest sort, the little boy was carried away to the times, at the close of the past century, when Great-grandmother Sarah, the wife of Nehemiah, ruled as its mistress. She had died at the great age of ninety long before he was born, but Grandmother Hannah had known her, and could speak from close knowledge. She had been a large, swarthy woman, a trainer of horses and as good a manager of men. She smoked tobacco constantly, and since she was so much with rough, homely folk, she could swear with the best and bring to the mark the most unruly servant. Even in her old age, a widow and the only overseer of the farm, she would take a daily course on horseback through her farmlands, and woe to the laborers she found wanting in their duty! Then oaths of the most colorful vehemence roused the countryside; there was no silencing her till she had had her say. But with all her roughness she had her tender side which she showed to her Negro slaves. She owned some twelve or fifteen of them. Every night, Grandmother Hannah told Walt, to that very kitchen, the young darkies would come trooping for their evening meal. Right here, in front of the hearth, they squatted on the floor in a circle, laughing and chatting, their wooden spoons clattering against the bowls as they ate their supper of Indian pudding and milk.

Except for the absence of slaves, life was not much different

13

on the farm. Of course most of the servants had gone, and large parcels of the land had fallen into other hands, but one had still a great deal to be thankful for. Pork and beef and poultry were not wanting for the dinner table. There were always logs enough for the huge winter fires in the hearth, and cider aplenty to cheer up the long evenings for the menfolk. Women, of course, then as now, drank a little tea with a bit of sugar.

In a decent household there was never time for idleness and mischief, for everyone had his special task to do, even the children. The menfolk, of course, did the work proper to them, out in the fields and the stables. They grew the grains and the vegetables, they pressed the cider, they built the sheds and did the heavy chores. The women made sturdy homespun for their clothes and their family's. They cooked and baked, they nursed the sick and helped their neighbors in childbed. They even sewed shoes and did a bit of repairing when the cobbler was not about. But the strong winter boots and the shoes for the men were made by the shoemaker who would come round at a certain season and board here and there till he had provided the neighborhood with the year's supply of footwear. Bought boots were a luxury and one had to go to the city for them. On the whole a household was like a little community. It had to be able to run itself. Everyone in it had a share of responsibility, and all were liable to the head of the house. If a woman was left a widow, she had to be able to take the husband's place and keep the family together. Certainly the Whitman women had not failed in their duty. A large, vigorous breed, they raised families of sons and lived, most of them, to a great age.

When Walt was not in West Hills or Cold Spring, he was off exploring the shore by himself. From his earliest childhood he had had the sound of the sea in his ears. He had listened to the far-off pounding of the surf on stormy nights, and the weird shriek of the wind on the waves. From the hilltops he had caught the shimmer of the water on his rambles and his heart beat with a strange yearning. Often, before his family had moved to Brooklyn, he had gone with the men and women on bathing parties, or accompanied the men alone when they went clamming or fishing, or cutting salt hay. The tang of the south-side meadows was one of his earliest memories which in his later years filled him with a keen nostalgia. The sea was in his blood, the blood of

Dutch Kossabone, Old Salt, related to my mother's side, far back.

How early did he learn the Indian name for Long Island, Paumanok, that was to ring a great bell rousing his sleeping imagination? Paumanok, the fish-shaped land, the water-bitten, water-tortured, water-loved land. The Indians had long ago found it and possessed it. Off at the extreme end of it, at Montauk, they were now concentrated, a weak settlement of Red Men and half-breeds, gradually becoming extinct, the ocean alone beating a dirge for the dying of a race. The fine grazing lands of the peninsula had been taken away from them by the rich farmers of the eastern towns. Hired herdsmen now lived in it, their rude shacks the only habitations in that place. Sometimes the fishermen would meet them, wild, barbarous creatures as untamed as their horses. Every day, toward sundown, the land would be covered as far as the eye could reach with droves of sheep and long lines of cattle returning from the pastures. Then the air, laden with the sound of the sea, would be soothed by the mellow clanging of cowbells till darkness fell and all was still but for the never-ceasing throb of the surf.

On the south side the meadows of salt hay spread for miles, the horizon boundless behind them, changing with the ever-changing sky. Kill-calf and huckleberry varied the landscape, sometimes a clump of locusts or an apple orchard. Then at night on the Hempstead plains glowed the fires of the charcoal burners like mysterious beacons in that solitary expanse.

Young Walt knew every dent of the Paumanok shore and

15

learned to know it better as he grew older. With the men he would go fishing as far as Montauk, but most often alone he would wander for miles upon the sands, his trousers rolled up, his feet naked to the lapping of the waves. He knew the farmers, the herdsmen, the bay-men, the pilots of the boats that went far out to sea. He talked with everyone, and everyone responded to the bright-faced boy whose gray-blue eyes had in them the colors of the sea.

Winter or summer he frequented his favorite inlets. With a chum or two in the cold autumn mornings, at low tide, he would go digging for clams, barefoot over the stiff sea-grass. Sometimes with eel-spears and baskets on their hand-sleds they would race across the frozen meadows to the shallows, cut holes in the ice and try their luck. What rejoicing rang through the air when they struck a bed and filled their baskets with fat, squirming, gray-green eels!

But best of all he liked the summer when he could feel the warmth of the sun on the hard sand beneath his feet, or plunge into the waves and lie floating on his back, watching the clouds change in the sky. Water, air and sun, he took them into himself, washing his large young body, filling his lungs, glowing in the life-giving light. And as his body developed, his imagination grew also. The wrecks off Hempstead beach had their stories to tell; the lighthouses piercing the darkness with their signal lamps wakened him to awe, intensified by the low, lost, intermittent sob of the bell buoys. He soared with the water birds that made their home in the bays and learned from the life about him more than from any book. He knew joy and gladness and the exultation of a healthy body, but he learned also that all was not happiness in life, that parting and sorrow, too, formed the heart of experience.

Once Paumanok,
When the lilac-scent was in the air and Fifth-month grass was
    growing,
16

Paumanok

Up this seashore in some briers,
Two feather'd guests from Alabama, two together,
And their nest, and four light-green eggs spotted with brown,
And every day the he-bird to and fro near at hand,
And every day the she-bird crouch'd on her nest, silent, with bright
    eyes,
And every day I, a curious boy, never too close, never disturbing
    them,
Cautiously peering, absorbing, translating.

Shine! shine! shine!
Pour down your warmth, great sun!
While we bask, we two together . . .

Till of a sudden,
May-be kill'd, unknown to her mate,
One forenoon the she-bird crouch'd not on the nest,
Nor return'd that afternoon, nor the next,
Nor ever appear'd again.

And thenceforward all summer in the sound of the sea,
And at night under the full of the moon in calmer weather,
Over the hoarse surging of the sea,
Or flitting from brier to brier by day,
I saw, I heard at intervals the remaining one, the he-bird,
The solitary guest from Alabama.

Blow! blow! blow!
Blow up sea-winds along Paumanok's shore:
I wait and I wait till you blow my mate to me.

Yes, when the stars glisten'd,
All night long on the prong of a moss-scallop'd stake,
Down almost amid the slapping waves,
Sat the lone singer wonderful causing tears. . . .

Although he was only a child when he listened to the song of
the grieving bird, Walt knew it was something ineffable he was
hearing. Not alone to its lost mate was the mourner singing,
but to the boy whose spirit stirred for the first time to the

evocation of wonder, whose sensitive being awakened, gropingly, uncertainly, to the potentialities within him.

And with the bird's song sighed the voice of the sea, the two, the chant of mourning and the whisper of the waves, mingling indissolubly in his imagination—

Delaying not, hurrying not
Whisper'd me through the night, and very plainly before daybreak,
Lisp'd to me the low and delicious word death,
And again death, death, death, death,
Hissing melodious, neither like the bird nor like my arous'd child's
    heart,
But edging near as privately for me rustling at my feet,
Creeping thence steadily up to my ears and laving me softly all over,
Death, death, death, death, death.

Chapter III: The effect upon me of my early life

SCHOOL could have had no charms for the youthful wanderer after the magical days and nights on his beloved Paumanok. He went because he had to go, like other boys of his age, but no teacher, no schoolboy friendship, left any impression upon him. It was part of the routine of life, like having breakfast in the morning and going to bed at night. The real business of his existence would come later. Meanwhile he acquired his real education after school in his interminable wanderings. The public schools he attended held only his growing, lazy, inattentive body.

One June day in 1829, however, something happened that startled the boys out of their seats. A dull roar as of an earthquake shook the building to the very foundations. Then all was still again. When school was let out, the streets in the neighborhood were buzzing with excitement as people came and went in the direction of the Navy Yard close by. The frigate *Fulton*, anchored there, had blown up. Later, when the papers came out, the details were known. A sailor, it seems, nursing some private vengeance, had set fire to the powder magazine, destroying the ship and killing forty-three men and officers. It was the most sensational disaster that had occurred in Brooklyn in a very long time and the whole town was aroused.

Walt showed as much interest as any, in fact, more. A beautiful steam-frigate had been wrecked, heroes had perished. It was a disaster to fire his boyish imagination. No wonder, therefore, that several days later—school or no school—Walt saw to it that he should be among those who followed the hearse of one of the *Fulton* officers to the grave.

The cemetery, one of the many small burial grounds with which Brooklyn was studded, lay not far off on Fulton Street opposite the Globe Theatre. Walt knew it well, though he had never had occasion before to accompany so distinguished a corpse, in so impressive a ceremony. Through the streets lined with people filed the procession, the sailors in their dress uniforms marching hand in hand, two by two. The banners, held aloft, were not streaming in the wind but, shrouded in black crape, punctured the air in signs of mourning. Even the beat of the drums came muffled and dead, a subdued background for the wail of the bugles playing a slow, solemn funeral march.

The coffin was lowered into the grave; the soldiers fired the last salute. Nothing could have been more awe-inspiring than that final leave-taking of a hero. Boy-like, Walt responded. What was his shock when a few minutes later, while he was still in a pleasing melancholy over the dead march and the stirring ritual, he saw that same band skip out of the graveyard to the tune of a lively jig!

The boy's sensibilities were offended. As many times later, he protested inwardly against the superficial formalism that took the place of real feeling. At a much earlier age than Keats he had been more than half in love with death which, for so young a boy, he faced not only fearlessly but even with a yearning to know its secret. The whisper of the sea, the song of the bird, were more than the projections of his boyhood wonder in an effort to throw light on the mystery. Both stood rather for the outward symbols of something as wonderful, as affirmative as life. If, like the boy Shelley, he haunted the places of the dead, it was not with the young atheist's zeal to disprove the secrets of Christianity, but to make for himself a faith anchored in the valor and greatness of living. It was still too early for revelation, but intimations, as yet hardly conscious, were beginning to break upon his receptive mind, already alive to spiritual values.

That same year of 1829 was to bring the boy in the presence

of another of the personalities that had a lasting effect upon his development. One winter evening, toward the close of the year, Walter Whitman, returning home from his day's work, threw down on the kitchen floor the armful of kindling he had brought, and said to Louisa, "Come, Mother, Elias preaches tonight."

The name of Elias Hicks had often been mentioned in the Whitman family. Indeed, as a young man Grandfather Jesse had frequently been in the company of Elias, a carpenter at the time, fond of sleigh-riding and jovial songs, though much troubled in his mind about spiritual matters.

Not till he was twenty, however, did Hicks fully realize his mission, when he gave up his carpenter's trade and took up farming in the Hempstead section of Long Island where he was born. His parents were Friends, but until the crucial year he himself had taken little interest in religion. His closeness to the soil, however, and the solitary hours in the fields during which he came face to face with himself and his spirit, helped him to know the thing that was working within him. For years he wrestled with himself and the light pointing the way he should follow, but it was not till 1779, at the age of thirty-one, that he took his bundle and his Book and set out as an itinerant preacher.

From Vermont down to Maryland he went, rejecting openings leading to the ministry so that he might be free to express the God within him. Not everywhere was he well received, for although the persecutions that had marked the first landing of the Quakers in New England had ceased, there was still a difference of opinion on what a man might and might not utter as the promptings of the Inner Light. Like the New England Puritans whose General Court lost no time in pronouncing the Society of Friends "a blasphemouth sect" there were still many too ready to believe that if any voice spoke through an inspired man, it was not necessarily the voice of the Lord.

More generally than one might have expected in the enlightened nineteenth century, the Quakers were held suspect for having no set creed, no church and no ministers, and for holding their meetings as the spirit prompted them, under the direction of whatever member felt upon him the impulse of God. The feud, however, that had existed in the early days between the New England Church and the Quakers had ended. Devoted men and women no longer died by the rope for not worshiping God in the Puritan way. On the other side the Quakers, no longer exasperated by unjust laws, moderated their sometimes sensational protest. No prophets in winding sheets now broke in upon Church lectures, crying out upon the elders as hypocrites. No more bottles were broken over the heads of ministers as in the case of the Rev. John Norton of Boston, whom two Quaker women had treated to such summary symbolism "as a sign of his emptiness." No virgin, like the pure Deborah Buffum of Salem, found it necessary to walk through the town naked, her face blackened with ashes, to expose the bareness of the religion of the Church. The Quakers were tolerated.

Although it was comparatively safe to worship as one pleased, it was another matter for even a man of God to interfere with economic tradition. Elias Hicks, therefore, showed remarkable courage when he preached against slavery not only in the North but in Maryland itself. For years he raised his voice like an angry prophet, with such eloquence that even those who did not believe with him agreed that a divine breath inspired him. Tall, majestic, intense as a flame, he preached in a ringing voice, the deep black eyes in the ascetic face suddenly glowing as if from the radiance of the light within. He spoke simply, in the language of the Bible, with a poetic figurativeness that all could understand. At times his body was possessed by emotions so strong that those who sat near him saw it quiver. Then, after he had spoken, he collected himself with a brusque shock and became human.

The effect upon me of my early life

At the time Walt was taken to hear him as a special reward for having been a good boy, Hicks was a patriarch of eighty-one, gaunt, spare, a taper consumed to the wick. The grand ballroom of the Morrison Hotel on the Heights, resplendent with lights in the crystal chandeliers, teemed with people, young and old, the faithful and the curious. All of Brooklyn's fashionables and first citizens—Pierrepont, Judge Furman, General Jeremiah Johnson—fine ladies in their veils and furs, Navy Yard officers in uniform, had turned out to hear the man, sitting there on the platform amidst a group of elderly Friends, with his thin white hair over his shoulders, and on his head the broad-brimmed hat which he would take off for no man. How otherworldly he looked! How grand and noble in the simplicity of his drab cloth!

Walt did not once take his eyes off him. Suddenly the old man rose, stood for a moment silent while the people held their breath, and then, his hat still on his head, he spoke slowly, in a thrilling, resonant voice: "What is the chief end of man? I was told in my early youth, it was to glorify God, and seek and enjoy him forever. . . ." On and on he spoke, now pleading, now tender, now wrathful. At one point he took his broad-brim from his head and dashed it on the seat behind him, speaking earnestly all the while, as the people listened, many of them— the little boy saw and marveled—with tears in their eyes. The ten year old could make little of the prophet's vehement speech, but he never forgot the solemn and somber figure, lighting up miraculously with the flame within him.

How much did the boy know of Hicks' story? He must have been told of the preacher's humble origins, no better than his father's, in fact, the same, but that Walter had farmed in West Hills and Hicks in Jericho. He must have known that he had helped to free the Negroes born in New York by preaching for the passage of a certain act, just a few years before he, Walt, was born. Probably he had heard too of the prophet's personal sorrows, of the loss of his four sons, which perhaps gave his face that terrible, austere look. And, surely, in a house wherein both sides had connections with the Quakers, he must have heard talk of the split which Hicks had brought about in the Society because of his opposition to formalism. The Whitmans, though not really members, stood of course with the Hicksites, the liberal branch.

As he grew older, even more than the Sunday schooling to which he was exposed in the old gray Dutch Reformed Church on Joralemon Street, Walt was influenced by the winds of doctrine blown to him from the Hicksite quarter. The old prophet himself died a few months after that meeting at Morrison's Hotel. His spirit, however, lived on in the Whitman household. Unwittingly, as he had been assimilating his experiences of nature, Walt was drinking in the outpourings of the prophetic fount, diluted, it is true, through his parents' comprehension, but still near enough to the source to retain their purity.

Vaguely at first, with a child's understanding, he apprehended what every good Quaker should believe—that the inner Deity is a surer guide than churches, doctrines or even the teachings of the Bible. In a sense, therefore, every man is holy, and every body sacred for being the lamp through which the Inner Light may burn. All are sharers in the common divinity, the poor, the ignorant, for there is no vessel so mean that it may not receive the divine Host, and speak for Him. "The prophet . . ." Whitman was to write, "means one whose mind bubbles up and pours forth as a fountain, from inner, divine spontaneities revealing God . . . The great matter is to reveal and outpour the Godlike suggestions pressing for birth in the soul. This is briefly the doctrine of the Friends or Quakers."

Meanwhile in the country at large all sorts of stirring things had been happening. On July 4th of that same eventful year another railroad, the Baltimore and Ohio, had been opened, and the first successful trip made by an American locomotive, a new name for a new and wonderful mechanical mode of travel. The whole country seemed to want to bind itself together more than ever, to bring the farthest states as near as possible to one another. Everywhere canals, following the success of the Erie, cut through the separating land: there were the Delaware and Chesapeake, the Delaware and Hudson and the Oswego; there were the Farmington in Connecticut, the Cumberland and Oxford in Maine. Arteries of water, arteries of rail carried the prosperity of the nation to the farthest reaches. A living body, the country was thriving and growing large. Some dreamers even saw it stretching from one ocean to the other, a giant among the powers of the earth.

In Washington, in 1829, John Quincy Adams grudgingly made way for Andrew Jackson as president. An exciting election, it seethed with clashes and demonstrations. In a frenzy of enthusiasm an uncontrollable horde of backwoodsmen and mountaineers in their motley costumes crashed the White House cheering, "Old Hickory! Old Hickory!" Feelings ran high. For the first time in history the outgoing president failed to attend the inauguration of the new. Some said Adams was in bed, ill, but the well informed told that until midnight of the previous day he had been up signing appointments to deprive Old Hickory of patronage.

But the general, the hero of Florida, knew his tactics. With the cry, "To the victor belong the spoils," he made a clean sweep of more than a hundred and fifty opponents, and instituted the system of rotation in office. Then, because the Cabinet was not as co-operative as he could have wished, he surrounded himself with confidential advisers who came to be known as the Kitchen Cabinet, while the official members blunted their quills in the chores of mere clerks. His own pen, however, he worked overtime, vetoing more bills in the first few weeks of his administration than his predecessor had done in as many years. He had also another astute trick for unpopular legislature. He would postpone action until Congress adjourned, and then he failed to sign the bills. They might as well have been in his pocket, forgotten. The Pocket Veto thus became a well-known term. His was dictatorial procedure, but in the eyes of his supporters Old Hickory could do no wrong.

One may be sure that Jackson's stormy career was closely followed by the Whitman household, good Jacksonians all. To them he was a great man, a brave one and a sage, just as he was to the new generation that saw in the changing economic and social conditions the logical working out of the Jeffersonian dogmas. With greater faith in America, inspired by material prosperity, they were beginning to turn their eyes away from the Old World, fixing them more than ever hopefully upon the almost untouched resources of the New. Confident in themselves, happy in their leadership, they began to pull away from the leading strings of European influence. With the rest of the country the Whitmans felt the change and attributed it to their President, brusque, rough, domineering, but straightforward and aboveboard. He was a man after their hearts. They admired and approved.

Once in 1833, the ubiquitous Walt caught a glimpse of the hero during Jackson's grand tour of the North. The day was sweltering, one of the worst of the summer. Nevertheless Brooklyn boiled with people concentrated in the streets near Fulton Ferry, the gateway of all wonders. In a fine carriage drawn by spirited horses, sat the President, a grand and terrible old man, doffing his broad white beaver hat to the right and to the left as the people cheered, the boy Walt no doubt louder than any. The rest of the family must have envied him this moment in the immediacy of greatness when he recounted it later.

Impressions, vivid pictures, mixed emotions, sights and sounds stored themselves in Walt's awakening mind. He was no longer going to school. The household, now quite a large family of boys and girls, required some supplement to the elder Whitman's uncertain income. Jesse, the firstborn, was already going to work. Walt, a year younger, found himself a job in a lawyer's office on tree-lined Fulton Street. He was only eleven when he left school, but big for his age and, according to the views of the day, old enough to contribute toward the support of the family.

Lawyer Clarke took an interest in the lad, and finding him bright, gave him a subscription to a circulating library. (Are there predestined benefactors assigned to open library doors to budding poets? At any rate Lawyer Clarke belongs with that benevolent stranger who, when he realized that the wildly gesticulating Blue-Coat Boy, Coleridge, had not tried to pick his pocket, but was merely talking to himself, rewarded him with a library card.) He also put him at a desk near the window, showed him how to improve his penmanship, and gave him lessons in composition.

Walt did not remain long with the lawyer for in a little while he was running errands for a doctor in Brooklyn. Probably the attractions of a desk with a view of the street struck him as far less alluring than the opportunity of free-footing through the street itself. He had learned to enjoy reading, however, not systematically or with any fixed purpose, but for the pleasure in the book itself. The bookshelf had never occupied a large place in the Whitman home. Indeed books, a luxury, were scarce. Out in West Hills, Walt had taken his turn poring over the varied pages of the yearly almanac. Then there was the Bible, and doubtless also Paine's *Age of Reason*, with little else besides except for the copies of *The Free Enquirer* which had begun to come into the Brooklyn home after Frances Wright lectured in New York toward the close of the 'twenties. The magazine was read religiously by every member of the household old enough to appreciate it, for Frances Wright and Robert Dale Owen, co-editor with her on the magazine, wrote in the free-thinking tradition of Jefferson and Paine—and the Whitmans were faithful. One of the most vivid impressions Walt received as a

27

very young boy was the vision of Frances Wright—"glorious Frances" he was to call her—speaking from the platform. Like Elias Hicks she glowed with the ardor of her message, but hers was a religion of another kind, a faith based on the love of man for man, aspiring toward universal brotherhood. Walt was to hear of her again in his young manhood. "Her very appearance seemed to enthrall us . . . She possessed herself of my body and soul."

But to the lad of twelve there opened still another world in his discovery of the *Arabian Nights* and the works of Scott. He reveled in the fanciful tales of the wily Scheherazade, but more than any other reading he loved the romance and adventure of *Ivanhoe*, of *Kenilworth*, *The Fortunes of Nigel* and *Heart of Midlothian*. Over and over he read the novels, the last of them more than a dozen times, and began to build his own small library, putting at the base a bulky volume of Scott's poetry. He was boy enough, however, to enjoy the lusty yarns of James Fenimore Cooper, especially *The Red Rover* that used to "stir him up clarionlike." As yet he was only satisfying the boy's need for imaginative adventure, told in a language that he could understand.

Real adventure the streets supplied him. What excitement in the pages of a book could compare with the hurry of Manhattan's broad avenues, the crowds of people, the carriages, shop windows, the riots and parades? What gilt-lettered binding promised as much as the closed door of a theater in the daytime, so hushed, so deserted, yet so full of wonder and enchantment when the lamps blazed at night and the carriages drew up with their prancing horses and beautiful women? So far he knew that world only from the outside. What description in print could stir one as much as the actual sight of the rivers round Manhattan, and her ample bay with its ferries, its sloops, its skiffs and schooners, the swift yachts, and the incoming ships that had made their way across the Atlantic? What poem more exhilarating than the Battery against the open sea and sky, washed by the breezes and loved by the fashionable lounger as by the idling, dreaming boy whose glimpse of the ocean from a Long Island hilltop had given him his first intoxication?

Yes, books were wonderful but life was more wonderful still, plotting in its everyday run meetings more thrilling than any contrived by an author in a novel, bringing one, as it were, face to face with the past and the future. Lafayette, Andrew Jackson, Elias Hicks, Frances Wright—what character in a book had given him a thrill comparable to that produced by the living presence?

And so he read and ran his errands and swam in the life of the city as zestfully as he had swum the tides of Paumanok. He saw strange things and had curious meetings, but everything he accepted with boyish avidity. They were all part of life and he was just discovering what it was to live. It was early for him to put off childish things, to leave school and go to work. But then, was there not the good American tradition, to which doubtless his mother Louisa subscribed, that with ambition and hard work anyone could reach the top of the ladder of success? At that time particularly, when the great American fortunes were being amassed, talk abounded in Franklinian maxims, and already signal instances were at hand for citation, most notable of all that of John Jacob Astor.

Everyone knew the story of his phenomenal rise. The son of a butcher of Waldorf, Germany, he had come to America in 1783 with a view to bettering his luck. The voyage in steerage had been long and painful. At the end, however, arched a very material rainbow, with a still more material pot of gold that he had as good a chance as any to attain. A collection of seven German flutes was all he brought to propitiate fortune. He knew into what family to marry, however. Down in Queen Street a modest shop with the name of John Astor on the shingle displayed flutes, guitars and pianofortes. Little by little he went into fur trading, then real estate. Before the new century was well on its way he was sending his ships to Europe and Asia with his merchandise, and founding his own trading post on the Columbia River—a small town that he called after himself, Astoria. Meanwhile his investments in real estate multiplied like the Belgian hare. No one knew how much money he accumulated—enough, in any case, for people to apply to him the recently coined word, "millionaire." Some said that he could scarcely read and write and that he ate peas with a knife. Nevertheless he had become a legend.

On a January day in 1832, while Walt was walking on the West Side near Houston Street in Manhattan, he saw a bent but stout-built old man in rich furs, with an ermine cap on his head, being led, almost carried, down the steps of his high front stoop. The servants guided him from step to step, and then lifted him into a sleigh drawn by a pair of the finest horses Walt had ever seen. There they tucked him in like a baby, enveloped him in rich fur robes, arranged him and made him comfortable. Finally the driver cracked his whip and the sleigh swished away. The millionaire was going for a ride.

Long the boy gazed after him, the old man who was fond of saying of his dollars that "the first hundred thousand were the hardest." There was another side to the picture of success. Walt never forgot it.

Chapter IV: The plague spot of the nation

LOUISA'S frequent childbearings told upon her health. Although of a hardy constitution strengthened by an athletic girlhood on the Van Velsor farm, she became so run down that the house in Brooklyn had to be given up and the family returned to West Hills. Walt, as a wage earner, was considered capable of fending for himself and so remained behind. The pleasant job of errand boy, no longer suited to his increased responsibilities, was abandoned and he apprenticed himself to a trade with a future that would also take care of him for the present. How he found the new place, or what decided him upon it is uncertain, but in 1832-33 he was one of the printer's devils in the composing room of the *Long Island Patriot*.

Those were still the large, unhurried days of old-fashioned community life, even in the heart of Brooklyn. At each trade employer and employees formed a close family, every member of which took an interest in his fellows and looked upon the "boss" both as a guide and a friend. Often, indeed, under the system of apprenticeship, the employer found himself in the position of another father, accountable both for the spiritual and the physical wellbeing of the young people in his care.

Samuel E. Clements, the owner of the *Long Island Patriot*, a Quaker from the South and as proud as Lucifer of his origin, took his duties seriously. Every week, when the paper was off the press, he would take a group of the boys out riding, Walt among them. There were still many pleasant country drives, those days, near the business center of Brooklyn. Fulton Street itself presented a rural landscape with its mile of tall elms, while on the Heights the fisherman would often be seen with his basket and tackle, seeking out some leafshaded nook along

31

the water's edge. Mr. Clements had no aversion to mingling instruction with pleasure. On Sundays he would shepherd his flock to "a great old rough, fortress-looking stone church," and an odd group they made, the tall, lanky hawk-nosed Quaker in his long-tailed blue coat and gilt buttons, and his bright-faced "devils" mending their walk to his solemn gait. He was a kind old man who provided well for his young charges, some of them away from home for the first time. With the other apprentices Walt boarded with Mr. Clements' grand-daughter.

It must have been one of the trials of his boyhood for Walt to be cut off from his mother. The silent bond between them had tightened with the years. The hardworking, uncomplaining woman who with uncanny sympathy let him have his way knowing intuitively that it was best for him, had by this time become the pivot of Walt's life. Between him and his taciturn father a barrier persisted which nothing could remove. Not that there was any active unfriendliness between them. They simply could not draw toward each other with the understanding that had made Louisa know, when Walt was still a child, that whatever he did was right. Walter, on the other hand, as the head of the family, had discipline to maintain, had even to speak harshly and to inflict punishment whenever necessary. Moreover he was often away from home on his jobs, whereas Louisa remained constantly with the children, tending to their needs and nursing them when they were sick. However the rest of the brood may have responded, Walt's feeling for his mother was rooted in the very quick of his being. He was fond of his brothers and sisters, of Jesse, the oldest son, of Mary and Hannah Louisa, and of Andrew, George and the young Thomas Jefferson—Jeff, as they called him; but his life was lived more or less independently of theirs. He had made no friends among the boys at school. No chum, except on fishing expeditions, ever accompanied him on his Long Island jaunts, or on his roving about town. No one of his age shared his dreams or experiences. The only human being who had any inkling of what he was about and received his rare confidences was Louisa. He felt no need for anyone else. Even so early his devotion to his mother had become the center of his emotional life.

He was growing too fast. By the age of fifteen his boy's body had shot up as tall as a man's. Broad of shoulder and long of limb, he stood a head taller than others of his age. His face, however, remained as rosy and smooth as a woman's; there was something unmasculine in his indolent walk. But with his vivid eyes and glowing cheeks, he attracted attention wherever he went.

In the composing room of Mr. Clements' paper he learned his craft from an old printer, William Hartshorne, a veteran of the Revolution who befriended him. Walt took readily to printer's ink, though unlike Shelley who had helped to set up the atheistical tract that caused his expulsion from Oxford, he had no thought of printing anything of his own, revolutionary or otherwise. Enough for him to become expert with the type and listen to the reminiscences of Hartshorne. To the list of those who had known Jefferson and Paine he added Hartshorne who had seen Washington. In the presence of such men the impressible Walt felt he touched hands with the heroes of those glorious days when history was being made.

History, however, is made every day, and seldom more passionately than it was in Whitman's own, even though the *Patriot* and Colonel Spooner's *Long Island Star*, to which Walt was graduated, carried little in their columns of what was happening in the nation at large. Though a man of principle and a humanitarian strongly agitated by ethical issues, Colonel Spooner, a Whig in politics, had his own views on contemporary events, and one may be sure he aired them wherever there were ears to listen, no doubt even those of the printer's devil whom he liked but whom he found inclined to idleness.

At the outset of 1831 the smoldering question of slavery

33

burst into flame in America. There had been sparks of protest, especially in New England, from the time ships had begun arriving with the black cargo of the Guinea trade, but it was not till William Lloyd Garrison sounded the call to freedom in his *Liberator* that the institution of slavery became a vital issue.

From the first, conscientious men had been appalled by a system that converted human beings to articles of merchandise falling under a code of instructions. A good load of Negroes brought high prices in the markets. It was to the advantage of captains and traders alike for the merchandise to arrive in as fine shape as possible.

"As slaves like other articles when brought to market," read a set of instructions to the captain of a slaver in 1785, "appear to best advantage . . . too critical inspection cannot be paid to them before purchase; to see that no dangerous distemper is lurking about them, to attend particularly to their age, to their countenance, to the straightness of their limbs. . . . Male or female slaves, whether full grown or not, we cannot particularly instruct you about; and on this head shall only observe, that prime male slaves generally sell best in the market. . . . When you consider that on the health of your slaves, almost your whole voyage depends . . . you will therefore particularly attend to smoking your vessel, washing her with vinegar, to the clarifying your water with lime or brimstone, and to cleanliness among your people, as well as among the slaves. . . ."

A prudent captain generally paid heed to these regulations with their false tone of humanitarianism. Often, however, especially after the decision of the Supreme Court of Massachusetts made the traffic illegal by abolishing slavery, conditions on the slavers were so inhuman, what with crowding and unsanitary quarters, that of a full hold of slaves not more than a third would arrive for the markets. Nevertheless the commerce proved so profitable that each seaport town had its brigs engaged in the brutal trade. In 1790, when the first census was taken, Massa-

The plague spot of the nation

chusetts alone of all the states in the Union returned only free persons.

"It is reported," Dr. William Bentley of Salem wrote in his diary in November of the same year, "that Sinclair (a slave trader) has returned from a Guinea voyage with a loss of all his crew. Notwithstanding the laws of the Commonwealth, there is not one man of spirit to stand forth and make inquiry into these detestable practices."

One man finally did stand forth, but only after the eighteenth century had closed and the nineteenth drew on toward the first thirty years. William Lloyd Garrison was only twenty-four when he sounded the call that roused the sleeping conscience of the nation. As a boy he had been a printer, but when in his young manhood he found he had much to say, he turned to writing. His earliest venture, in the anti-slavery paper of Benjamin Lundy in Baltimore, brought him a jail sentence for libel when he denounced a certain Mr. Todd for transporting a cargo of Negroes from Baltimore to New Orleans. Garrison's imprisonment roused New England. Whittier, Henry Clay, men and women who until then had given little thought to the question, found themselves taking sides with Garrison. On his release public sentiment was ready to listen.

He spoke, in the first issue of the *Liberator* that heralded the new year: "I am aware that many object to the severity of my language, but is there not cause for severity? I *will* be as harsh as truth, and as uncompromising as justice. On this subject I do not wish to think, or speak, or write, with moderation. No! no! Tell a man whose house is on fire to give a moderate alarm; tell him to moderately rescue his wife from the hands of the ravisher; tell the mother to gradually extricate her babe from the fire in which it has fallen—but urge me not to use moderation in a cause like the present. I am in earnest: I will not equivocate; I will not retreat a single inch—AND I WILL BE HEARD."

35

He was fearless and he spoke from his heart to the heart of the people. And he was heard. From his poor hole of an office in Boston that contained both his printing press and his bed, the *Liberator* went forth speaking for the millions inarticulate in their bondage. Samuel E. Sewall at once organized an anti-slavery group. Little by little other societies sprang up until they numbered in the hundreds, each becoming a working center for liberation. Lewis Tappan, Lucretia Mott, Whittier, labored indefatigably. The abolitionist movement became a force to cope with.

Immediately the opposition set up bulwarks of its own, not only in the slave-holding states of the South but in the North as well. For Garrison, with the impatience of the reformer, demanded the immediate and unconditional liberation of the Negroes. Tremendous interests were involved. In the first place the slave-owners would not willingly surrender property in man power worth millions of dollars. Besides, if they did free the slaves, what was to become of the emancipated hordes? If the Negroes were sent out of the country to found their own nation as some idealists proposed, where could the paid workers be found to take their place? Again, if they were allowed to roam at large who would provide for them—and who quell the insurrections that would surely break out?

As if in confirmation of their fears trouble loomed when Nat Turner of South Hampton succeeded in rousing a large following of slaves under the banner of revolt. Quickly and ruthlessly the insurrection was smashed. Together with seventeen of his unlucky followers Nat Turner was hanged. But he and his men did not die in vain. In the Virginia legislature a debate, carried on for several weeks as a result of the tragic incident, far from defending the position of the slave owners, exposed the evils of slavery, responsible for national disharmony.

Such agitations had their echo abroad. In Parliament, during the discussion of the bill proposing reform of the rotten borough system, Sir Robert Peel rose up and denounced it as a call to revolution. The people must not be given too much power. See what evils resulted in America! "The United States," he said, "has been rapidly undergoing a change from a republic to a mere democracy. The influence of the executive—the influence of the Government—has been daily becoming less, and more power has consequently been vested in the hands of the people."

Those in America who believed as he did called upon the legislatures for suppressive measures. So violent became the feeling against the Abolitionists that many states passed penal laws. Northern governors, like Edward Everett of Massachusetts and Marcy of New York, approved. The South posted rewards as for escaped criminals, for the apprehension of Garrison and Whittier. The *Liberator*, the *Freeman* in Philadelphia, and the New York *Emancipator* came out at the risk of their editors' lives. No Northerner of any prominence could any longer travel safely in the South. Almost daily the papers reported one or another arrested, flogged, imprisoned in a Southern state. Nor was hysteria less violent in cities comparatively unaffected by slavery. In Boston, Philadelphia, in Cincinnati and Utica, abolitionist meetings were broken up, private houses searched, public meeting halls burned, newspaper offices raided and destroyed. In New York the house of Lewis Tappan was sacked by angry mobs. In Cincinnati the office of the *Philanthropist* was wrecked. At Alton the Rev. Elijah P. Lovejoy was murdered for trying to save his press from destruction. Vainly young Abraham Lincoln, elected to the legislature of the state for the second time, condemned this atrocity and inveighed against the proslavery tendencies of Illinois. There, as in every state where slavery was an issue, violence left its trail of blood. In Boston itself Garrison was dragged through the streets at the end of a rope, and only by miracle escaped death when three sturdy supporters carried him to jail where alone he could be safe from the mob.

But from the blood of the martyrs, as persecution increased, the Abolitionists gathered strength in a struggle that was to last for more than thirty years. Each side claimed right for its own. At Faneuil Hall in Boston, at a meeting called to protest the violation of the principles of liberty in the murder of Lovejoy, the two views had a chance to be heard. Lovejoy, declared the Attorney-General of the state, James T. Austin, "died as the fool dieth." Those who killed him were, in his opinion, as great in their patriotism as the men who had dumped the tea into Boston harbor on another historic occasion.

Cheers came up from a large part of the house, cheers that turned to hooting when Wendell Phillips, young and untried, took his stand to answer him. For a long time the jeering persisted, but he held his ground, shouting above the noise until all were forced to listen. "When I heard," he commented on Austin's speech, "when I heard the gentleman lay down principles which placed the murderers . . . side by side with Otis and Hancock, with Quincy and Adams, I thought those pictured lips"—he turned toward the portraits round the hall—"would have broken into voice to rebuke the recreant American, the slanderer of the dead."

His words were shining swords, and it was with words that the Abolitionists carried on their fight. Although their violence was verbal only, they spared nothing, neither Church nor Constitution when either served the ends of injustice. "The nation was deaf in regard to the evils of slavery," explained the Boston sibyl, Margaret Fuller, "and those who have to speak to deaf people naturally acquire the habit of saying everything on a high key."

Poets, clergymen, men and women of good will with nothing to give but their passion for justice, which they would have defended with their lives, joined the abolitionists movement, pitting their spiritual strength against the moneyed interests of both North and South. With the poet Whittier, Longfellow and Bryant espoused the cause; Emerson devoted to it his best thought. Women like Lucy Stone, Lydya Maria Child, Abby Kelley and the two sisters Sarah and Angelina Grimké, left their homes to speak from public platforms, shocking convention but helping the fight. Fugitive slaves were brought there, and from faltering lips people learned the barbarities of slavery. Everywhere, in defiance of authority, the Abolitionists held their meetings, which terminated often in physical violence when the other side had no other argument to offer. Their platform was free for all, even for the slave-holder who could come there to defend slavery—and be answered with words that left him speechless. Gradually but inevitably, despite the good that the cause accomplished, the nation was being sundered.

How did Whitman respond to the talk he surely must have heard in the newspaper offices where he was employed in Brooklyn and, at sixteen, in New York? What side engaged his sympathies? Did he answer the pleas for slavery in the South, and did he sharpen his wits with potent arguments in the debating societies which he began attending so assiduously? With New York as one of the battlegrounds of the question, Walt must have participated in many a heated session.

In 1835 and part of the following year, he spent most of his time in New York. He had jobs as compositor in the printing offices, on and off, but the evenings were his. The doors of the playhouses that had always lured him became familiar places— the old Park Theatre on Park Row, the Bowery, the Broadway. Then he discovered Italian opera which was to be one of the deepest pleasures of his life. Conscientious and thorough, anxious to miss nothing, he would prepare himself for the performance as for a rite. There was nothing headlong about Walt, even in his enjoyments. Was it *Richard III* or *Lear* that the theater bill announced? Before curtain rise the cautious enthusiast would read the play carefully. Were they giving *Lucia*, from his cherished Scott, or Rossini's *William Tell* at the Park Theatre? He would read the English translation of the libretto. once and then again, that he might know what the long arias were about, and follow the gist of the complicated plots. He learned by heart long passages from Shakespeare, and the melodies of operatic favorites.

All of a sudden, at the height of his discovery of metropolitan culture, he returned to Long Island. Was he out of a job, or did he want to be nearer his family? His mother, after her illness, had given birth to her last child, Edward. He was a few years old when Walt returned home, but already one could see that he was not like other children. Scarlet fever, complicated by paralysis, had left him lame and in a retarded mental state. Louisa felt especially tender toward Eddie, as they called him, and Walt understood. With a peculiar desire to conceal the truth—was it from himself or to spare Louisa?—he convinced himself that Eddie was only crippled. Anyone else who saw the child knew that he was hopelessly feebleminded.

Walt did not remain long with his family but found himself a place teaching school in Norwich, one of the small villages on the Island. Within two years he had changed his situation five times. Teaching in a country school when one had pulsated to the rhythm of the biggest city in America had little attraction in itself and became less attractive for the fact that no matter how often one shifted, only the locale changed. Babylon or Long Swamp, Smithtown or Whitestone, the boys offered no novelty, the houses in which he "boarded around" remained the same. Lover of people that he was, however, Walt gained pleasure and experience from his contact with the simple folk with whom he lived and whose sons he taught according to his lights.

The boys liked him, though his ways of teaching struck them as peculiar. He did not go by the book. Instead, he would stand before the class and talk on the lesson, on books, or more often

WALT WHITMAN AT TWENTY-ONE
From an old newspaper clipping

"The rather long-faced, dreamy-looking youth . . . with side-whiskers and a wispy chin-beard . . . could hardly be called a political gladiator."

about the things he had seen or done. Never strict with his boys, some of whom were nearly his own age, he managed nonetheless to maintain discipline. "Did I say he had his own notions how to punish a scholar?" I. A. Platt recalled after Walt was famous. "If he caught a boy lying he exposed him before the whole school in a story. But the story was told without the mention of any names. No punishment beyond that. He had such a way of telling his story that the guilty fellow knew who was meant." It was good psychology and certainly advanced for the times. Walt, the country schoolteacher, had his first trial at innovation.

Whenever he could, and it was often, he went to West Hills and about his beloved Paumanok. Usually he took a book with him, fiction chiefly, for since his first taste of Scott and Cooper, he had become an omnivorous novel reader. Shakespeare whom he had seen brought to life by the magic of the stage he loved and studied. At about this time a volume of Jefferson's writings also fell into his hands; through it and his reading of Paine, the liberal ideas among which he had grown, imperceptibly gained clarification. He was struggling to find himself.

In spite of his more or less steady employment people regarded him as an indolent fellow. Accustomed as they were to the dawn-to-sundown life of the farmer, they could not understand why a hale young man should suddenly drop the fork with which he was helping in the fields, and wander off to lie on his back, to gaze at the sky for hours together. It was unnatural. In the schoolroom, too, he had fits of abstraction that puzzled his pupils. "He warn't in his element," Sanford Brown, a farmer's son remembered. "He was always musin' and writin', 'stead of tending to his proper dooties. But I guess he was like a good many on us—not very well off, and he had to do somethin' for a livin'. But schoolteachin' was not his forte," he added, using a word he had probably learned from Walt. Yes, folks used to say he was idling when he lay out in the fields.

"But I guess he was then workin' with his brain, and thinkin' hard."

Walt was indeed thinking hard. As he sat by a stream fishing, or as he stared at the clouds floating overhead, his thoughts were occupied by an absorbing ambition. It was well enough to teach school and awaken young minds; but there were other minds he wished to reach. The scraps of paper he filled in the schoolroom, the penciled notes pinned together which he carried in his pockets, had germs of ideas that sought expression. Nothing stupendous, nothing even original. They were only such ideas as might find space in a little country newspaper. But even that meant a public.

He must have saved his salary and obtained help besides, for one day in the summer of 1838 he went to New York and bought a small printing press and type. Back in Long Island, he also acquired a horse. With what assistance he could muster in the unsophisticated district of Huntington he started a weekly newspaper which he named *The Long Islander*.

He was like a mother with a firstborn. He wrote, he edited, he set the type himself, and when the edition was ready, he gave a whole day and a night to distributing it through the neighboring villages. It was an ideal life. During the week he worked upon his paper, out in the open as much as possible. Then on Saturdays, mounting his horse, he distributed the bundles through Babylon and Jericho, in Smithtown and Comac, places with names in which their history was implicit, the history of God-loving farmers, simple in their faith, rugged in their living. They learned to expect their editor at the close of each week. In one village Mrs. Brown would prepare such a dinner as she knew the hearty young man would like, with plenty of meat and a pie still warm from the oven. In another a goodwife would make some special tidbit. Plain but large, their hospitality enfolded him like a comfortable old coat. He could be Walt to them, a rough ready fellow like the rest, whom they could invite to the hayfield or for rides through the brush. Then, too, there were occasional evenings, and the girls.

He liked to be with them, but as mothers of marriageable daughters could not help noticing, he paid no particular attention to them. His brother George, like all inquisitive younger members of the family, saw it too, and so did his pupil, Platt. "The girls did not seem to attract him. He did not specially go anywhere with them or show any extra fondness for their society," he recalled. George corroborated him almost word for word. "I never knew Walt to fall in love with young girls . . . He did not seem to affect the girls."

Parsifal or Launcelot? A "pure fool" or an honorable knight for whom life held in wait some overmastering Guinevere? However it was, Walt, for the time being, found in the uneventful execution of his duties all that he required without engaging his heart. Nevertheless he sensed in his way of living a lack which expressed itself in an indeterminate yearning for someone to share his capacity for love. He longed for a human being other than his mother on whom to fix his affection—it mattered not whether man or woman. A curious sexlessness entered his desire, as much of the spirit as of the body, a circumstance extraordinary in a healthy youth of twenty. Unconscious suggestions of the anomaly forced themselves upon his attention, and as is usual with sensitive spirits, he sought expression outside the medium of everyday prose, which would have put too baldly what he but vaguely understood. Not that what he now began writing could have been dignified with the name of poetry even by the most indulgent. Whatever his models, they were not to be found in the thousand-page volume of Scott, nor in Shakespeare and the Bible. Their lachrymose sentimentality usually closed the last column of the last page of the newspapers whose editors felt that journalism, as well as life, had need of a drop of poetry in it.

O mighty powers of Destiny!

invoked the plaintive Walt with proper deference to abstraction—

When from this coil of flesh I'm free
When through my second life I rove,
Let me but find one heart to love
As I would wish to love. . . .

For vainly through this world below
We seek affection. Nought but woe
Is with our earthly journey wove;
And so the heart must look above
Or die in dull despair.

To die in dull despair was assuredly a drastic alternative for a young man who had not yet seen enough of life to look above for compensation to disillusionment. Outwardly, as everyone could see, from his family to James Brenton whom he was now helping with the publication of the *Long Island Democrat*, he led a healthy though not too energetic existence, full of sunlight and air and plenty of time for himself. His own *Long Islander*, which for nearly a year he had published with success and even profit, he gave up as suddenly as he had started it. He found it more to his liking to continue teaching school and publishing his occasional "shies at poetry" in another man's paper.

Mr. Breton, nicknamed "Dr. Franklin," was not too exacting an employer, albeit he could have wished that Walt spent more time in the typesetting room instead of loafing under the apple trees or with his legs stretched out in Mrs. Breton's living room where she could not pass him without stumbling. For it never occurred to Walt in his abstraction to remove his feet from the way of a bustling housewife. His mother had always let him be, having learned early that it was easier to walk round that monument in her parlor than to expect it to remove itself.

44

The plague spot of the nation

Walt's verses which appeared from time to time in the *Long Island Democrat* became, if possible, more tearful and undistinguished than his complaint to Destiny, which had also found hostage in its pages. With the lugubriousness of the graveyard poets who had wearied a generation with their complaints on the futility of existence Walt, finding no satisfaction for his yearning, dwelt on the thought of death. It was beautiful death, heart-easing death, the cure for the "many sights of woe" that filled the earth. Even though his vital nature would have resisted any threat of extinction with every fiber of that splendid body, Walt invited:

> So welcome, death; whene'er the time
> That the dread summons must be met,
> I'll yield without one pang of awe,
> Or sigh, or vain regret.

Indeed, said he on paper, he would welcome the final rest as would a child who, weary of roaming through field and wood all day,

> throws him sleepy, tired and sore
> Upon his bed and rests him there,
> His pain and trouble o'er.

He enjoyed imagining the circumstances of his demise. Not in a rich bed, not amid the thunder crash of war, but out in the open would he wish to die, at the close of day, in a place where "sweet shrubs grow."

> At distance through the opening trees,
> A bay by misty vapours curled,
> I'd gaze upon, and think the haven
> For which to leave the fleeting world.

Tentatively Walt was giving voice to the mystery of the sea's message, whispered long ago to the heart-stilled child. But what a travesty of the meaning, what a false rendering of the true song! Never had poet made a more unpromising beginning.

Chapter V: Transcendentalism

BOSTON, the recognized mother of culture in America, had been groping for nearly a quarter of a century for the lever with which to raise the materialism of the post-Revolutionary era and make the world look upward. It found it in Transcendentalism. The word itself was to remain unintelligible to the masses, but very early its influence became as pervasive in the life of the spirit as the light of the sun in the physical world. Boston was proud. Boston's Brahmins held up their heads a little higher. Boston intellects exerted themselves more than ever for the further uplifting of humanity.

Like all growths Transcendentalism sprang from a minute seed—a deviation of interest on the part of the scholars from the prevailingly classical orientation of the previous century to an awareness of new philosophical currents of thought in Germany. To a knowledge of Plato and Aquinas they now added a familiarity with Kant and Hegel. German became the coming language of the schools, and German philosophical mysticism, strained through the intellects of Coleridge and Carlyle, the nectar of the Transcendentalists. A school, without being formed, made itself felt.

In 1824 George Bancroft, fresh from the German universities, published in the recently founded *North American Review* his translations of Schiller and Goethe. They were only the minor poems of the two literary titans. But Boston's expert minds needed no more than to sample a drop to know the true vintage. By 1831 interest in German had grown so great that Harvard College created a professorship in the language and its literature. Other colleges followed its example. They were not, however, as fortunate as Harvard, which boasted as the representative of the new thought Professor Charles Follen, a political refugee from Germany, and in himself symbolic of the unfettered intellect. Believing in his mission Professor Follen not only indoctrinated the Harvard students but spread his views among the people of Boston in a series of crowded lectures. The hungry sheep, this time, looked up and were fed.

Before long not only the lecture rooms but the press and the breakfast table sounded with the names of Kant and Jacobi, Fichte and Novalis, Schelling and Hegel, Schleiermacher and De Wette. Social conditions received a goodly share of criticism, their very virtues stigmatized as but the shadows of the light that might be. Transcendentalism captured the imagination. Everywhere, at first in cultivated New England, and then farther afield, people were giving it thought.

"They see," Margaret Fuller explained, "that political freedom does not necessarily produce liberality of mind; nor freedom in church institutions, vital religion. And seeing that these changes cannot be wrought from without inward, they are trying to quicken the soul, that they may work from within outward. Disgusted with the vulgarity of a commercial aristocracy, they become radicals; disgusted with the materialistic working of a rational religion, they become mystics. They quarrel with all that is, because it is not spiritual enough."

And Margaret Fuller knew what the movement implied. Although she wrote comparatively little for publication, her indefatigable pen kept the fertilizing idea flying through the mails to her hosts of correspondents, while her equally tireless tongue plumbed what seemed unfathomable subtleties in the classroom and the popular *conversazioni* where people enjoyed meeting to exchange ideas. Short, fat, decidedly unattractive, Margaret Fuller nevertheless set herself up as the high vestal of the fire of learning, of which Emerson was the Apollo. In her opinion the flame could not soar but through her feeding of it. She showed her pride in her trust in the very way she held her head, in the startling opening and shutting of her eyes, which often made her listeners stare at her more with alarm than with admiration. She would leave none in doubt of her importance. "There are . . ." she said, "in every age a few in whose lot the meaning of that age is concentrated. I feel I am one of those persons. . . . I feel chosen among women."

Working in her own unmethodical way Margaret Fuller did more perhaps than any other individual except Emerson toward stimulating interest in the movement and spreading the idea which soon began to mean all things to all men. Emerson, never a blind follower of any cult, found in it the springboard of his faith in the dawn of a spiritual awakening. To George Ripley, William Channing, Theodore Parker, F. H. Hedge and others of their aspiring humanitarianism, it provided an instrument toward the building of a more equitable social order. To the common people the transcendental wine, diluted with the waters of Spurzheim's popular phrenology, gave a mild exaltation in themselves and their potentialities. Faith in self, from its Emersonian summit to its subsequent vulgarization in the phrenological cabinets that sprang up everywhere, became the watchword of the idealist movement. One and all plunged into the exhilarating current in which Swedenborg and Spurzheim, Carlyle and Fowler, Coleridge and the merest charlatan, swam happily together. Imperceptibly, however, the world was absorbing the doctrine of the godlike quality of the human spirit.

Although much had been said and written since the first glimmering of Transcendentalism, it was not till 1837 that its meaning had rung across the the country in the accents of its ex-officio leader. Originally a minister known to a select coterie of admirers for his courage and independent thinking, Ralph Waldo Emerson had forsaken the pulpit because he differed with the orthodox in the observance of the communion service and could not therefore continue to administer the rite. While alienating many, his intransigent sincerity won him the esteem of a wider public. After a stay abroad where he communed with the master spirits of the Old World, he returned stronger than ever in his belief that man's soul must make its way untrammeled by tradition. Instead of the pulpit he mounted the dais, to speak on the philosophy of history, the conduct of life, on humanity, heroism and the meaning of culture. From Unitarianism he escaped to the Transcendental.

He delivered his message with great personal charm which helped to carry over the ennobling precepts he never wearied of reiterating. As he stood behind the lectern, a plain, lanky figure, his otherwise cold face made human by the glint of humor in his eyes, he looked a homely Prometheus, bearing the spark for the intellectual hearth. First in Boston and then throughout the country, when he began to publish his small but all-encompassing volumes, his philosophy made itself known. It was Transcendentalism, but passed through his highly original mind and weighed in the balance of a profound culture that knew no limits for its expansion.

He had no self-consciousness in speaking of the soul; he was on familiar terms with the oracle within. So could all men be, he promised, would they but realize the high powers, the dignity, of that source of all knowledge and all truth. In their mystical aspects the philosophy of the New England sage and the religion of the Jericho Quaker wore one and the same garb. But here the likeness ended. For to Emerson the soul was the backbone of the individual, the keystone of the temple of self-reliance. Strengthened by it, man could behold the facts of the universe, bring them to coherence, and help construct a better future; he could nourish cheerful hope and hurl in the teeth of unbelief the reality of the good, the true and the beautiful. Simply, piquantly, often with rare beauty, he translated the abstruse doctrine into human terms for all to grasp. The soul left its lofty seat to mingle with humanity which learned to seek "an ampler ether, a diviner air."

Quite early Emerson had shaken off the cerements of the past and the reverence for all that had come from Europe in culture and in life. Transcendentalism for him must wear the domestic homespun. In the epoch-making lecture, "The American Scholar" which he delivered on the 31st of August, 1837, for Cambridge, he spoke without faltering. Still more plainly he repeated his message a year later at Dartmouth. The man of the New World must forsake the empty ways of classical and European tradition; he must take his place in the front ranks of the tumultuous army of the doers and workers; he must leave the ivory tower and come down to earth; he must *do* as well as dream, and he must think for himself. "Our day of dependence, our long apprenticeship to the learning of other lands, draws to a close. Neither Greece nor Rome, nor the three unities of Aristotle, nor the three kings of Cologne, nor the College of the Sorbonne, nor the *Edinburgh Review,* is to command any longer." It was heresy, but what daring, what sublime heresy! "Let him not quit his belief that a pop-gun is a pop-gun," he said in homelier terms, "though the ancient and honorable of the earth affirm it to be the crack of doom!"

Trust in himself and faith in the good of Nature: with these two man could be the master of the universe. In his addresses, in his writings, in his advice to his disciples, Emerson repeated his credo, with a conviction so fervent that his thoughts took wing and soared, and his prose came as poetry. "Whilst a man seeks good ends, he is strong by the whole strength of Nature. . . . Character is always known; thefts never enrich; alms never impoverish; murder will speak out of stone walls. The least admixture of a lie . . . will instantly vitiate the effect. But speak the truth, and all Nature and all spirits help you with unexpected furtherance. Speak the truth, and all things, alive or brute, are vouchers; and the very roots of the grass underground there do seem to stir and move to bear you witness."

But always, whether in the same or in different words, he exhorted and continued to exhort, "Trust thyself: every heart vibrates to that iron string," making each listener believe that "Every man is a divinity in disguise."

Whatever the deep convulsions that shook American society, a wave of reform swept the country through the early 'forties, luminous at the crest with the struggle of democracy in the Abolitionist movement, and for spiritual values in Transcendentalism, and carrying at its ebb the temperance and salvation societies active in every metropolis. Each man saw according to his sight, some envisioning a practicable Utopia in communistic experiments such as Dr. George Ripley's in West Roxbury, others deeming it best to clear the foundations of prostitution and similar evils before sinking the cornerstone of the new edifice. Brook Farm or the missions at Five Points, each represented a link in the great chain of democratic unity.

With such ferment in the air, no wonder Walt Whitman, schoolmaster and journalist, was seized with the general intoxication for reform. He need not have read Emerson to be filled with the transcendental spirit which went beyond the written word, no more than it was necessary for him to attend the experience meetings of the Washingtonian delegation— the first of its kind in the United States—for him to form his own opinions of drunkenness. In his usual easy pace he taught his boys in Jamaica or Woodbury, and wrote his articles for Mr. Brenton's paper. He felt mature and responsible with his two jobs, and the better to impress the public, he adopted his first costume.

An old newspaper clipping preserves the looks of the twenty-one year old Walt for posterity. The rather long-faced, dreamy-looking youth whose hair half covers his collar, with side whiskers and a wispy chin-beard coming to a point at his knotted cravat, can hardly be called a political gladiator, or for that matter a gladiator of any sort. His lips, full and sensual, are uncovered. The eyes, almond-shaped and slightly out of alignment, look out dully, and are surmounted by arched, quizzical, dark, not too full brows. The long wide-nostriled nose is the only strong feature in that strangely lackadaisical face. He is wearing a black felt hat, which leaves uncovered his mixed dark and light hair. A black, slope-shouldered suit, the collar, cravat and the cane he carries mark him, of all unsuitable roles, a dandy, more likely to be encountered on the sidewalks of Broadway than in the quiet meadows of Long Island.

Mr. Brenton, perhaps out of regard for Walt's bearded looks, allowed him a few columns of space in the *Democrat* in which the young man could write as he pleased. Walt assumed a gently didactic personality. Under the heading "Sun-down Papers —From the Desk of a Schoolmaster," he proceeded to set his readers right in their way of living, delivered gentle sermons, but more often took them into his confidence on his outward life and inner aspirations. For the seeds had been planted within him, and the slow, too slow, germination had set in. Dull, sometimes, sloppily written and occasionally boring, his articles nonetheless foreshadow *Leaves of Grass* as the living embryo the mature man.

At first, taking his magisterial role seriously, he was chiefly the reformer, pointing the dangers of indulgent habits. "Amidst the universal excitement . . ." he wrote in the issue of April 28, 1840, "with regard to the evils created by ardent spirits, it seems to have been forgotten that there are other, and almost as injurious, kinds of intemperance. The practice of using tobacco, in any shape, is one of these." Gravely he expatiated on the theme; then, like a father who would temper his reproof with a smile, he ended with a pun. "It has been said by some satirical individual, that a fishing rod is a thing with a hook at one extremity and a fool at the other: it may with much more truth be affirmed, that a segar, generally has a *smoky fire* at one end, and a *conceited spark* on the other. . . ."

Tobacco, wenching, alcohol, even tea and coffee called forth

52

his paternal admonitions. Gradually, however, the desk of the schoolmaster found him penning articles on subjects close to his heart. He had tasted printer's ink and had found it good. He had also discovered in it a permanence that far outlasted monuments of marble and bronze. He dreamed, and while dreaming, outstripped his own ambitions. "I think," he confided to his readers on September 29, 1840, "that if I should make pretensions to be a philosopher . . . I would compose a wonderful and ponderous book. Therein should be treated on, the nature and peculiarities of men, the diversity of their characters, the means of improving their state, and the proper mode of governing nations. . . ."

Here were the first womb-stirrings of the plan of *Leaves of Grass*, to its very details. Was it too large a dream for a young schoolmaster? Perhaps. "Nobody, I hope," he forestalled, "will accuse me of conceit in these opinions of mine own capacity for doing great things. In good truth, I think the world suffers from this much-bepraised modesty. Who should be a better judge of a man's talents than himself? . . . Yes, I *would* write a book! And who shall say that it might not be a very pretty book? Who knows but that I might do something very respectable?"

But Walt was no Bryant who could produce his greatest poem in his youth. He needed time and the light of revelation, albeit the first gleams struck so early on his vision. Confidence in his powers was already his, that confidence which the world was to mistake for egotism. But he knew enough not to trust it too much, or to give it such free rein that fame became the goal, and not achievement. Some months earlier he had expressed himself in verse on the theme.

> Shall I build up a lofty name,
> 'And seek to have the nations know
> What conscious might dwells in the brain
> That throbs aneath this brow?

Easily could he build up that name, he implied; but was the

praise of the populace worth it? Was it worth their deafening shouts?

> Fame, O what happiness is lost
> In hot pursuit of thy false glare!
> Thou, whose drunk votaries die to gain
> A puff of viewless air!

No, not for him such vanity. Better to let him rein in his Pegasus till it could fly toward something worthier than a puff of air.

So for the present he continued teaching school while setting down the outlines of what was to be the gospel according to Walt Whitman. He did not wish for riches in his scheme of life. "It is a very dangerous thing to be rich," he warned in the same article that confessed his ambitions for authorship. "Life . . . is a long journey. . . . What wise man thinks of cumbering up this journey with an immense mass of luggage? . . . There is no freight car to the hidden land."

Rather than acquire wealth he would loaf, looking at the world and his fellows and treasuring the joys without price that his loafing brought his soul. "How I do love a loafer!" he exclaimed. "Of all human beings, none equals your genuine, inbred, unvarying loafer. . . . All the old philosophers were loafers. . . . What was Adam, I should like to know, but a loafer? . . . Who dare aver that he dealt in stocks, or was busy in the sugar line? . . . There have always been loafers. . . . Without any doubt, when Chaos had his acquaintance *cut*, and the morning stars sang together, and the little rivers danced a cotillion for pure fun—there were loafers somewhere about, enjoying the scene in all their accustomed philosophic quietude. . . ." Even before he invented his famous phrase Walt knew how to loaf and invite his soul.

One emotion was ever active in him, his love of his fellows; and that love he wished all men to have for one another. True,

54

it may have been one with the humanitarian tendencies of the times, but with Walt it was a doctrine so personal as to be almost part of himself, like his very heart. "I would have men cultivate their dispositions for kindness to all around," he said in July of the following year. "I would have them foster and cherish the faculty of love. To be sure it may not bring in a percentage like bank stock, or corporation scrip, or bonds and mortgages, but it is very valuable, and will pay many fold. It is a faculty given to every human soul, though in most it is dormant and used not. . . . It leads us to scorn the cold and heartless limits of custom, but moves our souls to swell up with pure and glowing love for persons or communities." But let none interpret such love to be the currently fashionable languishment of the romancers. "By 'love' as I have used the term . . ." he hastened to explain, "I do not mean the sickly sentimentality which is so favorite a theme with novelists and magazine writers. What I would inculcate is that healthy, cheerful feeling of kindness and good will, an affectionate tenderness, a warmheartedness, the germs of which are plentifully sown by God in each human breast; and which contribute to form a state of feeling very different from the puerile, moping love, painted by such trashy writers as Byron and Bulwer, and their more trashy imitators."

His scornful lashing of the older writers betrayed the youth. So early, however, he had formulated that love which, after he had learned the language of the phrenologist, he was to call *adhesiveness,* the love of comrades. Stammering and prosaic, the true Whitman accents were yet unmistakable. One theme was still lacking to complete Walt's gospel, the theme of patriotism with its concomitant of democracy. That too lay hidden in the pages of the *Long Island Democrat.*

> O my soul is drunk with joy,
> And my inmost heart is glad,

he rhapsodized in his "Columbian's Song,"

> To think my country's star will not
>   Through endless ages fade,
> That on its upward glorious course
>   Our red-eyed eagle leaps,
> While with the ever moving winds,
>   Our dawn-striped banner sweeps:
> That here at length is found
>   A wide extending shore,
> Where Freedom's starry gleam,
> Shines with unvarying beam;
>   Not as it did of yore
> With flickering flash, when Caesar fell,
> Or haughty Gesler heard his knell,
>   Or Stuart rolled in gore.

No link with the bloody past of Europe would Walt admit in America's forging of democracy. Freedom's starry gleam, from the moment it had broken upon the young Republic revealed to the world a fact as new and wonderful as had been the discovery of the western continent. On that fact Walt was to feed his undying faith in democratic America. Though separated by birth and culture, the sage of Concord and the carpenter's son of West Hills had arrived at the same hope.

But Whitman, with subliminal wisdom, knowing himself unready, let the hope grow hidden and unexpressed till the time should come.

THE NEW ORLEANS WOMAN?
From a tintype in a Whitman notebook, Library of Congress

"One knows that such a mouth, such eyes and hair, must have come with a skin of 'rich olive.'"

Chapter VI: The politician and the artist

B ESIDES, Walt had begun to take an active part in politics. He was a full-fledged citizen now, entitled to cast his first vote. Even the fault-finding Mrs. Brenton could have had little to say about her boarder's laziness in the fall of the year 1840.

Like his father Walt was a Democrat, of the party of the "sainted Jefferson" and of grand Old Hickory who in spite of the disastrous bank failures which the opposition blamed on him, had left office an even more popular man than when he had come in. To Walt the Democratic party, the party of the Locofocos, as the Whigs nicknamed it, stood for whatever was noble and progressive in the republican form of government. Jackson embodied its greatest virtues, Jackson, the "terrible old man" whom the Whig moneyed interests abominated but whom the people adored.

Of course there had been much to criticize in his sweeping methods soon after he entered the White House, but the corruption he destroyed, as he had destroyed other more material enemies of the republic, had smelled to heaven. Many had found his unrelenting ferocity toward the United States Bank destructive to business. Certainly the bank had made vast loans to commerce and agriculture; but it had also lent as freely to speculators, till inflation showed its plethoric bulk in almost every enterprise. Jackson, clearsighted where others blinked, saw the bank as an unhealthy corporation and a dangerous political engine and determined to crush it by withdrawing from it all government funds. "No power on earth—so help me God!" he solemnly swore, "shall control the key to the nation's funds but the United States government itself."

57

For his pains Old Hickory, through Mr. Clay's indignant eloquence, found himself written down in the Senate books in a
resolution of censure as having "assumed upon himself authority and power not conferred by the constitution and laws, but
in derogation of both." In vain he protested; his enemies for
a time proved stronger than himself. They almost justified
themselves to the nation in the panic of 1837 when banks failed
all over the States and depression settled its lethargic length
over all enterprise. He was no longer in office, but his friends
still fought against the injustice done him. The very year of
the panic Senator Thomas H. Benton put through the Senate,
after three years of futile endeavor, the famous Expunging Resolution, vindicating Jackson against the condemnatory sentence.
It could not have made him more popular than he was with his
loyal supporters. To them as to Walt, then and as long as he
lived, Old Hickory remained "true gold . . . unmined, un-
forged, unanything, in fact—anything wholly done, completed
—just the genuine ore in the rough."

It was therefore to be expected that Walt should throw himself on the side of Van Buren, renominated by the Democrats,
against General William Henry Harrison.—What! did the
Whigs think they had another Old Hickory in him?—The
eager young Democrat mounted the stump to speak for Little
Van in Queen's County. It was no easy contest. President Van
Buren had inherited Jackson's worries as well as his office, and
by the unreasoning logic of the multitude, was held equally
responsible with his predecessor for the depression that had tied
up the nation during his own administration. Even the three
thousand miles of railroad where none had been before Jackson
came to office, militated against Little Van by transporting thousands of his political opponents from all over the country, to
speak and electioneer in Harrison's interest. In fact, in May of
that year, no fewer than twenty thousand Whigs collected in
Baltimore, to mass their strength for their candidate. Another

era had dawned in national politics. No more scanty local meetings. From now on, thanks to the greater mobility made possible by the railroads, the gatherings were to number in the hundreds of thousands in the vital centers of the nation.

Walt, however, as a tyro in his party, exercised his robust legs in his county, and addressed the ears of his fellow Long Islanders. The Whigs, unfortunately, in spite of the temperance reform, offered more potent arguments, suggested indirectly by the Democrats themselves in one of their leading papers when they mocked: "If someone would present Harrison with a barrel of cider he would sit down on a log content and happy the rest of his days." Immediately the log cabin and the hard cider barrel became the emblems of the Whig campaign. Floats passed through the towns with miniature log cabins upon them, while at the street corners barrels ran with more infectious enthusiasm than even that fiery orator, Webster, could inspire. "Tippecanoe, and Tyler too," rang the Whig war cry, against which Little Van could show only the record of a not too prosperous administration. The middle States almost unanimously gave their majorities to General Harrison. With their cider barrels and their songs about the Eagle of Tippecanoe the Whigs succeeded in bringing about a virtual revolution when, with the election of Harrison, they broke the forty-year tenure of the Democratic party.

In the disappointing outcome Walt enjoyed one small personal triumph. The town in which he had fought, during the campaign, an acrimonious debate with the Whig son of Rufus King for attacking the Democratic Party, remained staunchly by Van Buren.

Alas, the Whig victory proved all too short-lived, like their president. It rained on inauguration day. The aged general caught cold and took to his bed. Day in and day out the office seekers clamored at the door of the sickroom, giving him no peace. The cold proved to be pneumonia. A month after enter-

59

ing office the Eagle of Tippecanoe died, as much a victim of the politicians as of the deadly germ. Vice-President Tyler succeeded him, and for a time matters proceeded as the Whigs desired. When, however, the subject came up of re-chartering the old United States Bank, they were hardly prepared for Tyler's decision. The measure had passed both Houses by a close vote. What was the consternation of the Whigs when Tyler vetoed it! Disillusioned, they had no choice but to withdraw their support from the administration they had floated into office on rivers of hard cider.

Alive to the new developments, Walt left the limited boundaries of Queen's County for New York where, in the spring of 1841, he edited the *Aurora*, a small factional paper in which the political-minded young editor aired views irritating to the more conservative citizens. Fairminded, he now supported the much-hated Tyler.

Tammany, meanwhile, had found Walt a valuable worker. He had shown results in his electioneering. Moreover he could wield a pen, and occasionally make speeches. Indeed, Walt began harboring a secret hankering for the platform. He had an imposing presence and a good voice, and he had ideas which he thought worth expressing. The party may have given him more than one opportunity to raise his voice in its behalf, but the record of only one of the political speeches he delivered has survived—not from the platform, but from the soapbox.

On the 29th of July, 1841, Tammany called a mass meeting in the Park to hearten its cohorts. Ten thousand persons listened to the call, among them the reporter of the *New Era* who, pleased with the address of Walt Whitman, quoted it in part. Brief and to the point, it ended on an inspirational note: "We are battling for great principles—for mighty and glorious truths. I would scorn to exert even my humble efforts for the best democratic candidate that ever was nominated, in himself alone . . . The guardian spirit, the good genius who has attended us ever since the days of Jefferson, has not now forsaken us. I can almost fancy myself able to pierce the darkness of the future and behold her looking down upon us with those benign smiles she wore in 1828, '32, '36 . . . Again will she hover over us, encouraging us amid the smoke and din of battle, and leading us to our wonted victory." Yes, there was fervor, together with statistics. Yet there was too a genuine idealism breaking through the cloudy rhetoric of the political speaker, an idealism confirmed by the name of Jefferson which like that of God, Walt would not have taken in vain.

The city once more engulfed him. No longer a boy, he entered into its storms and excitements with the urgency of his vigorous manhood, yet not, on the physical plane, without that caution which, like the guiding compass of the mariner, oriented his life toward the safer shores. Incapacity or timidity? Which of the two prudently held him in check? To his friends, years later, he held up a lusty god proliferating the earth, a prodigy who, in his words dictated to John Burroughs, had "sounded all the experiences of life, with all their passions, pleasures and abandonments." He was young and in perfect bodily condition, he explained, and New York offered plenty of opportunity.

No doubt like all youths independent of family ties and eager for experience, he tried his manhood as occasion presented itself. He would have been indeed abnormal had he not done so. But it was a far cry from the curious nocturnal adventurer to the all-fructifying Zeus of an unconvincing legend. To begin with, Whitman was at that time ridden by a highly developed moral purpose than manifested itself in everything he said or wrote. Considering his devotion to his mother, her image could not but have interposed itself between him and his temptations. Again, the Whitman of twenty-two was no rebel but a conformist, adhering with as much outward decorum as the most hide-

61

bound citizen to the moral code of his day. Walt Whitman, the opposer of conventions, the revolutionary, had yet to be born.

There was still another curb. Physically sound though he was, with a magnificence of body that an athlete might have envied, Whitman had also the tenderness of a woman and a woman's yearning to give and take affection with no thought of ultimate physical fulfillment. His desire rose above sex. Whether love were passion or friendship, a woman's or a man's, the fact of its being satisfied his need. In his tentative probing of his psychological makeup he had already discovered its essence. To him the Byronic storm and stress of passion were as alien as the mawkish sentimentality of the ladylike writers whose sighs and tears filled the magazines. Nothing excessive entered into his understanding of the emotion, nothing weak or sickly. Love as he knew it was as life-giving as air. "A healthy, cheerful feeling of kindness and good will," the schoolmaster had called it, "an affectionate tenderness, a warmheartedness." A spiritual emotion, it was not shared solely by men and women in the accepted romantic reciprocity, but equally by all men and all women. No boundaries existed, but like the light of heaven, it was for all humanity.

In that light he basked wherever he found it, whether among the bus drivers of the many lines that threaded their way through the city, or with the chance acquaintance, the woman who thought that love could be bought and sold. Not till long afterward did he put into words the all-inclusiveness of his doctrine of love in his verses "To a Common Prostitute." Already however, he was practicing it.

Be composed—be at ease with me—I am Walt Whitman, liberal and lusty as Nature,
Not till the sun excludes you do I exclude you,
Not till the waters refuse to glisten for you and the leaves to rustle for you, do my words refuse to glisten and rustle for you.

It was this spirituality, which made even the lowest partake of the bountifulness of love, that gave the lie to Whitman, the sounder of life's "passions and abandonments"—except in his imagination. More often his communion with the actual mate was deferred to a more perfect future.

My girl I appoint with you an appointment, and I charge you that
    you make preparation to be worthy to meet me,
And I charge you that you be patient and perfect till I come.
Till then I salute you with a significant look that you do not forget
    me.

As his political activities, labors of civic devotion, brought no financial returns, Walt began writing for the magazines. Good names appeared in the contemporary reviews, Lowell's, Whittier's, Longfellow's. Edgar Allan Poe had first attracted notice through the prize he won for a story in a competition. Not long since he had published his *Tales of the Grotesque and Arabesque*; he was now a contributor to the newly established *Graham's Magazine*, a periodical of high literary pretensions. In Boston the *Dial*, the organ of the Transcendentalists, had been launched with Margaret Fuller at the helm. Only the initiated gained admittance to its pages, but their word, at least wherever the *Dial* was read, spelled law. Bronson Alcott enlightened himself, if not the world, with his "Orphic Sayings"; Margaret Fuller gave a piece of her mind to critics; Theodore Parker expatiated on "The Divine Presence in Nature and the Soul"; Emerson contributed his poem, "The Problem," his essays finding wider circulation in the volume of 1841. Nathaniel Hawthorne had made his literary debut with the extraordinary stories that for a number of years had been appearing anonymously in the *Token*, till Park Benjamin revealed the incognito by mentioning the author by name in the *American Monthly* and bestowing upon him unprecedented praise when he pronounced him the equal of Washington Irving. The year Walt was making his political speech in the Park, Hawthorne, pitchfork in hand, was attacking a hill of manure to which, for the good of his soul, Dr. Ripley had set him in the Brook Farm paradise. Out on the Pacific, Herman Melville, exactly Walt's age, was absorbing materials for his masterpiece, on a year-long whaling cruise. Not many months earlier Dana had stirred up interest in the sea with his lusty *Two Years Before the Mast*. James Fenimore Cooper, involved in endless lawsuits, brought out his novels of adventure with astounding regularity. He had recently published *The Pathfinder* and *The Deerslayer*. Walt saw him in a court room in Chambers Street, and thrilled at sight of the man who had brought to his boyhood the first glimpse of American romance.

Every day, however, the nation was living its own adventures. For years, since Jackson's expeditions in Florida, wars had broken out intermittently with the various Indian tribes. With undemocratic ruthlessness the government shifted whole populations of natives from place to place, causing the death of thousands on the way. Indian champions spoke up against such cruelty, and when they were not heard, resorted to action. Like an unspent fire the Seminole's rancor flared in rebellion and was quenched in blood, as troop after troop was sent to Florida. In 1835 the war resumed a serious aspect when chief Osceola's wife, the daughter of a slave, had been seized in his absence and returned to her mother's master. From that moment Osceola vowed vengeance on the white usurper. Gathering his tribe together, he opposed with violence the government's removal of the Seminoles west of the Mississippi. A treaty was offered, but on the continued quibbling of the agents the enraged chief drove his knife into the table and swore: "The next treaty I will execute with this." He lived up to his oath to the letter. General Wiley Thompson seized him and put him in chains. With his own hands, after regaining his freedom, Osceola scalped him. Major Dade, who was leading an expedition from Tampa Bay was ambushed at Wahoo Swamp with a loss of nearly all his men. Hardly a year passed from then on without some outbreak, aggravated when the Creeks in Georgia and Alabama united with the Seminoles against the white settlers. By 1841, when the Indians had been brought somewhat under control, the government sadly computed that the cost of the wars, so far, had been more than forty million dollars—twice the amount paid for Florida and Louisiana together.

To compensate for such losses the United States engaged in constructive enterprise, as when, in August of 1838, Commander Charles Wilkes raised the American flag over his little squadron in the harbor of Norfolk, Virginia, on the first exploring expedition undertaken by the government. Ninety thousand miles the intrepid fleet sailed to the southern ocean and the mysterious pole, along a coast no civilized man had ever seen, then in the Gulf Stream to strange harbors and exotic islands. Tribes of savages for the first time saw white men, and for the first time Americans looked on primitive peoples whose skins were not black but ivory, men with pleasant-looking countenances who had not learned the use of clothes in their mild climates, and wore a single sandal, a patch of sealskin on one shoulder of their naked bodies, a flower, or perhaps a band of color. To Terra del Fuego sailed the expedition, to Callao and the Tahiti Islands, some till then unknown, and onward to the Samoan whose women, less beautiful than the Tahitian were, as in civilized communities, also more virtuous. With scientific passion Commander Wilkes's men climbed mountain peaks to determine their height, and plumbed depths of till then undiscovered lakes. They explored the craters of extinct volcanoes and took specimens of mountain palms and arborescent ferns. But their red letter day dawned when three ships of the squadron, proceeding separately to the southward after leaving Sidney, came upon the icy barrier that had concealed the unknown Antarctic Continent.

Like passages out of the *Ancient Mariner* read the descriptions of the virgin land, surrounded by its clear green water.

65

Three hundred fathoms the sea was sounded without touching bottom. High and rounded and shimmering with snow, the first promise of land rose out of the water. A chain of perpendicular icy cliffs protected it; icebergs blocked the way of sailing ships. Undismayed, Commander Wilkes's men penetrated the barriers of ice, climbed the rounded hill and raised the flag on its summit. The New World had discovered a still newer world.

America itself, however, was still *terra incognita* in its vastness, as Wilkes showed when, on the return voyage of the expedition, he investigated the northwest coast. But there the glory of discovery belonged to John Charles Frémont. Already a number of exploring groups had been sent to the West toward the region later known as Oregon. In 1842, as the government thought it expedient to acquaint itself with the land between the southern geographical boundary of the United States and the Rocky Mountains, Frémont was chosen to head the expedition with the object of finding the latitude and longitude of the South Pass, the great crossing place of the Rockies on the way to the Pacific. Many sufferings the party endured, and unimaginable hardships, but the object was gloriously achieved. As Wilkes had planted the flag on the icy peak of the Antarctic, Frémont raised it among the clouds where even the eagle had not dared venture, on the loftiest crag of the Rockies.

Patriot that he was, Walt kindled with pride at the nation's triumphant assertion in every field and reserved judgment on troublesome domestic problems. He was concerned with Walt Whitman. He knew he wanted to be a writer. Had he not taken his readers into his confidence about the book he would give the world some day? Meanwhile he had to make his living, and he had experienced enough to know that though the muse may be a pleasant companion, she is not a provident one—no Louisa who kept the family going comfortably whether the purse were fat or lean. He had had jobs here and there; he had tried his hand as editor of his own paper. He was not satisfied. Like all aspirants in the process of finding themselves, he veered between the security of a salary-paying job and the unchecked flight of the "free-lance." Riches, he knew, were not for him. He despised them as dangerous and soul-killing. Want, however, can kill the body as well as the soul. The best compromise would be to earn enough for one's keep while leaving sufficient leisure for the soul's ranging. In other words, work for the physical necessities, but keep the spirit free.

He had more or less permanent employment between 1841 and 1845. The records are not clear. But there is no doubt that in the New York that held more enchantment for him than any pleasure-domed Xanadu he worked a little, wrote whenever the spirit moved him, loafed much, and invited his soul. The bus drivers, "a strange, natural, quick-eyed and wondrous race" knew him well and made place for him beside them on the fleet of Yellow-birds and Red-birds and other stages of the street lines weaving through the carriage traffic of Broadway, Fifth Avenue, Madison Avenue, Fourth, Knickerbocker and busy Twenty-third Street, east and west, from river to river. Walt knew them all by name. He had only to stand on the curb and hail them with his large salutation, arm high, hand uplifted, for the Balky Bills, the Tippys, the Yellow Joes, Big Franks and Patsey Dees to welcome him up with a shout.

> Toward you all, in America's name,
> I raise high the perpendicular hand.

Bus drivers, boat pilots, peddlers, tramps, any honest friendly face readily received Walt's *salut au monde*.

He spoke to them and they returned his cordiality with the bluff comradeship of the class from which he sprang. Very early in his dealings with people he learned the difference between the lettered fool and the illiterate sage, the gowned scholar whose learned lumber could not make him a raft to keep afloat on the stream of life, and the plain farmer, Elias Hicks, who with scarcely any learning, lifted one heavenward with the power of his mind. Walt never apologized for his choice of companions. They were his equals. As he drove down Broadway on a cool June night, Pop Rice or Old Elephant telling with inimitable gusto some masculine yarn above the city's roar, Walt knew that not only Rabelais and Cervantes, but Homer and Shakespeare, would have relished such company. They would have enjoyed these men's "immense qualities—largely animal—eating, drinking, women." They would have admired the personal pride of these untaught workingmen, their comradeship, affection, their good will and sense of honor. Walt felt no discrepancy, therefore, when he returned their entertainment by declaiming at the top of his voice some passage from *Julius Caesar* or *Richard III*. Shakespeare had addressed himself to such men, among others. He had not written for the universities.

Walt went often to the theater, his boyhood love, using his connections with the newspapers for free passes in return for a notice. The life of the stage appealed to him; he would have wanted to be another Booth. One season, for his pleasure and perhaps to test his ability, he joined an amateur dramatic company and trod the boards. Nothing came of his efforts except that he acquired favorite plays by heart. No, acting was not for him.

Without pursuing any definite direction, in fact, by following whatever way chance opened before him, Walt was preparing himself for the goal. He was too easy going to make a decision and stick to it. Besides, life spread before him, endlessly wonderful, with exhibitions to see, libraries to browse in, and streets to walk, with their unexpected adventures. He lived, but he also found time to write. So far he had taken his shies at poetry and written the gentle sermons he called the "Sun-down Papers." He had attempted nothing more lofty. With a side glance at what other authors were producing for the magazines he tried the short tale at which Poe and Hawthorne had worked with such success, and furbished up to more ambitious form the verses he had published for the *Democrat.*

In August of 1841 he had the thrill of seeing his short story, "Death in the Schoolroom" in the pages of a literary magazine. The *Democratic Review* enjoyed a certain prestige as well as a good circulation. Inclusion in its pages meant a long stride forward for the beginner, no matter how he rated the merits of his fellow craftsmen. Whitman was pleased not alone with his work but with its success, for to believe him, his sensational story made a considerable impression upon its readers and was reprinted in other periodicals. The *Democratic Review* in any case must have been satisfied with its reception, to judge by the frequent appearance of Walt's work in its pages through that year and the next.

But Walt was no *littérateur.* If, with his fondness for foreign terms he did not hate the word, he had contempt for the thing it represented. Nothing repelled him more than the tradition of the man of letters. Suspiciously he looked upon the New England group, upon the cold intellectuality he saw in some of its exponents, and was convinced that his place was not with them. Margaret Fuller he admired, and for Emerson, whether or not he had read the recently published essays, Walt had the regard which everyone, friend or foe, bore his courageous enlightenment. For Emerson's voice, if not heard in its fullness, was borne far and wide by the echoes of his detractors as well as by the zeal of his disciples. In all probability Walt had not heard its living accents, but the gist of its meaning thrilled the air. He may not have read his exhortations to the writer to come out of the world of books and join the ranks of the doers; he may not have listened to the actual words, "Inaction is cowardice," but the lessons implicit in Emerson's message he had by heart. He belonged with the army of workingmen and doers; he was one with them in the turmoil of life—at least he felt himself to be. Hence it is not surprising that when he made his first attempt at fiction he saw to it that the reader understood it to be no figment of his imagination, but, as he scrupulously labeled it, "a fact."

Fact or fiction, "Death in the Schoolroom" was a poor story by any standard, except for its intent. What reader with any imagination could have taken the misfortune of little Tim Barker at the hands of the cruel schoolmaster for anything but the drabbest of fact? Who could have had any doubt that the unskillful narrative of the starved boy, dying of fright, followed the uninventive ways of reality? What innocent would have mistaken its fumbling awkwardness for art, even though the closing sentence was calculated to hit one with the force of a Poe—"Death was in the schoolroom, and Lugare had been flogging a CORPSE." The capitals only served to stress the author's lack of confidence in his effectiveness. But he had driven home his moral point—the lack of understanding where it was most wanted.

Obviously Walt was playing the sedulous ape, and clumsily at that. Of all impossible models he chose Poe, the pure artist who with no concern for ethics wrote for the story's sake only. "Bervance" which appeared in the December issue of the *Democratic Review* revealed the influence strongly in the theme of madness which Walt chose to treat. The closest parody both of style and content followed in the poetic allegory of "The Angel of Tears." It was Poe with a moral, a typically Whitmanesque moral, however, and one which gave perhaps the earliest expression to the tolerance which is one of the glories of *Leaves of Grass*. The formulation came haltingly, in the stammer of Moses before his tongue knew the release of the divine coal; the spirit, however, had breathed upon Walt's soul. "Oh, it is not well to look coldly and mercilessly on the bad done by our fellows. That convict—that being of the bloody hand—who could know what palliations there were for his guilt? Who might say there was no premature seducing aside from the walks of honesty—and no seed of evil planted by others in his soul during his early years? Who should say he was not so bred that had he at manhood possessed aught but the propensities for evil it would have been miraculous indeed? Who might dare cast the first stone?" He spoke as one whose message is caught in his throat, but he knew he had the power and the voice which would one day ring out crying:

I am he attesting sympathy . . .
I am not the poet of goodness only, I do not decline to be the
poet of wickedness also. . . .
Through me many dumb voices,
Voices of the interminable generations of prisoners and slaves,
Voices of the diseas'd and despairing and of thieves and
dwarfs . . .
Through me forbidden voices. . . .

But how weak a piping he made in prose!

However, he continued publishing in the hospitable *Democratic Review* such sketches and stories as "The Tomb Blossoms" and "A Legend of Life and Love." Walt Whitman, or rather W.W. as he signed himself with extraordinary self-effacement, began to make himself known to the readers of other contemporary periodicals like *Brother Jonathan, The Columbian Magazine, The American Review,* and later the *Broadway Journal.* Stolidly he continued hewing his slices of life and buttering them generously with edifying homilies. Besides Poe, he flattered by imitation Hawthorne and Dickens who arrived on his first visit to America in 1842. No critic with a gleam of foresight could have anticipated any career but that of a hack from Walt's mediocrity, yet shortly a brief novel of his was to be advertised as the work of "one of the best Novelists of this country."

Chapter VII: Franklin Evans

EVER since six reformed tipplers in Baltimore had founded their Washington Temperance Society after a hell-raising sermon on the evils of drink, every center in the United States had been drowned in a flood of tracts and repentant tears. The name of the society might have raised a smile in the knowing, for the Father of his Country had never been one to set down any rules for abstinence. It was a patriotic gesture on the part of the temperance reformers who wished to cover their enterprise with the American flag. Jefferson's name had at first been suggested, but Washington's had won out. The Washingtonians were well content, never having seen any of the articles of agreement drawn up between Washington and his servants in a less enlightened era, when drink was considered as necessary as food. What would they have said to the document in which Washington pledged himself to provide his gardener with "a decent suit of clothes, befitting a man in his station; to consist of a coat, vest and breeches," and also with "four dollars at Christmas, with which he may be drunk four days and four nights; two dollars at Easter to effect the same purpose; two dollars at Whitsunside to be drunk two days;—a dram in the morning and a Drink of Grog at Dinner at Noon"?

Luckily for their missionary zeal Messrs. Hawkins, Pollard, Shaw and Casey who preached for the cause, never saw such damning evidence of Washington's non-temperate outlook, though even in that they might have found matter for their exhortations in churches and saloons, on city squares and in dens of iniquity. Drunkards and outcasts of the worst type, however, reformed and joined the movement, preaching in their turn while their wives, mothers and sisters, not to be outdone, sang hymns in the doorways of saloons, like the fine ladies of Boston and the society matrons of New York. Such harmonious pleas might fail, perhaps, in reclaiming the unregenerate, but even they often found that their dram had the salt taste of tears, prompted by music, heavenly maid, as much as by the potency of the spirits. Except for these lost souls, the temperance missionaries made converts by the thousands, the regenerate ones elbowing one another in their anxiety to be among the first to sign the pledge. Pageants, processions with banners, bands of music, festivals and children's "cold water armies" filled the land with "the feast of reason and the flow of soul."

In 1842, at the height of the temperance excitement, Walt Whitman was approached by none other than Park Benjamin and his associate, James Aldrich, to write a short novel for the worthy cause. Walt, whose purse was suffering from chronic leanness, lent a willing ear. Benjamin and Aldrich owned the *New World*, a cheap family journal that came out every Saturday for the edification of the citizenry. Now and then as an added circulation bait the *New World* issued novelettes or special features in brochure form which it sold at a nominal price. The list of subscribers gave evident proof that more than most journals of its kind it reached the masses. The cheapness of its rates brought it within the range of even the poorest.

Mr. Benjamin's offer sounded alluring. He would pay seventy-five dollars down for the story and fifty more if it should have a large sale. Walt considered the proposal, but not too long. He needed the money. More than that, he yearned to reach the widest possible public. Dickens, whose sketches he read with avidity the moment they reached the American press, had from the first struck him as a truly democratic writer who strove to make himself understood by the lowest common denominator —human beings, too, although social distinctions might place others above them. He was ambitious to be like Dickens. He would seek to amuse as well as to edify—for he could never

73

divorce the function of the artist from that of the reformer—
and he would endeavor to appeal to the masses. What better
way than to write for them the temperance novel—a subject
worthy of Dickens? Walt closed the deal with Mr. Benjamin
and set to work.

It took him three days and the help of "a bottle of port and
what not" to produce the odyssey of *Franklin Evans, or The
Inebriate.* In a double sense he worked ardently on it, although
(to take advantage of his pun) Walt took in more ardency than
he gave out in the writing of his longest work so far. What happened in the course of his labors to reduce Dickensian aspiration to a low level of sensational journalism, and his fervor for
reform to "rot, rot, of the worst sort"? That he had no such
opinion of his work after finishing it is evident in that he had
Park Benjamin publish it on schedule, and that he reprinted
it himself with slight changes four years later. Indeed, he did
not blush when the *New World* shrieked in an advertisement
on Saturday, November 5, 1842:

> Friends of Temperance, Ahoy!
> Franklin Evans
> or
> *The Inebriate*
> A Tale of the Times.—By a Popular
> American Author.

Had "Death in the Schoolroom" brought Walt so much to
the fore than he could justly be described as a popular American author, or was he allowing himself to be invested with the
tinsel of popularity to bait the reading public in a good cause?
Surely, compared with the favorite hacks of the cheap magazines W.W. or Walter Whitman was unknown. On the other
hand where did he stand when placed with Dana, Poe and the
no longer anonymous Hawthorne?

The note accompanying the advertisement glossed the decep-
tion while adding to the deceit. *"Franklin Evans,"* it explained,

"was written expressly for the *New World* by one of the best Novelists of this country, with a view to aid the work of Reform, and rescue young men from the demon of Intemperance. . . ." All is right in love and the war for Reform. What harm in a little self-puffing in so laudable a fight?

Long afterward when Walt looked back upon his novelette from the height of real accomplishment he saw it as unworthy of him and grew angry whenever anyone brought it up in conversation. But the young author who wrote an introduction for the finished work looked upon it less critically. To him it was a stone well aimed at the Goliath of drink; he was a David meeting the enemy as he had never been met before. More important still, he was waging the contest for the people. He wished that point to be driven home.

"Its being written *for the mass*," he enlarged, "though, the writer hopes, not without some claim upon the approval of the most fastidious; and, as much as anything else, the fact that it is a pioneer in this department of literature—all these will give THE INEBRIATE, I feel confident, a more than ordinary share of patronage. For youth what can be more invaluable? It teaches sobriety. . . . It wars against intemperance. . . . My book is not written for the critics but for THE PEOPLE."

What a shadowing forth of the Whitman technique for the conquest of his public! Not for the cold intellectual was he writing, but as he capitalized, for THE PEOPLE. If the fastidious approved, why, welcome to them; he excluded no one. He looked upon his book as an original venture (how often was he to insist upon such originality in his subsequent work!) and hence worthy of support. With stupendous ignorance he flung to oblivion Lucius Manlius Sargent's *My Mother's Gold Ring* which by that time had attained the rank of a classic in temperance literature, and swept to the dust heap the writings of such men as Pierpont, Woodward, Channing and others who were impressing themselves upon the public mind. It gave Walt pleasure to consider himself a pioneer in every undertaking. Neither self-deception nor arrogance entered into this notion of himself. He willed it to be so, and therefore it was. He received impetus from the belief that he was the first to set his foot on the spade for the turning of new soil.

Of the countless homiletic productions hurled at the head of that guilt-haunted decade, few could have been as stupefying as Walt's "pioneer in this department of literature." He took with no grain of salt his function as reformer. Never a humorist, he saw that not the faintest glowworm flitted through his Inebriate's dismal swamp. Franklin Evans had a course to run, and he ran it through with no deviation, to the final, staggering moral. The drunkard, now reformed and therefore impelled to tell his tale, recounts it as if it were a series of experience talks well seasoned with hortatory pleas. "Reader!" he exclaims after his fall from grace, "perhaps you despise me. Perhaps if I were with you at this moment, I would behold the curled lip of scorn, and the look of deep contempt. O pause, stern reverencer of duty, and have pity for a fellow-creature's weakness!" With the repetitiousness of a litany, the stern reverencer's lip of scorn is admonished not to curl as with appalling stubbornness the Inebriate persists in his dissolute ways.

In the narrative the Dickensian play of contrasts works overtime: the rich criminal gorges at the banquet; the hapless stealer of a loaf dies at hard labor. Innocent childhood begs for its drunken parent; guilty experience inducts simplicity to its own evil practices. No doubt Walt believed he was writing a social document. He relied too much, however, upon his notion of what constituted social realities and too little on actual experience. But then, as he declared, he was not writing for critics.

While battling for one reform Walt saw no harm in tackling another by the device of carrying Franklin Evans to the South. The slavery question, far from arriving at a solution, bristled with graver issues every day. The rift between the opposing parties widened as time, instead of healing it, threatened the safety of the Union. In 1840 the first national convention against slavery had met in Albany; it succeeded only in highlighting the irreconcileable differences between North and South.

Walt, the frequenter of lectures and debating societies, had imbibed opinions and prejudices, neither of which could have been called convictions. He had listened to the pros and cons, and had been agitated by the seriousness of the conflict, but he had not yet formulated his personal ethic on the question. Both his great-grandfather and his grandfather, as he knew, had owned slaves. He also recalled a childhood friend, the freed Negro Old Mose, whom he always thought "very genial, correct, manly and cute," attributes which by the stress he laid upon them, betrayed a latent patronage of the "inferior" race.

Not that Walt would have meekly accepted such a charge. Nevertheless in almost every opinion of the Negro that he set down in prose, there is to be found an involuntary admission of his feelings on the race. "The South was technically right and humanly wrong," he summed up his view of the issue that bled the nation. Only in the poetry wherein the prophet spoke, did Whitman transcend the plodding follower of orthodoxy that he could sometimes be. "Poor wretches," he once exclaimed, long after the war had been fought and won, asserting the equality of the Negroes as human beings. "They are invariably —invariably—almost without exception—a superstitious, ignorant and thievish race." And this after he had heralded a more perfect world in his verses:

I will sing the song of companionship . . .
I will write the evangel-poem of comrades and of love,
For who but I should understand love with all its sorrow and joy?
And who but I should be the poet of comrades?

I am the credulous man of qualities, ages, races,
I advance from the people in their own spirit,
Here is what sings unrestricted faith.

77

Early in his career Walt's two distinct personalities asserted themselves: the cautious follower of the trodden way and the liberated poet for whom no height reared inaccessible. In his most trivial writings the dichotomy appeared, nowhere more clearly, perhaps, than in his treatment of the slavery question in *Franklin Evans*. Walt had never been South when he wrote his novelette. But he had known Southerners, and he had read about their institutions. The humanitarian in him saw, as he admitted more than once, the evils of slavery; yet when he came to write about it he emerged as the apologist of the slave-owner. Indeed, the French plantation keeper in *Franklin Evans* is made to judge the Negro slave far more fortunate than the European workingman. "He beheld, it is true, a large number of men and women in bondage, but he could not shut his eyes to the fact that they would be far more unhappy if possessed of freedom"!

Oddly, in the midst of his unconvincing apologia, Walt introduces a striking description of a Creole slave-girl, the most complete and satisfying portrait he had so far painted of a woman. Youths and boys he had described more than once, as in "The Last of the Sacred Army" where he spoke of "boys, beautiful creatures struggling on," and in "A Legend of Life and Love" in which he portrayed one of two brothers: "He was a beautiful youth. Glossy hair clustered upon his head and his cheeks were brown from sunshine and open air. Though the eyes of Nathan were soft and limpid, like a girl's, and his cheeks curled with a voluptuous swell, exercise and labor had developed his limbs into noble and manly proportions."

The word picture of the Creole Margaret matched the rhapsody of Nathan and excelled in allurement the white rival whom Walt set against her. The type attracted him. "She was of that luscious and fascinating appearance often seen in the South, where a slight tinge of the deep color, large, soft voluptuous eyes, and beautifully cut lips, set off a form of faultless proportions—and all combined with a complexion just sufficiently removed from clear white to make the spectator doubtful whether he is gazing on a brunette or one who has indeed some hue of African blood in her veins. . . ."

Had Walt seen Margaret's counterpart in one of the "musical drinking-houses" which he depicted in such detail in his novel, or had she been one of the countless women whose beauty he had surreptitiously admired in the streets of New York? In spite of the diffidence that made Walt, the author, underline how near white her complexion really was, he dwelt too lovingly upon Margaret's charms for the description to be wholly objective. Had he like Franklin Evans been attracted by one of her dusky sisters and, more successfully than his hero, had he resisted temptation with the illiberal argument, "But she was not of my race. . . . What had I to do with such as she?"

His words were not without significance, at least in their indication of what type of woman could stir his emotions. If he had succumbed to any such charmer of flesh and blood he kept the knowledge from everyone. So secretive, so wary was Walt on the subject of women, that his brother George not only absolved him from any affair of the heart as if it had been an unnatural thing, but also defended him against any suspicion of the fleeting encounters of the street. "As for dissipation and women, I know well enough that his skirts were clean. I never heard the least bit about his doings with women. Any charge that he led a miscellaneous life is without bottom." He went farther to prove Walt's clean habit by calling on incontestable authority: "All those fellows intimate with Walt, at night, anywhere, anytime, will tell you the same thing." Walt built up his edifice of virility, and George tore it down. Maladroitly, and as it were by accident, George, however, stumbled closer than many on the key to Walt's mystery.

In due time *Franklin Evans* issued from Mr. Benjamin's establishment to enter the tenements of the American masses.

The reception proved unusually friendly. So well did the novelette sell that Walt received the extra fifty dollars which had closed the bargain. Encouraged by his success, he kept on writing, both prose and verse, and when impulse flagged, he did not scruple to unearth some past seedling which he then pruned and set in other soil. So it was that in March of 1843, while the money from *Franklin Evans* was still jingling in his pocket, he wailed in *Brother Jonathan,* in the same terms as in the *Long Island Democrat,* long since, that it was "not in a gorgeous hall of pride" that he wished to die.

Every piece of writing which he had thrown off so far came from the surface of the mind as reflections called forth from the outer polish and not the true metal. All the while, unformed yet alive, the book he had dreamed of carried on its silent growth below consciousness. Only Walt knew its stirrings. Years before he wrote down his caution to himself, he had been wise enough to "Keep the secret—keep it close."

Chapter VIII: Israfel and the New Adam

UP UNTIL 1845 Walt continued "free-lancing" while keeping the kettle boiling with the more certain income from odd jobs as compositor and sometimes editor in the ephemeral press of the day. In the estimation of the world he had hardly begun to make the grade for a man of his years, a fact that would have impressed itself on one more material-minded than the defender of loafing who had just got a job on the Brooklyn *Star* for the munificence of four or five dollars a week. True, he contributed little to each issue of a journal which he despised for its spinelessness as a political organ. But it gave him a chance to air his opinions on the welfare of the nation. Patriotism with Walt did not end with a lusty singing of "The Star Spangled Banner." It began where the lip service of the average citizen left off, and became at once a religion and a passion. What concerned the States and every human being who could be called an American was also his concern, and though in his public expression he colored general issues with the tints of his party, in more specific matters he spoke for himself.

The Whitmans, now that Louisa had recovered from her long illness, again left Long Island and returned to Brooklyn. The family needed a large house. The first-born, Jesse, was a man of twenty-seven; the youngest son, Eddie, a child of ten. Dutifully Walt came to live at home, to help tide things over with a good slice of what little he earned.

Everybody in that busy clan worked—everybody but Walt, thought George, who had his own opinion of writing and such loafing. Walter Whitman, at fifty-six, could show anybody what real work meant. He was an old man in his looks. His hair, which he wore like a shaggy thatch over his forehead, had turned gray; the tuft of his sideburns was white. The eyes had the deep-searching look of age combined with a bold directness; the firm mouth radiated with wrinkles from his long habit of keeping it closed against needless talk. He did not believe in talk. Much better to use one's hands and produce things that one could work with, houses to shelter one, tools for labor. Early in the morning, when the sun was hardly an hour high, he would start off to work with his dinner pail which Louisa or one of the girls had fixed up for him. When he came back it was already night. He was not working for himself at present, but soon he would again build houses and sell them as the town spread out. There was no age for the laborer. He worked as long as he could use his hands and his strength lasted. It was healthful outdoor work and he was not ashamed of it. In his striped carpenter's suit, with his bag of tools, Walter Whitman belonged to that army of workers that was beginning to know its strength. He had not read in vain the articles in Frances Wright's *Free Enquirer* and listened to her lectures in which she told of the nature and history of civilization and what hopes there were in the future for the mechanics and laborers. Her wonderful little book, *A Few Days in Athens* that taught, in a sane way, how people could get the most out of life, he may have read. Maybe the philosophy was too deep for one who had no booklearning, but Walt, his son, read it and made others read it to the end of his days.

Of the girls, one had taken Walt's place teaching school in a little village in Long Island. Jesse worked, and so did George and Andrew. Jeff, who was twelve years old, went to school and was learning to play the violin. Walt enjoyed listening to him from his room where he slept late when he was not needed at the newspaper. Little Eddie, too simple to go to school, remained with Louisa and helped with easy tasks. In the morning he would grind the coffee for breakfast. He was a goodnatured, harmless child who would never grow up. Walt, whose strongest family feeling went out to but one member, made room also for Eddie, his mother's chief concern. Jeff, too, he liked, for the boy's sedulous admiration of his big brother.

Back home, Walt had no more order in his life than he had ever had. He came down for breakfast whenever he pleased. He was no watcher of clocks. He went through his day without system, doing a job when he had one to do, but otherwise holding on to the wings of the hours, letting himself be borne along. No use telling him what to do or when to do it. With a curious deliberateness he let anyone advise him and then did as he pleased. "He would refuse to do anything except at his own notion," George said. The family, however, had developed a strange regard for Walt, this son and brother who, with his bearded chin and dandified clothes, somehow made them all look up to him. "He was like us—yet he was different from us, too." They came to him for his opinion, and George saw with awe that even strangers seemed to detect something in him out of the ordinary. So they all thought it best to let him follow his own way, hoping it might lead to a steady job with a good salary at the end of each week. They did not appreciate the satisfaction of seeing one's name in print, the rapture at the thought that people, utter strangers, were reading one's words, some of them with understanding, maybe with fellow-feeling.

More than ever he was writing with a purpose. It had been well to imitate the literary in allegories and poetic tales. But they were not for him. *Franklin Evans* with all its serious faults, had succeeded in embodying more of his intention than anything else he had written. He had had a message to give; well or ill, he had given it. Of the thousands who read it, many had thought it was meant for them. Yet there was, there must be, a directer way of communicating with the masses. What it might be he did not yet know. For the present he would speak forthrightly to them, with no attempt at art. He did it in the newspaper pieces in which he gave his reactions to national events—as in the dispute with England over the Oregon boundary—and in perfervid verses springing from the same source. Somewhere between the one and the other might be the way to reach the people.

Meanwhile he looked about for other channels for his writings. There was the *Broadway Journal*, edited by Poe in New York. Why not try it with an essay on something contemporary? Poe and he were worlds removed; but in some matters, strangely enough, they were in accord.

For months Poe had been waging war on the New England school, concentrating his attacks on Longfellow and the Transcendentalists. So notorious had the dispute become during the brief year of the *Broadway Journal's* existence that the "Longfellow War" loomed as much an item of news as the conflict with England, the newspapers vying with one another to be the first to take up and republish Poe's goading articles. Whitman, considering his intense nationalism, could not but agree with Poe. The New England school did not represent America. It looked back too longingly on Europe for inspiration, in spite of Emerson's call to the present and to America, in spite also of Margaret Fuller's warning that books which imitated the thoughts and life of Europe could not make the literature of the New World. The Transcendental renaissance, while awakening the intellects of New England to profounder values, had made them subservient to their foreign masters. Too much of their work sprang from books, too little from the large, lusty, expansive life about them.

Walt lifted his voice in the small chorus of yea-sayers of America in an essay which he called "Art Singing and Heart Singing," prompted by a vocal recital of the Cheney quartette which he had heard in Niblo's garden soon after their first appearance in New York in October of 1845. He had been strongly affected by the singers, three young men and a girl,

the children of a New Hampshire preacher, Simeon Pease
Cheney, who conducted singing classes in the country districts
of his state. Walt, with the rest of New York, enjoyed the native
singing of the New Hampshire troupe, but unlike the many who
had listened to them, heard in their song a note for all America.
He wrote his article and submitted it to Poe who published it
in one of the final issues of the *Broadway Journal* with the comment: "The author desires us to say, for him, that he pretends
to no scientific knowledge of music. He merely claims to appreciate so much of it (a sadly disclaimed department just now) as
affects, in the language of the deacons, 'the natural heart of
man.' It is scarcely necessary to add that we agree with our
correspondent throughout." O wonderful agreement between
the poet of "The Raven" and the poet-to-be of *Leaves of Grass*,
of Israfel and the new Adam!

In his article Walt went directly to the point. "Great is the
power of music over a people!" he cried. "As for America, we
have long followed obedient and childlike in the track of the
Old World. We have received her tenors and her buffos; her
operatic troupes and her vocalists, of all grades and complexions; listened to and applauded the songs for a different
state of society—made, perhaps, by royal genius, but made to
please royal ears likewise; and it is time that such listening and
receiving should cease. The subtlest spirit of a nation is expressed through its music—and the music acts reciprocally on
the nation's very soul. . . ." It was time the dependence ceased,
time that "all grades and complexions" gave way to the American, time that music written to please royal ears were made
to reach the soul of democracy.

The article was unusually well written. Had Poe's editorial
pencil lopped off excesses, pruned Walt's exuberance? Despite
the restraint of the form Walt's enthusiasm broke through,
overflowing in a wondrous vision of singing America streaming
cross country in a procession of youth like the Cheneys, "brown-

faced, stout-shouldered fellows," the girl "strangely simple, even awkward in her ways,"—young men and women, the present and future of America, chanting the native chants. "To our taste, there is something refreshing about all this," he declared of uncorrupted native simplicity. "We are absolutely sick to nausea of the patent-leather, curled hair, 'japonicadom' style." There at Niblo's, in those sun-browned young singers he had beheld America unadulterate, free of the artifice of an effete Europe. How beautiful in its naturalness! How full of promise for a native greatness! And what greatness, could the potential good of America be brought to fulfillment!

He looked about him, however, and saw everywhere the tyranny of a decaying culture, from the "japonicadom" style of dress that sickened him, to the architectural atrocities built by American millionaries in emulation of the gothic castles, Italian villas and oriental palaces of Europe. Even the municipal government had lost its head over foreign flim-flam when it planted in the outskirts of the city* its water reservoir in the Egyptian style. The city had grown considerably since 1840 when the solid, square structure thrust its crenelated top into the sky. Nevertheless sheep grazed peacefully round the asylum for the blind near Thirty-third Street, and now and then a cow leapt the fence of the home pasture to trample the flowerbeds of the latest millionaire villa down Fifth Avenue. Farmhouses still perched on rock ledges in the 'Thirties, yet only a thistle patch away flourished the literary salon in whose damasked, draped, gilt-furnished interior sat ladies in their Godey fashions, each occupying three yards of space with the flounces of their skirts. The time of emancipation had not yet come to Mrs. Amelia J. Bloomer of Seneca Falls and to her friend Elizabeth Cady Stanton, soon to stir up a revolution in feminine styles and women's rights. Subservience and revolution—both existed in the city nearing its half-million souls.

* On the site of the New York Public Library at 42nd Street and Fifth Avenue.

Walt was all for revolution. Although, Tammany man that he was, he sometimes saw little beyond the demarcations of the party, he responded so eagerly to the political and social optimism of the day that with the drum pounding politicians in Washington he had no doubt that America's destiny was bounded only by the world. Progress, the catchword, rang through the air. How false of Walt had he not taken it up and sounded it in his way!

Soon after the publication of his essay, late in November, 1845, Walt went to see Poe in the office of the *Broadway Journal* in the neighborhood of Duane and Pearl Street. Poe had liked the article; he had taken the trouble to say that he agreed with its author. Walt, therefore, saw no harm in seeking to advance himself in an interview with the editor. What were his feelings when he, the unknown journalist, stood face to face with the most famous poet of the day? And how did the slight, large-headed, seraph-faced Poe react to the fine-looking bearded youth who filled the doorway with his bulk? Walt recorded that Poe was very cordial to him, in a quiet way, and that he appeared well in person and in dress. He found him "very kindly and human, but subdued, perhaps a little jaded."

As it was, when the two great poets of America met for the first and last time, Poe was still staggering under the sudden fame that had come to him after the publication of "The Raven" in the New York *Mirror*, on the 8th of February, 1845. For four years he had been working on the poem. He had carried it with him from office to bar-room, reading it to anyone who would listen. He had labored on it late into the night while Mrs. Clemm, his mother-in-law, sat quietly by, rising now and again to look into the bedroom where Virginia slept, then going into the kitchen to brew Poe another cup of the black coffee with which he plied his already overwrought nerves.

At thirty-six, Poe was a spent man. Burdened with poverty, he found that popularity brought no relief. The millions who recited "Once upon a midnight dreary, while I pondered, weak and weary . . .", who listened to the gossip of excesses and dissipation, knew nothing of the squalid life he had led from boarding house to boarding house, in the bare cottage at Bloomingdale Village, two miles north of the reservoir, where Virginia, slowly dying of consumption, might at least have air. They knew only that the author of the fantastic tales, the perpetrator of the balloon hoax, was an unreliable, irritable drunkard, incapable of keeping any place or any friend.

By the *literati* of New York, however, during the past year, especially by the poetesses, he had been pampered as the lion of the season, not alone because of the furore of his poem, but because he could give them a friendly puff in the *Broadway Journal*. They were romantically thrilled, too, at the thought of his lovely consumptive wife—the "lost Lenore" whose death he had forevisioned in "The Raven." Willingly would they have taken Virginia's place on earth as his inspiration.

Throughout the winter Poe was to be seen of an evening at the home of some member of the "starry sisterhood," especially the Waverly Place salon of Anna C. Lynch who cultivated the French manner of speech and the Greek fashion of leaning her slender height against the mantel as if it had been the lintel of some antique temple. Mrs. Elizabeth Oakes Smith came to the gatherings, the ethereal Mrs. Fanny Osgood the poet, Ann Stephens and, shining with white arctic light, Margaret Fuller, the star of Boston, who had condescended to leave her orbit to write literary criticism for Greeley's *Tribune*. Here, too, came lions of the first pedigree, the austere Bryant who had begun his poetic career with a poem on death, Fitz-Greene Halleck, the formidable Dr. Rufus Wilmot Griswold, and Bayard Taylor. It was Poe, however, with his melancholy eyes and strange aura of tragedy who caused the most dizzied fluttering in the muses' dovecotes. Never too strong, he was further weakening himself in tantalizing platonics with various members of the sisterhood,

ANNE GILCHRIST
From a photograph

*"When Whitman set eyes on her . . . she was a woman of forty-eight, with
not a silver thread in the dark hair framing wing-like a plain face. . . ."*

only to drown his conscience over Virginia in drink that acted more powerfully upon him than a poison. No wonder Walt found him "perhaps a little jaded." Others, who had come upon Poe at his desk unexpectedly, had been known to flee in terror from a violent maniac.

Nothing came of Walt's interview. Within a few issues the *Broadway Journal* breathed its last and Israfel again became an outcast upon a world he had never known. Politics, reform movements, the throes of a country giving birth to the future, hardly touched him. He was a stranger in the life of men, singing songs that had nothing to do with their mortal passions. Clearsighted, he had discovered and avowed that limitation in himself.

> If I could dwell
> Where Israfel
>   Hath dwelt, and he where I,
> He might not sing so wildly well
>   A mortal melody,
> While a bolder note than his might swell
> From my lyre within the sky.

Did he, who saw where others were blind and heard music strange to worldly ears, see in the diffident young man before him the poet who would be sounding the bolder note he had not plucked? Futile speculation. Yet there was something epochal, as of two planets clashing, in that meeting arranged by the ironical gods in the dingy office of a New York journal.

Chapter IX: Editor of *The Eagle*

THE fates favored Walt with the coming of the new year
for while he was still contributing articles to the poorly
paying *Star*, he obtained an excellent "sit," as he termed
it, on the Brooklyn *Daily Eagle*. It was a young paper entering
upon its fifth year, though viewed in the light of the meteoric
press of the day, it ranked as a fixed star. The first and last of
its four pages were filled with paying advertisements. The inner
sheet carried, besides the news and "the latest intelligence from
Europe," the editorial opinions of the Democratic-Republican
party of which it was the official organ.

Isaac Van Anden, a rightist Democrat and a man of sound
principles, had founded it, like most papers of the time, with
no false pretenses about its political connections. He had placed
at its head William B. Marsh, an able editor, trained at the
school of Horace Greeley. Although, during the years of Marsh's
editorship, the *Eagle* had failed to gain a large circulation, it
had managed nevertheless to acquire a reputation not only in
New York, but throughout the country. Marsh died suddenly
in February of 1846 and Walt Whitman, not quite twenty-
seven, succeeded him.

He was not too young for such a post. Greeley, only eight
years his senior, counted as an old campaigner whose editorials
molded the opinions of the nation. Even though the *Eagle*
could hardly be compared with the *Tribune*, Walt's position
was nevertheless one of equal responsibility. With the free hand
Van Anden gave him, it was for Walt to make of his post whatever he chose.

He tackled his job with a will, aware of his good fortune and
anxious to do his best. The *Eagle* became his fledgling and he

90

the mother-bird whose duty it was to nurture it, indeed, to keep it alive. In a sense the paper that bore the name of America's symbolic bird, assumed the place in Walt's life of an eidolon, a representation of the storms and strivings of the nation. Through it he could reach the hearts and minds of the people whom he would seek to enlist for the building of the country's greatness. Eagerly, therefore, he went out as reporter to hunt material for the *Eagle's* pages. As editor he addressed himself to work not only for his party's advantage but for the larger good of the States. As essayist he endeavored to edify while amusing, and as critic he strove to deflect the taste of the public from foreign artifice to domestic virtue. The *Eagle*, in fact, soon resembled its editor as a child its parent.

The two or three printers working under Walt who marked his aldermanic pace, his disregard of the clock and his apparent lack of system, privately made a joke of him. "Boss" Van Anden, too, looked quizzically upon the shoe-leather his editor wore out on the city pavement; but as the circulation not only of the walker but of the paper was stimulated, he made no complaint. Besides, Whitman had come to him as a reliable party worker with a good record; he knew he could count upon him at campaign time, to sound the trump of patriotic eloquence, summoning all good Democrats to close their ranks against the enemy. Only Henry Sutton, the fifteen-year-old printer's devil, gave him unqualified admiration. He liked the informal editor who called him Hen, treated him as an equal, and often invited him out on exciting jaunts. For as it had now become a habit with him, Walt did more of his actual work on his tireless feet than at the infrequently occupied editorial desk.

Back and forth across Fulton Ferry, to the remotest slip uptown whither the Wall Street steamboats, the *Champion* and the *Cleopatra*, chugged their way up the Hudson in a race, then back again to Fort Greene in Brooklyn or the shores of

Coney Island, journeyed the ubiquitous Walt by water, omnibus, and more often, on his own Shank's mare, gathering material. People in the home section and farther afield came to know the florid young man with his square-cut beard, wide-brimmed black hat, knotted cravat and cane. He visited the current exhibitions, the police courts and jails, attended the lectures at the Brooklyn Institute, once the Apprentices' Library whose foundation stone he had seen Lafayette lay; he ambled through playgrounds and city streets whose romping children woke a melancholy yearning in his heart—twenty-seven and unattached. One little scamp on Cranberry Street, for reasons known only to his whimsical brain, always greeted him as "Uncle Tom." Walt put him and his companions into one of his earliest articles. "Ah, beautiful creatures!" he sentimentalized. "What wonder is there . . . that the Beloved of God chose ye to image the Kingdom of Heaven? . . . Who can be harsh and bitter with children? and yet far, far too many are so." On another occasion he broke into verse. Whenever, gloomy and weary, he said, he wandered and saw the gayhearted children,—

> Methinks white-winged angels,
>   Floating unseen the while,
> Hover around this village green,
>   And pleasantly they smile.
>
> O angels! guard these children!
>   Keep grief and guilt away:
> From earthly harm—from evil thoughts
>   O shield them night and day.

No fluttering school-marm could have done worse.

But let none make the mistake that Walt plucked exclusively the tenuous harpstrings. Wide awake, for all his hate of hustling, he let nothing escape him, as the pages of the *Eagle* bore witness through the two years of his stewardship. Like the patriotic bird he spread his wings across the nation, his all-seeing eye piercing the remotest distance, his cries of warning or of praise sounding bold, if unmelodious, in every issue. With his typical absorption in whatever he did, he gave himself wholly to his job. He had a busy time of it, whatever the other men of the *Eagle* might have thought, and he enjoyed his busyness.

Patriotism, however, came foremost, whether he advised his family of readers on personal hygiene or pointed out the pitfalls in the electioneering practices of the opposite camp. Altogether he was an honest, right-thinking citizen who took a fatherly interest in his fellow-Americans whom he loved and therefore chastised with the tempered severity of the New Testament. Together with the look of maturity that he cultivated, he fostered the didactic strain in his character. He was happiest when he could teach. Not yet could he assume the title of the Answerer, however. As editor of the *Eagle* he was but a slightly older schoolmaster with a firmer voice and strengthened convictions. Now the whole nation was his schoolroom.

The Democratic-Republican Party thought so well of him that for a year he was elected to serve as secretary of the Central Committee. Brooklyn took him to its heart. Everywhere, at party functions, private meetings, parades and celebrations, Walt Whitman was expected. He lent himself willingly, going as joyfully to a Sunday school picnic as to the opening of a new park. Indeed, he took such pride in the beautification of the town, and was so insistent in his demands that historic sites be preserved, that civic bodies began to pay attention to him. Fort Greene Park, he rejoiced, owed its existence to his tireless campaigning. He had a special fondness for Fort Greene. It was there, on its hallowed ground, that he first heard the lusty voice of America chanting his words.

On the 2nd of July, 1846, an ode, boldly announced as the composition of WALTER WHITMAN enlivened the pages of

93

the *Eagle*, with the note that it was to be sung that Independence Day to the tune of "The Star Spangled Banner." Walt saw no reason why he should not publish his patriotic poem. It was his best effort, so far, and he was justly pleased. Moreover, through the considerateness of the *Eagle*, good patriots would be made familiar in advance with the words of the ode, if, as it often happened, the singer should be more concerned with tone-production than with the meaning of his song. As secretary of the Fourth of July Celebration Committee, Walt could be forgiven for not hiding his light under a bushel. Besides, another ode, by the Rev. T. B. Thayer, had also been accepted for a similar honor, and was going to be sung before the oration. His own, surely, would not suffer for coming later.

On the great day Walt did not let the rain dampen his patriotic ardor as it seemed to have done in many other celebrants. With the few faithful he plowed through puddles to the appointed eminence at Fort Greene. The singer, Mr. Freeborn, was there. There, too, the young lawyer, the envied of his competitors, who had been chosen to make the oration, and the lucky individual elected to read the Declaration of Independence. Walt's heart beat high. He too had brought his offering to the altar of liberty. It was a great moment for him when Mr. Freeborn hailed, in the notes of the national hymn:

O God of Columbia! O Shield of the Free!
  More grateful to you than the fanes of old story,
Must the blood bedewed soil, the red battleground, be
  Where our forefathers championed America's glory!
Then how priceless the worth of the sanctified earth
We are standing on now. Lo! the slopes of its girth
Where the martyrs were buried: nor prayers, tears, or stones
Mark their crumbled-in coffins, their white, holy bones!

Well for him to recall that the ground they stood on had been made sacred by the blood of the dead, that on that very dust, "hope weak, the foe strong," had walked Washington, the Serene One, "still faithful, still fearless."

> Say! sons of Long Island! in legend or song,
> Keep ye aught of its record, that day dark and cheerless?

he questioned, and being Walt Whitman, replied:

> Ah, yes! be the answer. In memory still
> We have placed our hearts, and embalmed there forever,
> The battle, the prison-ship, martyrs and hill,
> O may it be preserved till those hearts death shall sever. . . .
>
> And shall not the years, as they sweep o'er and o'er,
> Shall they not, even *here*, bring the children of ages—
> To exult as their fathers exulted before,
> In the freedom achieved by our ancestral sages?
> And the prayer rise to Heaven, with pure gratitude given
> And the sky by the thunder of cannon be riven?
> Yea! Yea! let the echo responsively roll
> The echo that starts from the patriot's soul!

Mr. Freeborn, the well named, had need of much musical skill to fit the words of Walt's ode into the tune of the national anthem. Walt's patriotism, however, made its way direct. The verses might halt, the words be poorly chosen, the very fervor walk on stilts. Of Walt's sincerity there could be no question. Patriotic verses, even the most conventional, are hard to write. Walt, on the whole, acquitted himself no worse than Poe who, for gifts of Gabriel Harrison's tobacco, wrote his only poor verses in the campaign song for the White Eagle Political Club of which his benefactor was president. If Israfel could fail, it was to Walt's credit that he could even partially succeed.

Many of his readers who knew him only by his writing may have looked upon their editor as a benevolent crank. They knew that he neither drank nor smoked, that he loved children and condemned flogging in the schools, that he advocated brighter street lights and less gloomy Sundays, cleaner cities and frequent baths. Indeed, on the subject of health and cleanliness he left no room for doubt. He disliked doctors and disapproved of medicine. "To give medicine for any given disease," he wrote on the 4th of June, 1846, "*because* that medicine has apparently cured the same disease in another person, is one of the most dangerous as it is the most common follies of the school faculty. It would be well if those that practice the healing art, (a ridiculous term, if we mean by it drugging sicker those who are only a little sick!) would go no further than they had a light to their steps. Their pride makes them ashamed to confess an ignorance, which none short of supernatural power could avoid. Blindly thus, they sacrifice human life to their own miserable vanity! This is monstrous, and has no excuse at all!"

Clearly, Walt had no use for the medical profession. To him nature was the great healer, a belief he held to the end of his life. In spite of irate letters from offended medicos, he refused to retract a word. Of bathing, however, he was an enthusiast. "We are glad enough," he wrote after his diatribe against medicine, "could we see bathing more generally practiced. Brooklyn would be a healthier city even than it is, if the semi-weekly bath, during the summer, were a rigid rule for *all* our citizens—for all ages and both sexes." It was good for the health and the complexion, he said. It made one beautiful. When, therefore, Gray's Swimming Bath opened in a fine building just east of Fulton Ferry, Walt announced it with an editorial fanfare. At last Brooklyn bathers would not have to ride across the ferry to keep clean. "We shall now be able to reap all the advantages of the custom to which the building we allude is to be appropriated, without going away from our own shores."

Needless to say he was among the first to avail himself of Mr. Gray's civic enterprise, seeing to it at the same time that his young devil, Hen, learned by his example the benefits derived from the daily bath. Toward noon, after he had read proof on the *Eagle* articles, he set out with Hen for Mr. Gray's establishment. There he undressed while the boy waited, and went in for a swim. Methodical even in his pleasures, he remained in the water exactly twenty minutes, then stood under the shower while Henry worked the pump. "His arrangements are of a superior cast," he praised Mr. Gray's bathing contrivances. "To young men—particularly to the heads of families having children—a family of boys—do we advise the procurement of a season ticket. How many of the fine promising lads who are yearly drowned in this neighborhood, would have been saved, if they were furnished with bathing accommodations in the way we advise." Indeed, why could they not have in Brooklyn a couple of free baths? "They have them in many European cities, of not near our size, where the conveniences of getting water are not near as complete as here." What a pang it must have cost to admit that Europe could have had even so slight an advantage! But he admonished only to improve.

After his bath, taken "without going away from our own shores," he left the boy Henry to paddle about by himself, and promptly boarded the ferry for Manhattan. His day's work at the office was done. He must now dig up material and enlarge the mind. What contrasts the city afforded! Here the sumptuous palace of the newest millionaire, there the crowded jail. On one street the beggar stretching out a lean hand, unheeded, and just around the corner a luxurious palace where God was worshiped by a congregation of the élite. In his benevolent didacticism Walt saw sermons in the stones of the street and strove to find good in everything.

How difficult it sometimes proved he betrayed in his articles. *Vagrom Woman* he headed one sardonic item. "Ann MacDonough had occasion to bless her lucky stars on Christmas for being sent to the county jail for vagrancy. This will just about carry her comfortably through the cold weather. Happy Ann!" That was all. Words could not have been scathing enough to condemn such social injustices. Walt, however, relied upon his reporting to have its effect. Outwardly objective, it was like a harmless-looking parcel filled with explosives. Sometimes, wrought up by what he saw, he flung moderation to the winds and wrote with a spluttering pen. The opening of Grace Church in New York provoked one such outburst, followed by another, still more vehement.

According to the papers, the church had been inaugurated amid imposing ceremonies. Walt went to see for himself, although, as he warned his readers, he did not "look with a favorable eye on these splendid churches." Elias Hicks, after all, had required no palatial temple to deliver his promptings from within. What Walt forgot was that neither had Hicks scorned a candelabra-lighted ballroom as a place fit to receive the word of God.

What Walt saw when he went to the scene affected him to jaundice. Inside and out he found Grace Church a showy piece of architecture. What wonder, he thought, if the congregation paid more attention to the columns and carvings than to the preaching? One Sunday he attended the services. Never, he was shocked to see, had he witnessed such crowding and jamming as he found at the portal—not even at an opening of the Park Theatre or an Elssler's benefit. "People pushed and shoved each other—and the owners of the six-hundred-dollar pews had to worry their way through a mass of staring commoners, before they reached those genteel lounging places. The situation of the fat old doorkeeper was no sinecure . . . He eventually sent for a small force of the police, and we suppose succeeded in keeping 'the enemy' at bay . . ." That was the place where people were expected to worship! That was religion! Those worldly men and women, one must believe, had come there to turn their thoughts heavenward! Walt, who needed no temple to commune with the Spirit, looked at those fashionables and scourged them with his words, and vigorous words they were.

"The eye and ear cannot go amiss of the unhallowed intruders, the haughty bearing of our American aristocrats (that most contemptible phase of aristocracy in the whole world!), the rustling silks and gaudy colors in which wealthy bad taste loves to publish its innate coarseness—the pompous tread, and the endeavor to 'look grand'—how disgustingly frequent are all these at Grace Church! Ah, there is no religion *there!*"

To good purpose had he read Tom Paine. Yet something other than unorthodoxy and radicalism entered into his writings. More and more he gave expression to the spirit of the age with its strivings and its paradoxes: the hysterical shouts for liberty while the heel of imperialism trampled it, the campaigns for reform while the greatest reform of all, in social equality, was daily violated. Complexities and confusion clouded the minds of the most clear-thinking. The very men who were working for the best of causes often destroyed them by making fanaticism out of their faith. With a fine detachment in his best moments, Whitman stood above the battle; then he saw beyond the present to the farthest age. Too often, however, with the limited outlook of his contemporaries, he let the immediate problem obscure the lasting truth.

All manner of unfortunates, the criminal waiting for the hangman, the despised immigrant, the women slaving in sweatshops to earn from twenty-five to fifty cents a day, even the starving of Ireland and Scotland, had their advocate in the *Eagle* editor. Of them he sometimes wrote with the quivering pen of the future "Fanny Fern." He championed also the cause of the Negro (unlike the author of *Franklin Evans*), devoting in one of his earliest editorials many paragraphs to the horrors of the "middle passage." Writing in the blackest of ink, he described the hell-holes that were the transport ships, and the brutal crossings. "Still the black-hearted traitors who ply this work, go forth with their armed bands and swoop down on defenseless villages, and bring their loads of human trophy, chained and gagged, and sell them as so much merchandise."

But he had written those words on March 18, 1846. A month later the United States was at war with Mexico, precipitating a renewal of the still graver internecine warfare between North and South. Almost at once Walt abandoned the issue, to take it up again at the close of the year in another editorial denouncing the extremism of the Abolitionists.

The Hutchinsons, a group of native singers like the Cheneys, had been hissed by "certain zealous persons" when they sang "Liberty, a nation's glory!" at a concert that Whitman attended. "Is not Liberty a nation's glory?" asked the irate music lover. Why should the Abolitionists have hissed? "Come, now, let us be candid on this subject. The mad fanaticism or ranting of the ultra Abolitionists has pretty well spent its fury—and, by the way, has done far more harm than good to the very cause it professed to aid." Perplexing inconsistency! On the one hand he expressed his loathing of the plague spot of the nation, on the other he flinched at the method employed by the Abolitionists to extirpate it. Throughout he persisted in his dualism.

> Do I contradict myself?
> Very well then I contradict myself,
> (I am large, I contain multitudes.)

In the meantime, far from abating, as Walt confidently asserted, the fanaticism of the Abolitionists had been raised to a peak of excitement by the events of the preceding months. The trouble had started early in 1845, during President Tyler's administration, when a joint resolution was passed in Congress for the annexation of Texas. There was much rejoicing in the pro-slavery party which saw in the measure a distinct gain. But the government knew it was heading toward war, and so did Mexico, which would not relinquish the territory it claimed as a portion of its own domain. Knowing that it could not carry on more than one war at a time, the administration settled its dispute with England over the Northwest boundary by forget-

ting its battle-cry of "Fifty-four-forty or fight," and agreeing to
the Forty-ninth parallel as the dividing line. "*Very* excellent
news," the *Eagle* editor hailed the resumption of amicable
relations.

But Mexico was another matter. At first commerce went on
as usual, American ships stopping at Mexican ports with cargoes
of all kinds, many of munitions made in the United States.
Hostilities had not openly commenced, reasoned the munitions
makers. At this juncture Tyler was succeeded by the shrewd
politician James Polk, who for fourteen years had been the
representative for Tennessee in the House. Immediately the
new administration set about making active preparations for
war. Troops massed within striking distance of the Mexican
border and the army was placed under the tried command of
General Zachary Taylor. From St. Joseph's Island he crossed
over to the mainland as far as the Nueces River, and there
more troops stationed themselves, to remain in winter quarters
till war broke out.

They did not remain long in idleness. Indeed, early in May
of 1845 the President had informed Congress that "a state of
war" existed, inasmuch as the Mexicans had invaded *our* territory and shed the blood of American citizens on United States
soil. Long before the open declaration of hostilities, lives had
been lost on both sides. From then on, till September of 1847,
the papers carried news from the front where Taylor and General Winfield Scott executed the orders from Washington. De-
feats and victories met with partisan fervor at home, as newspaper readers struggled with the names of foreign places where
the American army had set its foot: Palo Alto, Resaca de la
Palma, Buena Vista, Chihuaha, Cerro Gordo, Contreras,
Churubuscu, Chapultepec. Democratic imperialism made holiday in the headlines.

Loud and long screamed the Brooklyn *Eagle* whose editor
had been following the campaigns with mixed emotions, run-

101

ning atrocity stories reflecting on the enemy, and roundly declaring: "Yes: Mexico must be thoroughly chastised." True, a foreign nation was being dismembered, but then it was hardly civilized. Under the American flag its soil would bloom again, its people be renewed in the light of freedom. He was quick, therefore, to feature editorially any American victory. "HONOR TO THE HERO!" he commanded the Brooklyn burghers after General Taylor's triumph at Buena Vista. "Whatever may be said of the evil moral effects of war, it seems to us plain that such events as this victory at Buena Vista, and our former victories in Mexico, must elevate the true self-respect of the American people to a far higher point than heretofore."

Brooklyn patriots, at any rate, proved that their self-respect had been elevated when two weeks later, on April 15th, they held a demonstration in front of the *Eagle* office to celebrate the army's triumphs. A huge transparency decorated the second-story windows of the building. When, at eight o'clock, it blazed with the names of Monterey, Vera Cruz and other battles, the crowd below cheered tumultuously. "There is hardly a more admirable impulse in the human soul than *patriotism*," Whitman commented piously the following day. Most beautiful of all was "the patriotism of what are called by some 'the common people' who form the great bulk and strength of the state."

In spite of the spread-eagleism of his article a certain doubt of the right of the war for the first time broke through. "One's country, it is true, cannot always be perfectly just in every motion and action," he said. "Neither can one's parents or wife, or dearest friend. But to go against either of the latter, to revile them, or to oppose them, were hardly more infamous than to revile or oppose the cause of one's native land." Fearing that he might leave some uncertainty of his own feelings, he added, "Cold must be the pulse, and throbless to all good thoughts— no true American's will it be—which cannot respond to the valorous emprise of our soldiers and commanders in Mexico."

102

But he had had enough of war. As early as January of the year he had intimated a desire for peace, declaring the national honor avenged and the Mexicans sufficiently punished. Once more he exclaimed, "Heaven grant that we may now have peace!" Peace came, however, only after General Scott had entered the halls of the Montezumas in the Mexican capital. With imposing military honors the regimental flag was raised where the Mexican colors had flown, and soon afterward the Stars and Stripes replaced them—the first foreign banner to top the turreted fortress since the coming of Cortez. Fervently General Scott addressed his thanks to heaven for the signal triumphs of his army, gave praise for America the land of the free, and ended with a fatherly admonition to his comrades-in-arms against the evils of rioting, straggling and drunkenness. In the solemn ceremonies at home celebrating the victories, no speaker mentioned that when America captured the palaces of the Montezumas it was the first time that her army had set foot in conquest upon a foreign capital. Large were the victor's spoils. When the treaty was finally signed the United States, for paltry pecuniary indemnities, acquired the whole of Texas, New Mexico, and upper California.

To the popular mind the nation had covered itself with glory, and people read with tearful emotion war poetry like Charles F. Hoffman's on the capture of Monterey, with its mourning over the dead heroes:

> Our banners on those turrets wave,
> 'And there our evening bugles play:
> Where orange-boughs above their grave
> Keep green the memory of the brave
> Who fought and fell in Monterey.

A different tune, however, came from the homely harmonica of Lowell's *Biglow Papers* written when the Brahmin of Brahmins worked under the influence of his passionately Abolitionist wife, the former Maria White. For him the Mexican War had no redeeming features. He saw it, impure and simple, as foreign conquest for the benefit of the slave power.

> They jest want this Californy,

he wrote in pungent Yankee,

> So's to lug new slave-states in
> To abuse ye, an' to scorn ye,
> An' to plunder ye like sin.

Long before this, while the war was still in its initial stages, wise heads had seen that the problem of slavery or Free Soil, of federal versus states rights, had to be settled if the country was to be at peace with itself. On the 8th of August, 1846, in connection with a bill asked by President Polk for two million dollars to negotiate a treaty with Mexico, the Wilmot Proviso was passed by the House of Representatives, making it "an express and fundamental condition to the acquisition of any territory from Mexico, that neither slavery nor involuntary servitude shall ever exist therein." Two days later, however, on the last of that session of Congress, when the Proviso was to be considered by the Senate, John Davis of Massachusetts, in order to obstruct final action on the bill, filibustered until the meeting was over. Great consternation prevailed in the abolitionist North over the defeat of the Proviso, and it was then that the fight began in earnest. In the Twenty-ninth Congress the Democrats, as a result of the new tariff and the prominence given to the pro-slavery question in the conduct of the war, lost their majority and found their own ranks split by the implications of the Proviso.

Suddenly, on the 21st of December, 1846, the *Eagle* editor who had excoriated the Abolition extremists only a few weeks earlier, came out with a forceful editorial calling upon the Democrats to set down their feet in favor of the conditions of the Proviso. "If there are any States to be formed out of the

WHITMAN IN 1853
From a daguerreotype owned by Miss Bertha Johnston

"Whatever anyone else might think, the half-Quaker Walt had not the smallest doubt that the voice of God spoke through him."

territory lately annexed, or to be annexed by any means to the United States, let the Democratic members of Congress, (and the Whigs, too, if they like), plant themselves quietly, without bluster, but fixedly and without compromise, on the requirement that *Slavery be prohibited in them forever*. We wish we could have a straightforward setting down of feet on this thing, in the Democratic Party. *We must*."

Again and again Whitman returned to the fight and seemed to discern some encouragement for his side when the Senate of New York passed the so-called "anti-slavery resolutions" by an overwhelming majority, topped by the Assembly, where Democrat and Whig had united, as if in response to his adjuration that they set down their feet. But the Democratic Party itself, in fact, the very *Eagle* office, suffered a division which widened as agitation on the question increased. At first "Boss" Van Anden let his editor have his way, as he had from the outset. But Van Anden was treasurer of the local General Committee of the party, and the Committee, as he saw, was veering sharply away from the position which, through the editorials of Whitman, the *Eagle* expressed. It was time, Van Anden decided, to call his editor to party order.

He reckoned with the wrong man. With the stolid tenacity of the Dutchman Walt, now that his feelings about slavery were growing to convictions, stood firm and continued to write as his conscience dictated. He was a puzzled man endeavoring to find his way through the complexities of a nation which he loved and would save from disunion at any cost. For the Negro as a Negro he had no particular sentimental devotion; for the human being in bondage he had all the love and compassion of his generous nature. Slavery itself in the United States he looked upon as a vestigial evil which the great workings of democracy would get rid of, in God's good time. Meanwhile he had no patience with the hotheads of the North who by antagonizing the South in its fixed institution were stirring up

105

sectional feelings that, in their extremes, might endanger the Union. As for the war of imperialism with Mexico, he did not recognize it as such. By acquiring additional territory the United States was merely furthering the work of democratization of the world. He labored under a fallacious idealism, no doubt, but at the time, he thought it right. About the extension of slavery, however, he was clear. "As to building up the edifice of slavery any firmer—" he wrote, "spend the money and lives of the North . . . to make additional slave States, the thing is out of the question, and it seems to us no man worthy of the name of true Democrat could wish it."

Van Anden, however, had his own point of view, and it did not coincide with his editor's.

Chapter X: I am the Poet

FALSE indeed would Walt have been to himself and to his public had he not indulged in a ramblelogue or two during his editorship of the *Eagle*. One in particular, published on the 13th of June, 1846, he took great pains to make as edifying to his readers as it had been to him. Although years had passed since he had printed his graveyard verses in the *Long Island Democrat*, the mysterious fascination of death had lost none of its power over his imagination. The child who had haunted the family burial grounds, the Brooklyn schoolboy who had followed the funeral processions to the cemeteries, the sentimental young writer who had reflected on the blessings of death in his "Tomb-Blossoms" in the *Democratic Review*, had no morbid interest in man's passing away. Nothing of the macabre had ever entered his melancholy speculations. Even at the age when man, in the fullness of physical perfection, thinks of extinction as a certainty hard to reconcile with the newly experienced pleasures of life, Walt was writing: "The grave—the grave—what foolish man calls it a dreadful place? It is a kind friend, whose arms shall compass us round about and while we lay our heads upon his bosom, no care, temptation nor corroding passion shall have power to disturb us."

It was therefore in the spirit of a pleasure jaunt that on a bright June afternoon Walt jumped into one of the stages that started from Fulton Ferry, and set out for Greenwood Cemetery. He sat with the driver on the front seat—no other place ever satisfied Walt—and engaged him in conversation. James Gladding, however, had little of interest to impart to his passenger. He knew nothing of the history of the road he traveled every day, and had never had the curiosity to find out about an

107

ancient Dutch house that bore the date 1669 over the gable end. But the ignorance of his Jehu interfered not at all with Walt's enjoyment of the scenes met along the drive. How Brooklyn had grown since he had begun to exercise his vigorous pedestrianism on its roads and byways! Years ago, when he had first roamed over those ways, not a single house had stood where Atlantic, Butler and Court Streets now ran. Only huts, with here and there an old farmhouse had dotted the commons and the corn and potato fields. Beyond the city center, the road again wound through rural landscape until, four miles from the starting point, the stage stopped at the gate of the cemetery.

Before entering Walt took in the scene like one who, on beginning a book, turns over the pages to whet his appetite for the intellectual feast. Along the roads cut through the wide fields, he was sorry to see family parties driving in luxurious equipages instead of walking among the graves. Ruefully he saw that he was almost the only pedestrian. Still, there *were* people there, learning their lessons from the tombstones. "The effect were good, truly," he said to his readers the following day, "if the whole mass of our population—the delver for money, the idler, the votary of fashion, the ambitious man—if *all* could, ofttimes, move slowly through that Beautiful Place of Graves, and give room to the thoughts that would naturally arise there."

He, at any rate, devoted to those thoughts a full afternoon. "We like to walk aside from the beaten track," he said. Accordingly, leaving the carriages to their unadventurous road, he sauntered up knolls and into groves where, away from the more crowded acres of death, hid some lonely grave, made beautiful by shrubs and vines. In one such secluded spot, he came upon an enclosure containing a single grave, a child's, whose tombstone bore only the name "Rosa," and her age, eight years. Over the slab, from a rose-bush planted at the head,

108

leaned a single large pale rose. "Frail blossom!" sighed Walt, "thy parents' hearts yet ache, doubtless, as they think of thee!"

But he did not linger too long over the touching sight, nor sermonize unduly over the dark vault, not far off, made ready for another occupant. Wandering about, he paused by the side of a lake shadowed by woods and tangled shrubs. Here, near the shore, he came upon Indian Mound, the grave of a young woman, wife of the chief of an Iowa tribe. She had died in that neighborhood two or three years earlier. Walt had seen Do-Hum-Me before her fatal illness. He may even have been one of those who contributed toward the erection of the monument over her grave—a sculptured Indian, mourning.

Dutifully he gave scope to his thoughts. The spot was one of the loveliest in the cemetery. In that peace, by the quiet water reflecting sky and trees, away from envy, strife and cold misunderstanding, a poet might have found rest. Indeed, only a few feet away from the mound of Do-Hum-Me, one had recently been buried. Few had known McDonald Clarke, the mad poet, and those only to scoff. He had been miserably poor—no virtue ever among the living, however moving a text the biographer might make of poverty after the poet had died of it. Unhinged to begin with, Clarke had found no foothold for stability in the precariousness of his living. He became still more eccentric, so that people, unheeding the poet, noticed the madman, to make sport of him. Walt had seen him once or twice, and had been pained at the mockery his harmless aberrations excited in the heedless.

Now, by the dust of the unfortunate man, Walt took stock of the dead and of himself, the living, though, in his own case, only by inference. Scorned and laughed at, Clarke nevertheless had possessed a spark of the divine fire. "Whoever has power, in his writings," Walt wrote with meaningful generalization, "to draw bold, startling images, and strange pictures—the power to embody in language, original and beautiful and quaint ideas

—is a true man of song." So far he, Whitman, had drawn no startling images and strange pictures; but original and beautiful ideas had been starting to the surface of his mind from hidden depths. Now and then, like suddenly bright flowers, they broke forth in the dull fields of his prose. Was he a poet? Could he claim kinship with even so humble a son of song as Clarke? With amazing vividness, in the midst of an obscure essay on a graveyard, he drew the portrait of a poet—not simply McDonald Clarke who served as the model, but *the poet*, such a poet as perhaps he, Whitman, might be.

"Clarke was such an one; not polished, perhaps, but yet one in whose faculties that all-important vital spirit of poetry burnt with a fierce brightness. From his being out of the common channel; from his abruptness, and, if we may so call it, jaggedness of style—many persons have not taken the trouble to read the fugitive effusions which he gave to the world . . . He was very poor. Not of the earth, earthy—not engaged in the withering toils of traffic—not a votary at the altar of any golden idol—was he to whose memory we devote this passing tribute . . . Genius, after all, is a dangerous trait. Its fires, to be sure, sometimes enlighten and beautify, but quite often scorch, wither, and blast the soul of its possessor. Like Phaeton's privilege, the mighty gift conferred, may bring death and ruin."

Walt knew the glory of the gift of genius; he knew also its dangers. It was with his eyes wide open that he bent his head for the mighty gift conferred. No one, neither his mother who saw most deeply into his secretiveness, nor any other human being with whom he came in contact, marked the least difference in the outward man. But Whitman knew himself of the chosen. Not long after he had written his essay on the poet, he began to confide "original and beautiful ideas" to a small leather-looped notebook that he carried about with him jealously lest other eyes than his should fall upon it. They were strange, chaotic jottings—many of them observations in prose, some phrased with the sobriety of a newspaper editorial, others in the hortatory style of the preacher, still others in queer, fractured rhythms such as Elias Hicks might have broken into when, moved by the Spirit, he swayed back and forth, lending his body to the mighty shakings. Often the notes were admonitions to himself, like the opening stylistic direction: "Be simple and clear.—Be not occult," strikingly paralleled by a paragraph in the *Eagle* for July 20, 1847: "Don't attempt to be too fine in speaking. Use good honest English, and common words for common things. If you speak of breeches, shirt or petticoats, call them by their right names. The vulgarity is in avoiding them."

Had anyone found Walt's notebook of 1847-48, he would have been shocked by many of the writings. "Who is the being to whom I am the inferior?" read one bold note, capped by still another, "I never knew how it felt to think I stood in the presence of my superior." A further jotting helped to gloss what might have appeared arrant egotism: "Every American young man should carry himself with the finished and haughty bearing of the greatest ruler and proprietor—for he is a great ruler and proprietor—the greatest." "My life is a miracle and my body which lives is a miracle," he declared elsewhere, incorporating in the one sentence the mysticism of Hicks and transcendental affirmation. "But of what I can nibble at the edges of the limitless and delicious wonder I know that I cannot separate them, and call one superior and the other inferior, any more than I can say my sight is greater than my eyes.—"

"If I walk with Jah in Heaven and he assume to be intrinsically greater than I it offends me, and I shall certainly withdraw from Heaven,—for the soul prefers freedom in the prairie or the untrodden woods—and there can be no freedom where—" By its very boldness the thought cut itself short.

"Different objects which decay, and by the chemistry of nature, their bodies are [   ] into spears of grass—" read another

111

note, followed more explicitly by a pregnant suggestion, "Bring all the art and science of the world, and baffle and humble it with one spear of grass."

What genius—or was it madness?—was working itself out in these electric jottings, thrown off like the lambencies of a soul aglow? Why did Walt suddenly feel the necessity to write them down? What was he contemplating? Had the moment arrived for his spiritual simmering to come to a boil? Or had he heard the inner voice saying, sarcastic, *"Walt, you contain enough, why don't you let it out then?"* For some pages in the notebook there was nothing but blankness. When he wrote again it was to give the answer in the accent and form of the book by which he will always be known:

> I am the poet of slaves, and of the masters of slaves
> I am the poet of the body
> And I am
>
> I am the poet of the body
> And I am the poet of the soul . . .
>
> I am the Poet . . .
>
> Have you supposed it beautiful to be born?
> I tell you I know it is just as beautiful to die;
> For I take my death with the dying
> And my birth with the new-born babe.

He was a poet. So much Walt, at the ripe age of twenty-eight, had determined. Not a lecturer, not an actor, for all his well-thumbed prompt books, not a journalist, even though for over a year he had been occupying an enviable post on an important paper, not even a novelist, contrary to the advertisement of *Franklin Evans*. He was not only a poet but a new kind of poet. He had struggled within himself, as the groping repetition showed, before the directness of his statement of fact: "I am the Poet." After that he had only to go on, and he did go on, in the exalted pronouncement of the four lines on birth and death. By ten years the secret scrawl in Walt's notebook preceded Emerson's concise expression of transcendental mysticism in his "Brahma" which everyone was to find so baffling and so grand:

If the red slayer think he slays,
  Or if the slain think he is slain,
They know not well the subtle ways
  I keep, and pass, and turn again . . .

They reckon ill who leave me out;
  When me they fly, I am the wings;
I am the doubter and the doubt,
  And I the hymn the Brahmin sings. . . .

How had Walt come to the superb conviction: "I take my death with the dying. And my birth with the new-born babe"? True, the Transcendentalists had long stressed the relation of man and nature and God, a doctrine which by making man the sum and summit of all created things, conceived of him also as part of nature, the physical reflection of the mind of God. Again, just as nature reflected God, man's mind became the mirror of celestial good and divine love. Partaking as he did both of God and the physical world, man, therefore, identified himself with the manifestations of nature and the body and spirit of his fellow-man. For were they not all compact of the essence of godhood? "What is there of the divine in a load of bricks?" asked Emerson, answering succinctly, "Much. All."

Out of the orbit of Transcendentalism, as far as the movement itself was concerned, Whitman could have felt its influence only by reflection, which lends more veracity than critics are willing to grant to his repeated assertions, late in life, that Emerson's essays and poems had no direct relation to the inception of *Leaves of Grass*. He even told Burroughs that up to the time he published the quarto edition, he had never read Emerson at all, although in the *Eagle* for December 15, 1847, he quoted a paragraph from "Spiritual Laws," one of Emerson's lectures which he, Whitman, acknowledged to be as truthful as it was beautiful. There was nothing in that essay, however, which he could not have derived from the inspired words of the Quaker preacher whose personality had been so powerful a force in his growth. Certainly by the time he read "Spiritual Laws" he had already planted in his notebook the living germ of *Leaves of Grass.* In a general sense Emerson could have been called his master, but his influence exerted itself in the intellectual world only like the light of the sun, which gives hue to every flower, each in its kind. Walt Whitman, however, was a new genus.

Long ago, when Whitman had first thought of himself as the author of a book, he had said with callow modesty: "I would carefully avoid saying anything of woman; because it behooves a modest personage like myself not to speak upon a class of beings of whose nature, habits, notions and ways he has not been able to gather any knowledge, either by experience or observation." Though he had as yet but imperfect familiarity with the subject he would once have omitted, he now saw the fallacy of excluding half of the human race. The book he was planning must include all, as nature included all. He wrote among many other verses of his projected poem:

> I am the poet of women as well as men.
> The woman is no less than the man
> But she is never the same.

How negligible the assurance he felt about woman he betrayed in the ineffective conclusion. But the true knowledge was to come, even to him.

Nevertheless, although he was confessedly inexperienced about marriage, he had taken it upon himself in his editorial capacity to offer unbidden advice in the guise of a humorous essay on April Fool's Day, 1846,—the year before he elected himself the poet of women as well as men. Under the heading, "Motley's Your Only Wear," he dilated on the subject of what fools these mortals be, concluding, "As we must stop in the category somewhere—we wind up with that multitude (if it be not a bull to say so) of single fools, the bachelors and maids who are old enough to be married—but who, from appearances, will probably 'die and give no sign.' If seizing the means of the truest happiness—a home, domestic comfort, children, and the best blessings—be wisdom, then is the unmarried state a great folly."

Why, one might ask, did he then not follow his own advice? Men much younger than he were already fathers of families in those days of early marriages. What kept him, a lusty man, earning a good salary, from assuming the responsibilities he urged upon others? He answered for himself under an innocent generalization: "There be some, doubtless, who may not be blamed—whom peculiar circumstances keep in the bonds of the solitary, but the most of both sexes can find partners meet for all, if they will. Turn Fools, and get discretion," he concluded with sudden levity. "Buy candles and double beds; make yourself a reality in life—and do the state some service."

What were the peculiar circumstances to which he alluded, circumstances valid enough to keep people from marrying? That they were not social or economic he made clear by the assumption that "the most of both sexes *can find partners meet for them*." Nevertheless, he recognized certain circumstances, having nothing to do with economic responsibility, which were yet strong enough to create a bar to marriage—physical, perhaps, or more likely, psychic, since the *inability* to find partners *meet* for them prevented the consummation he charged upon the bachelors he addressed. Did he fall under the category of those who were not to be blamed for remaining single? In that case, what were *his* "peculiar circumstances?" Had he already

115

determined upon himself as the dedicated poet, wed only to his poetry? Had he sought and failed to find the one *meet* for him? Or was he aware of any psychic difference in himself that set him apart from the generality of his fellows? "Make yourself a reality in life," he admonished, "and do the state some service." Did the breeding of children constitute the most cogent argument for marriage? Was it solely a civic duty? What place did romantic love, which the poets had always sung, hold in Whitman's scheme? Why did he not, as the ardent patriot, "do the state some service?" If he asked himself those questions he must have answered them to his satisfaction, for long after he had urged others to marriage he was still a bachelor.

The subject continued preying on his mind, however. Ten months after the April Fool's Day article, he ran a brief paragraph, startling for its lack of connection with anything but perhaps the author's own thoughts: "Young man reader! if you have good health, are over twenty-one years old, and nothing to 'incumber' you, go and get married."

In the *Eagle* office, as matters of general policy pressed to the fore, the differences between "Boss" Van Anden and his editor grew daily more pronounced, especially over the issue of Free Soil on acquired territory. From the beginning, as Walt had shown in his editorials, he had been a Proviso man where the rest of the Democratic Party shilly-shallied. A loyal partisan, he had clung to the Jacksonian standard, salving his conscience as best he could over the discrepancy he saw between the ideal and practice in the workings of the Democrats. On the Proviso both the party and his loyalty tottered. "Set down your feet, Democrats!" had sounded in vain for half the members of the Democratic Party as the convention which met in Syracuse in the summer of 1847 clearly showed when, at its heated sessions, the machine defeated the proposals of the Proviso group to align the party with the advocates of Free Soil. Democrats split into Hunkers and Barnburners, the rightists and the radicals, from analogy to the farmer who burned down his barn to destroy the rats. Hunker stood for the stand-pat Democrat who accepted the whole "hunk" of party policy as handed down by the tried machine; Barnburner implied the hotheaded nonconformist who would destroy the party to do away with trivial abuses. A Barnburner, Whitman saw nothing trivial in the Free Soil question and therefore continued to use his paper as a sounding board for what he considered the right party policy. Van Anden gave him warning. Whitman persisted in his Barnburning activities. Free Soil, with its far-reaching implications, had become too serious to be subjected to party loyalty.

In editorials and subsequently in verse, Whitman showed the fine passion of which he was capable when treating a subject that engaged his convictions. Slavery must not spread through the land of the free; the dignity of labor must not be imperiled by the interests of the slave owners of the South. To Walt "the grand body of white workingmen," the backbone of the nation, represented one of the most important factors of the great democracy. Slavery menaced them by making them compete with labor in chains. "And this it is," he explained, "which must induce *the workingmen of the North, East and West, to come up, to a man, in defense of their rights, their honor. . . .*" He must spur America's laboring millions to make their importance felt.

In the middle of a common harangue Whitman, as if impelled by a realization of the poetic mission recently confided to his notebook, broke into an orchestration of sound, to be matched only by the overwhelming piling of word upon word in *Leaves of Grass.* "Let them utter forth then, in tones as massive as becomes their stupendous cause," he invoked the American workingmen, "that their calling shall *not* be sunk to the miserable level of what is little above brutishness . . . We call upon every mechanic of the North, East, and West—upon the carpenter, in his rolled-up sleeves, the mason with his

117

trowel, the stonecutter with his brawny chest, the blacksmith with his sooty face, the brown-fisted shipbuilder, whose clinking strokes rattle so merrily in our dock yards—upon shoemakers and cartmen and drivers, and paviers and porters, and millwrights and furriers, and ropemakers and butchers, and machinists, and tinmen, and tailors, and hatters, and coach and cabinet makers—upon the honest sawyer and mortar-mixer too, whose sinews are their own—and every hard-working man—to speak in a voice whose great reverberations shall tell to all quarters that the *workingmen* of the free United States, and their business, are not willing to be put on the level of Negro slaves. . . ."

Anyone who read the editorial of September 1, 1847, had a foretaste of the cataract-like power of the Whitman catalogue, that gushing and pouring of his immense apprehension of life breaking its confines to tumultuous expression. Now for the first time, amid the rhetoric of a political apostrophe, appeared the only poem he had so far published.

Neither Van Anden nor anyone else of the Hunker faction saw any reason to rejoice either in the form or the content of "American Workingmen versus Slavery." Four more months the refractory Barnburner was tolerated at his post, and then he suddenly found himself free to explore the city as he pleased without the routine of the daily visit to the *Eagle* sanctum. Neither the rows with Van Anden, nor the suasions of interested politicians had availed to make the stubborn Walt toe the party line. The final clash came when he assailed editorially the letter which General Lewis Cass had sent to A. O. P. Nicholson of Nashville in which the general, with ambitions toward the White House, skirted the dangerous subject of the extension of slavery by advocating the principle of local self-government in the acquired territory.

"All this might come with a better show of sense," wrote the clearsighted Walt on the 3rd of January, 1848, "if the legisla-

tive power of Congress over all its territories, were not as supreme while they *are* territories, as the State Legislatures over
their respective States . . . Is there a sane man who will say
that it is profitable so to introduce slavery?"

His outspokenness cost him his comfortable "sit"—but not
before he had kicked a meddling politician down the *Eagle*
stairs. Friendly papers took up the cudgels for the discharged
editor. Others, with political axes to grind, seized the opportunity to make the Hunker paper their whetstone. Several
weeks later, however, the *Tribune* contained a notice that "Mr.
Walter Whitman, late of the *Eagle*" was to have charge of a
new daily paper, to be published by the Barnburners in Brooklyn. But before anything came of the projected enterprise, Walt
was flying South on pinions free and with a good sum of money
in his pocket.

Chapter XI: O magnet—South!

CIRCUMSTANCE and change had begun to make themselves felt with the dawn of the year 1848. At first, despite the quarrels with Van Anden, Walt had seen little reason to fear for his position. Suddenly he found himself stranded, without a job and with no prospect of another. He had not let it interfere with his enjoyments, however. Several weeks after his last piece appeared in the *Eagle*, during an intermission at the Broadway Theatre, he fell to talking with a Mr. McClure, a Southerner on business in New York. Walt never hesitated to address anyone he met, whether the man were a laborer on a ferry, or the moneyed gentleman who, from his presence in the lobby of the opera, must obviously have kindred interests with him.

Stranger, if you passing meet me and desire to speak to me, why should you not speak to me?
And why should I not speak to you?

After the words of greeting Walt found that besides music he and the stranger had another interest in common; for as Mr. McClure was quick to tell him, he had come up North to look for someone to edit the paper which he and his partner, Hayes, were about to start in New Orleans. Walt and Mr. McClure took a friendly drink together. By the time they parted that night, Mr. McClure was convinced that none but Walt should be the editor of the *Crescent*. Walt had nothing to lose and much to gain from the journey South. Besides a remunerative position—a secondary consideration with one who despised riches—he would be able to see for himself the amplitude of his beloved America.

120

The paper was to begin publication in March. On February 11 he took the train for Baltimore. He was not alone. Since Mr. McClure had given him two hundred dollars for traveling expenses, much more money than Walt's moderate needs required, he was taking along Jeff, his adoring brother. The boy was fifteen years old. Next to Eddie, Walt had shown a protective interest in Jeff who, unlike the other sons, had been privileged to take violin lessons out of the family's scanty budget. Jeff, in return, looked up to Walt with the emulous affection of the younger brother who sees in the older man all that he wished to be.

Neither of the two had ever traveled far from home. The trip to Louisiana took on all the enchantment of exciting adventure. The trains, the passengers, the luggage, the crush and noise, the leavetakings and the scrambles for seats—there was nothing that Walt failed to observe and to record in his almost photographic memory. For him this was no mere trip to fill a position in a distant city. It was a voyage of devotion, an act that brought him close to the vast unknown of America, the America that must become as much a part of him as his own flesh. He had left New York with every nerve tingling to the knowledge that he was a poet. Not a thought in him but turned, from the impressions gathered and the moment lived, to the secret dedication of himself. He took his notebook with him. Everything in life must find its place in his large scheme, albeit so far he saw it indistinctly and with no form except a sense of its magnitude.

The ride by rail to Baltimore was made in a day. At seven the following morning they changed trains for Cumberland, one hundred and seventy miles distant. The travelers missed nothing of the landscape. Now, for many miles, the train seemed to follow the course of a narrow, endlessly winding river, turning where it turned, and chugging docilely along where it straightened. Walt marveled at the engineering feat when, as

121

they penetrated more deeply into the mountainous country, sudden cliffs, high as the Alps, rose now on one side, now on the other, in the bleakness of the wintry scene. What ingenuity it must have taken to hew through those mighty buttresses of nature! The enterprise paid enormous profits, however, considered the politically wise Walt, who thereupon began to speculate on the amount of talk it would take before the road was extended as far as Wheeling.

At Harper's Ferry the train came to a stop. No sooner had it pulled in than the station became a pandemonium of shouts and the clanging of bells as an army of hotel decoys made every effort to lure the hungry passengers to their particular resort for dinner. Little did Walt know on what ground he was standing, or what tragedy would there be enacted! With the quiet enjoyment of the traveler, he and Jeff had a substantial dinner for twenty-five cents, and leisure to look about them at the varied scenery, the abrupt hills and the houses clambering one on top of the other, to the summit.

Toward sundown they arrived at Cumberland. A prosperous town, with its newspapers and thriving hotels, it offered a novel spectacle in the droves of covered wagons that filed in from hundreds of miles west with their freight for the eastern markets. The huge, lumbering caravans of canvas-covered vehicles, built high at each end and low in the middle, with their teams of four or six horses, brought something foreign to the American landscape. Walt had never met a caravan on the Steppes, but that was how such a procession must have looked, he reflected. A Chinese junk which he had seen exhibited in New York not so long ago, had had the strange, scooped-in look of the Pennsylvania wagons. And all this in the United States which he had known only from the wide gateway of New York. Thrilling to the vastness and variety which he was now seeing with his own eyes, he was confirmed in his faith in America. Everything was to be found here where all, nevertheless, was

122

still undiscovered. The Old World and the best in it had been assimilated till all were part of the New, the olden beauty extant in some subtle variant which was yet distinctly American.

With mixed feelings Walt recognized the fusion the more he saw of the country whose greatness he had until then beheld only in imagination. Excited by the strangeness which gave his journey the novelty of travel in foreign parts, he could not for a moment forget that his excitement was perfectly legitimate. He had thought of Alps and Steppes at some aspects of the American landscape. Good. But he had thought of them only to show that we had such wonders here, too. When the time should come for him to "express" America, he would do it in American terms. Bearing his determination in mind, he made his notes, laboring for originality of style. The novelty was still too fresh, however. Originality, not yet mellowed by tranquil recollection, gave some of his first strivings a hideous vulgarity hardly to be reconciled with the Poet of the notebook. "Night now falling down around us like a very large cloak of black broadcloth, (I fancy *that* figure, at least, hasn't been used up by the poets) and the Alleghenies rearing them up 'some pumpkins' (as they say here), right before our nasal members, we got into the several four-horse stage coaches . . . whereby we were to be transported over the big hills. . . . Up we toiled, and down we clattered . . . over these mighty warts on the great breast of nature."

From Cumberland to Wheeling rumbled the coaches over the Alleghenies, the nine passengers in each passing the time in conversation. Walt spoke, or rather, listened to a garrulous patriarch, just returned from Washington, whither he had gone to claim a long-due reward for capturing a British merchant brig during the war with England. The brig, he narrated, had been lying in the New England waters. With his fishing smack he had captured her, brought her into port and had the satisfaction of seeing her cargo sold by the government for thou-

123

sands of dollars. Since he had had no privateering papers, he received no share of the sale, but he still had hope, after so many years, that Washington would give him his reward. "Poor old man," reflected Walt. "If he lives till he gets Congress to pay him, he will be immortal."

He liked the spirit of the man, however, who insisted on his rights even though his act of heroism would probably go unrewarded to oblivion. He talked sound sense besides on the Mexican war just ended, and advocated government pensions for the disabled veterans. It was a subject close to Walt who had written in the *Eagle*: "If we are to have war, the common soldiers, the *workingmen* of the army, should be well paid. They should have tracts assigned them from the government lands of the West. . . ." Peopled with heroes the West would bring forth heroes, like this grand old fellow who had brought thirteen children into the world, "All being alive and kicking!" Walt admired. He was meeting fellow-citizens face to face, men from the unspoiled West, and he loved them for their manliness and their habit of thinking for themselves.

Every ten miles or so the coaches stopped at the long, low roadhouses to change horses. Stiffly the passengers descended the steps, hugged their coats and shawls about them, looked up at the surrounding mountains and naked winter trees, and hurried toward that great hole of light in the moonlit vagueness which meant a welcome fire in the inn. For Walt the scenes in the waiting room held a peculiar interest. Where else had one such stupendous fires, such varied types, like those strapping drovers resting on the benches or sprawled before the hearth, as the red glow now lighted, now cast them back into the shadows? Here were pictures worthy of a great painter, "An *American* painter," thought Walt, "one who, not continually straining to be second or third best, in *imitation*, seizes original and really picturesque occasions of this sort for his pieces."

Outdoors nature lay in solemn enchantment. Standing at

the end of the long porch of an inn Walt, with the faculty that
had always been his, became the thing he saw. It was a majestic
sight. On one side reared a forbidding cliff; all about rose the
mountainous earth toward the starry winter sky. "The silence
of the grave spread over this solemn scene; the mountains were
covered in their white shrouds of snow—and the towering trees
looked black and threatening; only the largest stars were visible, and they glittered with a ten-fold brightness. One's heart
at such times, is irresistibly lifted to Him of whom these august
appearances are but the least emanation." *Night, sleep, death
and the stars* . . . Always his inmost self responded to the
grandeur of these appearances, the four universal strings from
which he was to draw his noblest music.

The last stages, after a stop at Uniontown in the gray dawn,
brought the travelers to Wheeling late Sunday night. In the
wharf the *St. Cloud*, steam up and lamps aglow, lay ready for
the voyage down the Ohio to New Orleans. Weary from their
jolting on the coaches, Walt and Jeff retired immediately to
their stateroom for a well-earned rest. The packet started off
almost immediately. When Walt awoke at the call of the breakfast bell at six o'clock the following morning, he found that
the ship had covered a good part of the distance to Cincinnati.

Daylight and a sound night's sleep buoyed up Walt for his
explorations. He overlooked no part of the boat. Not counting
his fellow passengers he found the *St. Cloud* tenanted by as
heterogeneous a collection of livestock as had ever boarded a
Noah's ark. Besides a dog, a permanent resident of the boat, he
came upon coops filled with geese, turkeys and other bipeds,
that sent up their protests in a discordant concert aided by the
bass of a number of hogs. During the frequent stops for the
exchange of cargoes (for the *St. Cloud*, a freight boat, took passengers only by courtesy), the quantity and genus of the livestock changed. Many other kinds of cargo, however, were taken
up at the various ports—here barrels of pork and lard, there

bags of coffee, rolls of leather, drygoods and other commodities. Walt, long familiar with the port life of New York, reckoned that the little *St. Cloud,* through the business tactics of her canny captain, managed to ship cargo enough for a liner.

He enjoyed life on shipboard. With the rest he got up shortly after dawn, ate his meals at the common table, read, and in the long nights talked with the smokers round the stove. There was no mingling of the sexes. Off in their part of the cabin the women sat for the most part listlessly, doing nothing—"And as far as I could learn, saying nothing!"

But even the women were shaken out of their torpor when the Captain, on crossing the falls of the Ohio just below Louisville, decided to go over the "boiling place" instead of taking the canal. At one stretch the Ohio dropped about twenty feet in the course of a mile. The intrepid Captain, guiding the boat over the shallow waters, was taking a great risk. More than once the bottom grated over the rocks and the pilots looked tense; but happily the *St. Cloud* made the dangerous pass without mishap.

At Cairo the muddy yellow Ohio gave way to the Father of Waters. They stopped long enough at the junction for Walt to express his disappointment in the town which, in spite of the outlay of money, remained a damp, unwholesome place. "It is doubtful whether Cairo will ever be any 'great shakes,' except in the way of ague," he punned irreverently.

The rest of the voyage proceeded uneventfully but for the stops at the ports which Walt always found of intense interest. Then one night, on the Mississippi, under the spell of darkness and the sea, he wrote a poem, not in the new rhythms he had recently confided to his notebook, but in the trite quatrains of his adolescent verses. A new sensitiveness, an awareness of things to come, almost a foreboding, brooded over the lines, as if some inner urge, or desire, or fear, had been made manifest in the mysterious night.

O magnet—South!

How solemn! sweeping this dense black tide!
  No friendly lights i' the heavens o'er us;
A murky darkness on either side,
  And kindred darkness all before us!

Now, drawn nearer the shelving rim,
  Weird-like shadows suddenly rise;
Shapes of mist and phantoms dim
  Baffle the gazer's straining eyes . . .

Oh, tireless waters! Like Life's quick dream,
  Onward and onward ever hurrying—
Like death in this midnight hour you seem,
  Life in your chill drops speedily burying.

What inner voice was giving him warning, and why this dwelling on death when free as never before, he could, if he chose, pour the "pent-up aching rivers" of his being into the fathomless ocean of life?

A few more stops, at Cincinnati, at Louisville, and the *St. Cloud*, rounding the last curve of the river, panted into the stone wharf of New Orleans, fabulous city of the South. It was late at night. For a long time, while the passengers and their luggage were being landed on the cobblestones, the *St. Cloud* kept her lights in festive brilliance among the phantoms of the moored ships about her. But no lights shone with more promise of romance for the young travelers than the dim lamps of New Orleans' historic quarter. How far away seemed New York where even then the *Eagle* was carrying on a squabble with the *Advertiser* on the dismissal of Whitman:

It is true, as you say,
We sent Whitman away,
But that is a private affair;
But since you have spoken
Know by this token,
You have no *wit, man,* to spare.

The consequences of that private affair were the most momentous in Whitman's life.

Chapter XII: From pent-up aching rivers

WHEN Jean Baptiste Lemoine, Sieur de Boinville,
chose the hollow of a three-sided bend of the Mississippi in 1718 for the site of the city he named after
the Regent of France, he must have had more than his share of
the prophet's second vision to see in that swamp overgrown
with willow and dwarf palmettos the capital of the province of
Louisiana. Hardly more promising as citizens of New Orleans
appeared the unruly riff-raff of galley-slaves, adventurers and
gold-hunters who under his direction cleared the land both of
its undesirable growths and the populations of serpents and
alligators that since Adam had been obeying unmolested the
biblical decree to increase and multiply. However, as the settlement sank its foundations deeper, the cluster of wretched
hovels put up by the founders, gave way to solid houses that
carried over the graces of old-world architecture. Then in 1788,
after the great fire reduced to ashes most of the old city, it rose
beautified without losing its ancient charm. Occupying as it did
a position of strategic and commercial importance, New Orleans spread from the original hollow which had given it the
name of the Crescent City from its curving river front, to an
extensive metropolis carrying as it were in its pocket the *Vieux
Carré*, or the old rectangle of the original town.

Until 1803 New Orleans with the rest of Louisiana had developed under the influence of France and Spain. But on the
30th of November of that year, in the council hall of the city,
the people of Louisiana relinquished their allegiance to the
King of Spain when the keys of the city were restored to the
French colonial prefect in a symbolic ceremony. Three weeks
later the keys passed into the hands of the Commissioners of the

128

United States by right of purchase of a large tract of the original province.

Under the new regime the city prospered, especially after Louisiana was admitted as a state into the Union. Without disturbing the *Vieux Carré* with its picturesque houses, its stuccoed walls and wrought iron lattices, the massive locks and hinges of the Spaniards and the delicate urns, fountains and statues of the French, the American quarter or New City, established itself in the south-west. Now with the balconies overgrown with roses and vines, New Orleans experienced the dignified residence of the business magnate whose taste, guided by money and fashion, succumbed also to the grace of what he saw about him. St. Charles Avenue and Canal Street with their fine new buildings and busy air of commerce, emphasized rather than marred the old charm of Toulouse Street and Dauphiné, Unzaga, Salcedo and Casa Calvo, names that were like the rubricated capitals on a page of history. Indeed, history had left still more solid records, like Lafayette Square and the bronze equestrian statue of Andrew Jackson in the Place d'Armes, showing the hero at the moment he made his triumphal entry after the Battle of New Orleans in 1815.

When Walt set foot in the storied city, Friday night, February the 25th, he had time only to find a room for himself and Jeff. After a makeshift arrangement the following day, he decided that the best was none too good; accordingly some time later, he settled in quarters at the Fremont in the American district. He could not have been better situated. Across the street the St. Charles Hotel teemed with the coming and going of visitors from all over the world. Rancheros from South America rubbed elbows with world-famous artists, attracted by the well-attended theaters and the opera houses, the boast of the Creole aristocracy which had made the city the capital of music in America. The first theater for such entertainment, the Théâtre de St. Pierre, erected in 1791, had been followed by the St. Philippe seventeen years later. The imposing building, modeled upon the eighteenth century opera houses in France, contained a parquet and two tiers of boxes where the Creole beauties and other members of Latin and American society could display their jewels against the protective bulwark of their escorts. No lady ever went to the theater alone. To provide privacy, and also to spare the feelings of those in mourning who sought the consolation of music, the Théâtre d'Orléans, when it was built, installed a few grilled loges.

The art of living developed to a high degree. During the season, while the coaches of society congested the avenues about the theaters, the district near the cathedral on Orleans Street in the old quarter swarmed with the city's population on their way to the famous quadroon balls in the Convent of the Holy Family. The brick building which had been given over to a Negro sisterhood, put aside its holiness for the occasion, and gaiety reigned in observance of the New Orleans tradition to tolerate everything but intolerance. Live and let live, though not formulated, became the rule of life among a people that had assimilated the pleasure-loving of the French and the romance of the Spaniard. Puritanism alone with its rigors and prohibitions was an alien thing. So much, indeed, had New Orleans adopted of the European way of life that during the holiday season thousands of visitors came from all parts of America to attend the colorful festivities.

The population alone was enough to give the city an exotic glamour. First came the Creoles in whom the European strain predominated through the mixture of blood of the French, the French Canadians and the colonists of the French and Spanish West Indies. For generations they had kept to themselves. Later, Spaniards of rank fused with the Louisiana Creoles, but the original stock retained the old Breton and Norman characteristics, the Creoles allowing the Spanish influence to make but few chinks in their armor of conservatism. Long after the

130

From pent-up aching rivers

French Revolution had lopped off aristocratic heads, wig and all, and discarded knee breeches for the proletarian culotte, the Louisiana Creole clung to the olden fashions. Far into the middle of the nineteenth century the silk stocking and silver knee-buckle, the peruke and the plumed headdress, were to be seen in the boxes of the opera houses. Only after Anglo-American modernity came in with the flood of immigration from the States did the Creoles show any sign of yielding, and then only to soften the ruggedness of the added element, the *Americain*.

Here and there the Spanish strain was observable in startling purity in some dusky face with liquid eyes and sharply defined features, clean as the edge of a cameo. More often it showed itself in a European cast in the bronze of an African face, as if some curious sculptor had experimented with his patinas. Although the lines of demarcation remained rigid between classes, the quadroon, the result of miscegenation, enjoyed privileges unknown to the rest of the Negro population with which, in spite of a limited legal freedom, it was linked. Yet even such infringements of caste the New Orleans code accepted as a proof of social tolerance.

Walt found himself in the magical city at the height of its holiday season. Balls, plays, concerts, carnival pageants spreading over a considerable period, gave New Orleans a liberating exhilaration that communicated itself to the staid Dutchman. Every day brought its adventures. At the time of his arrival the city was full of General Taylor's men released from the dangers of war and making the most of opportunities for pleasure unrivaled anywhere else in the States. Plain uniforms and epaulettes roamed all over town. Recklessness and gaiety, intensified after the privations of the Mexican campaign, became the order of the day. Walt mingled with the throngs. Among the stevedores, Negroes, boatmen, sailors of the crowded levees, he found the zestful life that stirred his blood. He talked with the quaint characters of the French Market, with the Negro and

Indian hucksters whom he found admirable specimens, with the handsome Creole mulatto woman, a noble creature of some two hundred and thirty pounds who gave him his breakfast of a biscuit and a large cup of wonderful coffee, poured out of a shining copper kettle whose proportions matched the vendor's. Early, as if with the air he breathed, he absorbed the easy tolerance of the people about him, together with the smattering of French which became for him the key to psychological release. The dominant conscience relaxed its vigilance, and Walt in New Orleans did as he saw the rest do. He who had once condemned coffee and all stimulants not only made a habit of patronizing the stand of the mulatto woman, but began to see the virtues of the imported wines and mild French brandies of the leisurely bar-rooms. Often the St. Charles saw him with the habitués relishing cobblers topped with snow and strawberries, in the popular New Orleans fashion.

And he began to notice women, not as in New York where the veil of a false idealization had blurred his vision, but as his imagination had shown him the seductive Margaret of *Franklin Evans*. He saw the type everywhere in the streets. Her eyes looked out from the face of the market women walking with the majesty of queens under the loads they balanced on their heads. He caught a glimpse of her behind a jalousie. He beheld her at her handsomest in the Old Cathedral, among others like her, dark-eyed Creole beauties, holding their gilt-edged prayer books in their hands "with an air that seemed to say that beauty was part of religion." More accessible, she was to be found in the flower girls, like the one who took her stand in front of the St. Charles Theatre next door to where Walt lived. Miss Dusky Grisette, he called her in the paper he devoted to her in the *Crescent*. "Her neat basket of choice bouquets sits by her side, and she has a smile and a wink for everyone of the passersby who have a wink and a smile for her." Surely Walt of the ready

132

greeting could not have snubbed one whom he took pains to describe with deceptive lightness.

"She can recommend a tasteful bunch of posies with all the grace in the world, and her 'buy a broom' style of addressing her acquaintance has, certainly, something very taking about it. She possesses pretty eyes, a pretty chin, and a mouth that many an heiress grown oldish and faded, would give thousands for. The *em bon point* of her form is full of attraction . . . The vermilion of her cheeks shows through the veil, and her long glossy hair is *nearly straight*." Again the italicized stress on the revealing circumstance: Margaret's skin "just sufficiently removed from clear white," and Grisette's "nearly straight" hair. Here it was, among the women of the South, with whose blood the tropical sun had mingled, that Walt found the beauty which could melt his long enduring resistance. Not for nothing did he set up obstacles of racial differences to his desire.

His contributions to the *Crescent*, which made its first appearance on the 5th of March after Walt had had ample opportunity to look about him, showed the erstwhile pugnacious editor of the *Eagle* in a woefully softened mood. It was a responsible job he had undertaken, and one which paid him so well that he who had never thought of accumulating money decided to save a thousand dollars to buy a farm for his mother. Editorially he still despised wealth, and seized the occasion of the death of Jacob Astor to preach a sermon on its inability to bring true happiness. What joy had there been in the mansion that bore the doorplate of "Mr. Astor"? "Ugh! the house gave one something of a chill when passing it, even in summer . . . The domestic affairs of Mr. Astor were never happy," he added in closing.

Money, domestic happiness: the contrapuntal themes made interesting music in the article of the bachelor who had counselled marriage to others. Was he now thinking of marriage for himself? And the plan to save money for a farmhouse—

was it motivated by the hope that he might bring a wife to live in the close domestic circle of which his mother was the center?

Whatever it was that had begun to leaven in him, it played strange tricks with his work, as the owners and the other editorial writers, Mr. Larue and Mr. Reeder, soon noticed. For the first two weeks Walt had given complete satisfaction. In fact, with his article in the daily *Crescent* wherein he defended the nude in such peformances as Dr. Collyer's "Model Artists" he had started a controversy, always a sign of lively interest. Walt had held to his guns, and unpopular guns they were in the middle of a reform-intoxicated century when the sight of a lady's ankle sent a flush to the masculine cheek. "The only objection that we conceive of to the undraped figure arises from an assumption of coarseness and grossness intended," he defended his article against the Mobile *Herald*. "Eve in Paradise —or Adam either—would not be supposed to shock the mind. . . . Amid all the works of that Power which, in the most stupendous systems and the smallest objects in them, shows such unspeakable harmony and perfection, nothing can compare with the *human* masterpiece, his closing and crowning work!" True, it had been a delicate question that the New York editor had taken up, but since it did no harm to the circulation of the *Crescent*, McClure and Hayes made no objection.

For some time they allowed him free use of the scissors in excerpting articles from the exchange papers which Walt later gave Jeff to sell for his own profit; they passed without blue-penciling his editorials and news stories; they even permitted without comment some feebly-written local color sketches of New Orleans characters. Then unaccountably, at least to Walt, the attitude of his employers changed. From cordiality it turned to singular coldness, and while they gave no direct reason for the change, they did enough by indirection to show that they had had enough of their importation. Jeff, poor innocent Jeff, who did all kinds of odd jobs for five dollars a week, received the full brunt of their irritability and was assigned much harder work than Walt would have permitted. The boy was not well. Besides feeling a terrible homesickness in the city that did not hold for him the attractions that it had for Walt, he was also suffering from the effects of the region, notorious for its epidemics of cholera. Walt, whose health was "most capital" who, indeed, felt better than ever before in his life, noted the iciness of the *Crescent* owners and wondered.

However, he did not let it affect the routine into which he fell, no matter where he was, making his work contribute to his pleasure and his pleasure to his work. He liked New Orleans. Here was a city where no blue laws existed, where on Sunday a man might dance and sing without being reminded that the Lord wants quiet on His day, where the opera began at six-thirty in the evening and lasted well into the night, where affairs of honor or of the heart were settled romantically at the Duelling Oaks, where women, whatever their color, were beautiful, and where love was love. Like recurrent motifs, women and love, with money and domestic happiness, came into his articles. He was in the throes of a powerful emotional upheaval. Mastered by it, he must speak out; but being Walt he made his confession cautiously and in terms so alien in their sentimentality that to this day his biographers are loath to use this leaden key to the secret of his heart. His sketch, "Samuel Sensitive" which appeared on the 2nd of May, and his article, "A Night at the Terpsichore Ball" of May 18, offer the two most positive clues, the one in a maudlin sketch of a lovelorn youth, the other in the first-person account of Walt's romantic encounter with a married woman at a masked ball. Alone, they are foundations too fragile on which to reconstruct his secret. Occurring when they do, however, and supported by other evidence, they add proof to the accepted theory of a New Orleans love affair.

It was his notebook, the book in which he had no need to be secretive, that received his whole confidence. For there he spoke not as Walt Whitman, the accidental man, but as Walt Whitman the Poet, who, as he had written, had "the divine grammar of all tongues." What he told might not be understood by all. But that was well. "The truths I tell you or to any other may not be plain to you, because I do not translate them fully from my idiom to yours.—If I could do so, and do it well, they would be as apparent to you as they are to me; for they are truths." Enough that for the present, he apprehended those truths himself.

And apprehend them he did with heart and brain and every one of his senses. By the wonder working of physical experience which in Walt involved the soul equally with the body, the giant, bowed in chains of puritanism and convention, now broke free and rose to the full immensity of his stature.

> I am the poet of sin,
> For I do not believe in sin,

he wrote, emboldened by his freedom. Generous in his no longer pent-up powers, he would have made all potent with himself, a man at last. Just as he had been reborn he would have all come to the utmost of their manhood.

> ### Strength
> Where is one abortive, mangy, cold
> Starved in his masculine lustiness?
> Without core and loose in the knees?
> Clutch fast to me, my ungrown brother,
> That I infuse you with grit and jets of life . . .
> I have stores plenty and to spare
> And of whatever I have I bestow upon you.
> And first I bestow of my love.

He too had been ungrown, till in a strange place and far

136

from repressing influences, he had had the strength to become
a man. The violence of the experience convulsed his whole
being. Daring conceptions, formless as lumps of lava thrown
from volcanic depths in the tumult of eruption, hurtled to his
consciousness. His shaken senses cried for appeasement which
could be found only in expression, after the flow and ebb of
passion. To whom could the poet speak the truths he had found
but to himself, until, in his function of "translator and joiner"
he had written them in the language of mankind? Hot as the
surge of desire, chaotic as passion, he wrote into his notebook
the paean of his awakened senses in words that borrowed from
the concrete and the mystical, till he scarcely knew his body
from nature's self, and his soul from God.

One touch of a tug of me has unhaltered all my senses but feel-
 ing . . .
They move caressingly up and down my body
They leave themselves and come with bribes to whatever part
 of me touches.—
To my lips, to the palms of my hands, and whatever my hands
 hold.
Each brings the best she has,
For each is in love with touch . . .
A touch now reads me a library of knowledge in an instant.
It smells for me the fragrance of wine and lemon-blows.
It tastes for me ripe strawberries and mellons,—
It talks for me with a tongue of its own . . .
The sentries have deserted every other part of me
They have left me helpless to the torrent of touch
They have all come to the headland to witness and assist against
 me.
I roam about drunk and stagger
I am given up by traitors,
I talk wildly I am surely out of my head,
I am myself the greatest traitor.
I went myself first to the headland.

Unloose me, touch, you are taking the breath from my throat!
Unbar your gates you are too much for me

Fierce Wrestler! do you keep your heaviest grip for the last?
Will you sting me most even at parting?
Will you struggle even at the threshold with spasms even more
  delicious than all before?
Does it make you to ache so to leave me?
Do you wish to show me that even what you did before was
  nothing to what you can do?
Or have you and all the rest combined to see how much I can
  endure
Pass as you will; take drops of my life, if that is what you are after
Only pass to some one else, for I can contain you no longer
I held more than I thought
I did not think I was big enough for so much ecstasy
Or that a touch could take it all out of me.

Never before had an American written so powerfully the language of the senses still reeling in the drunkenness of fulfillment.

Who was the woman whose power had overthrown the floodgates of his resistance letting loose the torrents of his desire? Was she some untaught flower girl wise only in the ways of nature, someone with a mouth "whom many an heiress would give thousands for," or the young lady he described in "Samuel Sensitive"—"with bright eyes, very bright, raven ringlets, very dark"? Was she the married woman at the masked ball, "she whom I have seen so often in dreams and imaginings," or some unknown Eve of mixed blood, like the octoroons he recalled with vivid emotion in his old age to young Traubel,—"women with splendid bodies—no bustles, no corsets, no enormities of any sort, large luminous bright eyes, face a rich olive; habits indolent, yet not lazy as we define laziness North; fascinating, magnetic, sexual, ignorant, illiterate; always more than pretty —'pretty' is too weak a word to apply to them"?

She could not have been of the aristocratic Creole class. Their women were too well guarded, and the boundaries of caste too rigidly respected, for any stepping up or down. The sense of family honor was so strong that many a man found himself challenged to the Duelling Oaks for a mere indiscreet glance at someone's wife or sister. At any social function of the élite, a man of so imposing a presence as Whitman, and so obviously a stranger, would have been the cynosure not only of the coquette, but of her watchful escort. Moreover, with the exception of the opera and the theater, he felt out of place at fashionable gatherings. At the by no means aristocratic ball in the suburb of Lafayette where he thought he had found the woman of his dreams, he chafed so much at the formality of white kid gloves that he burst through his too small pair.

Again, even if Whitman had fallen in love with a married or unmarried woman of family, as some of his biographers maintain against little evidence, he could not have pursued his passion without immediate discovery. Forty years after the event, when the mind of the old man wandered, he did say, among much that was contradictory, that he had had an experience of passionate love in New Orleans, but that it had ended quickly in an "enforced separation . . . the tragedy of his life." Who the woman was, he never told.

There is, however, pasted on a page of one of his notebooks, a tintype photograph of a young woman, treasured lovingly by the man who, before his death, took care to destroy all intimate records of his New Orleans sojourn. She is a girl of from twenty to twenty-five years old. Her face, of a distinctly southern cast, is framed in glossy black hair, parted in the middle and falling in curls on either side. Her "large luminous bright eyes" gaze not into the lens of the camera, like most of the early tintypes, but with a fervid intensity, a concentration of meaning, toward someone, perhaps Whitman, standing to one side when the photograph was taken. Her forehead is high and broad, the nose delicate yet wide-nostriled, the chin firm. The mouth gives the index of the whole face in the fullness of the lips and the negroid curve. Even from the faded color of the picture one knows that such a mouth, such eyes and hair, must have come with a skin of "rich olive." Under the loose jacket and the wide gathered skirt worn by women who refused to be enslaved by the wasp-waisted corset, one might guess a strong, sensual body, indicated by the rich, rounded throat and the powerful hands with their wrists of an admirable suppleness. She is not pretty. She is beautiful with the magnetic, sexual, earthy beauty of unspoiled womanhood.

She is not a woman of the upper classes; she is not of the Creole caste. Her clothes, in their inelegant simplicity and the cheapnes of the drab and plaid materials, are as far removed from the fashions of the day as she is, in her natural opulence, from the artificially constricted dressmaker figures that irritated Whitman with their "enormities." She is, in short, the octoroon he described so ardently to his young friend. "I slide my hand for the brown melons of your breasts," reads a vivid New Orleans note.

There is another clue to the social status of Whitman's beloved. Immediately before his rapturous outpouring on physical sensation come the broken lines:

It were easy to be beautiful with a fine complexion and regular
    features
' But to be beautiful
It were easy to shine and attract attention in grand clothes
But to outshine in sixpenny muslin

The duskiness of a southern face would not have been considered a fine complexion by an era that admired the alabaster brow and the throat of a swan, allurements which the feminine fair spent hours in secrecy to acquire. But to be beautiful—in the warm tones of the sun, that was true beauty for Whitman. As for clothes, in her sixpenny muslin the girl in the faded tintype outshines in her grave, concentrated passion the thousand vapid illustrations of the modish magazines.

Having found her, and through her the sources of his

strength, why did Whitman leave her? Who or what dictated
the enforced separation that was the tragedy of his life? No one
will ever know, but one may seek to pluck the heart of the mystery from what his abnormal vigilance overlooked in the records he left behind, albeit he did his utmost to lead one off the
track. "Far from her nest the lapwing cries away . . ." Like
Shakespeare's bird he cried most where his nest was not.

In the upheaval of his emotional life his work at the *Crescent*, never too good, deteriorated. McClure and Hayes, certainly, found little in their New York editor that they could
not have obtained more cheaply at home. The coldness between
them and Whitman turned to iciness. Soon they even avoided
the conferences they had been accustomed to have together on
the policies and management of the paper. Whitman, in his
perplexity at their revulsion of feeling, struck out at different
reasons but avoided the most plausible. They were Southerners,
imbued with the prejudices of their class. Rumors of his not
sufficiently clandestine affair, combined with the mediocrity of
his writings in the *Crescent*, must have made them leap upon
the first pretext to sever their relations with the least embarrassment to all concerned. It came on May 24 when Whitman
sent in a request for a small sum of money in advance. They
could make no more "advances" McClure answered coldly,
presenting a statement of what Whitman had already drawn.

Haughtily Whitman reminded them that far from his being
in their debt they were in his and suggested, with no thought
of being taken literally, that if they felt as they did, he would
be willing to dissolve the connection. With shocking alacrity
they accepted his resignation, waving aside the objections Walt
felt called upon to make. Three days later he and Jeff were
ready to leave New Orleans.

Before this, however, the enforced separation must have occurred between him and the woman he loved, for three days
would never have sufficed. They parted at the height of their

passion. Even though Whitman was to live for another forty-four years, the fire of his first and only experience of complete, generous, pure and exalting love (for it needed no sacrament to lend godliness to a relation which he saw as a holy one) burned in him to the end, infusing with life, ecstasy, sublimity and tolerance the book which more than his own body, was himself.

The reason for the parting will never be known. Perhaps the woman had ties she could not sever. Perhaps for the sake of the greatness she saw it in him to achieve she realized, with the uncanny wisdom of the "ignorant, illiterate," that his way must be traveled alone. Whatever the reason, they had to renounce a life together, an anchored home, and children. They made the sacrifice. One thing resulted. With his surrender of his love of the one, Walt turned to the love of the many. Since he could not belong to her, he would give himself to all, men and women.

> This is the common air . . . it is for the heroes and sages

he wrote before leaving New Orleans,

> It is for the workingmen and farmers . . . it is for the wicked just the same as the righteous.
> I will not have a single person left out . . . I will have the prostitute and the thief invited . . . I will make no difference between them and the rest.

A few years later, at the prompting of the past, and to record what he had long kept for himself alone, he wrote a poem, a half-confession of the love that changed his life. But he was not yet brave enough for the whole truth. He made of the experience of passion an experience of friendship with a man. "But now of all that city I remember only the man who wandered with me there, for love of me. . . ." It was the love that counted, no matter what the vessel, for its exaltation went beyond sex and became humanity. Ultimately he had the courage to set down the truth.

Once I pass'd through a populous city imprinting my brain for
    future use with its shows, architecture, customs, traditions,
Yet now of all that city I remember only a woman I casually met
    there who detain'd me for love of me,
Day by day and night by night we were together—all else has
    long been forgotten by me,
I remember only the woman who passionately clung to me,
Again we wander, we love, we separate again,
Again she holds me by the hand, I must not go,
I see her close beside me with silent lips sad and tremulous.

Chapter XIII: An end and a beginning

DIFFERENT from the journey South was the return home, as different as was the man from the immature youth who had set out. Winter had turned to spring; the efficient little steamer, *Pride of the West,* darted across the smooth water, making the voyage much more quickly than the commercial *St. Cloud.* It was just as well. The scene no longer had the excitement of discovery. Besides, Walt had other matters to think about. Jeff, now that he was on his way back, felt better and in gayer spirits. The homesickness of the past four months would be forgotten at the sight of his mother in her white cap and tidy black hair. She had not been well during their absence. For a long time not a line had come from home. It would be good to be surrounded again by familiar things and the faces of one's family, by the plain frame houses of Brooklyn, the Wallabout, Fort Greene and the ferries that had romance enough and to spare. It would be good to go back to West Hills and the haunts of fish-shaped Paumanok, good for Walt to recapture the healthful zest of his boyhood scenes and exorcise the enchantment of the South.

Walt felt unwell, whether from the rolling of the boat or from some other cause, he did not know. Certainly there were plenty of causes other than the mere motion of a steamer to make him uneasy. He had a secret which he must keep from all, especially from his mother. Would she guess what had happened to him during the few months of his absence? Would those shrewd, searching eyes of hers notice that the Walt who came back was not the Walt who had gone away? Guilt mingled with his uneasiness. In all probability, had Walt never gone away from Louisa's domination, he might not have known even the one love that marked the turning point of his life. In that family when a son married he was expected to bring his wife home to his mother, at least for a time, the new graft stemming off from the original stock as part of its own growth. How could Walt have brought to Louisa the woman he had loved in New Orleans? Would Louisa have understood where Hayes and McClure, men of the world, had failed?

One thing he knew, however, and that thing must have been brought home to him full force when, before the downrushing torrents of Niagara, he cried, "Great God! What a sight!" There was Walt Whitman. The dams of his soul at last sundered, he was free to pour out what had too long been held back. Thoughts, ideals, ambitions, his urge to help mankind, his humanitarianism, his pride of country, and most of all his irrepressible love, all were boiling and rushing in his spirit. Could he but harness their power, could he but direct into one channel that surging within him, he would set in motion some great good for the world. His renunciation, however painful—it remained the profoundest grief of his life—had brought him, though he did not then know it, his greatest gain. In losing his chance of happiness as a man, in surrendering himself, he had found the world. Psychologically, too, the experience had wrought a mighty good. With his emotional release, he himself was fertilized. The creative core that had long imprisoned tremendous potentialities, dormant like the buried seeds in ancient tombs, moved with life in rapture and pain; the time had come for it to burst forth. One notebook was filled. Eagerly he began another, putting down in it, thought on thought, as the leaves grow, the foliage of his tree of life. "Make full-blooded, rich, flush, natural works," he was to tell himself when he saw his conception clear. "Insert natural things, indestructibles, idioms, characteristics, rivers, states, persons. . . . Be full of *strong sensual germs.*" What a treasure for the world from one man's private loss!

At home it was as if the earth had never heaved, as it had for him, jolting him out of his orbit. Louisa, his father, his brothers, his sisters were as they had always been. Before his arrival he had had some moments of anxiety. But when he found himself in Brooklyn after sailing down the Hudson, strengthened by the grand and varied scenery, he knew he had worried needlessly. Nothing had changed, and no one perceived any alteration in him save for the healthy tan of his face.

Nothing had changed in the political life of Brooklyn, either, as he found out on opening the pages of the *Advertizer*. The feuds were still on, he gathered from the welcome the *Eagle's* rival gave him. "Whom should we meet, on the sidewalk of Fulton Street yesterday afternoon, with his brown face smiling like a wicker vessel filled with wooden particles cleft from timber, but our Barnburner friend himself? 'Rienzi has returned.' Dame rumor tells some tales of a forthcoming gazette, in which old Hunkerism is to be handled without gloves.— Put that and that together and see what it works out."

As it was, the rumor of the gazette had started soon after Walt had left the *Eagle*. Whatever ill feelings had cooled the relations between Van Anden and his Barnburning ex-editor, Walt's former boss did not long continue to bear him a grudge. When the first copy of the *Crescent* had been sent for notice to the papers, the editor of the *Eagle* compared it favorably with his own daily, discerned the hand of Whitman in some of the editorials, and ended with the wish that both Whitman and the *Crescent* flourish.

The political hatchets, however, were soon taken out by both factions and sharpened on the already much-used whetstone of the Free Soil issue. Hunker Democrats and Barnburners set to with a will, using as a pretext the Free Soil paper for which Walt began to raise money. Finding a willing and munificent sponsor in Judge Samuel E. Johnson, staunch in support of anti-slavery principles and anxious that they triumph in the impending elections, Walt took a basement office at 110 Orange Street, in the same building with Alden Spooner's *Star*, hired a force of brazen-lunged newsboys, and announced the *Freeman*, which came out on the 9th of September, 1848.

"Free Soilers! Radicals! Liberty Men!" it exhorted. "All whose throats are not quite tough enough to swallow Taylor or Cass! come up and subscribe for the *Daily Freeman!* It will be chock full of the right sort of matter. . . ." There was no mistaking the voice.

The *Freeman* started out modestly as a weekly. Later, if Van Buren, the candidate for the presidency endorsed by the Free Soil convention succeeded, it might be stimulated to become a daily, as the first issue promised. The opposing faction sputtered with wrath, but they might have spared their ire. On the very day the new arrival saw the light, a fire which had broken out in a neighboring building spread to those adjoining, enveloped a number of blocks whose frame houses offered excellent kindling, and lashed out as far as Orange Street. The *Freeman*, together with the building, went up in smoke.

But no such calamity as a fire could daunt a Barnburner like Whitman. Another plant was set up on Myrtle Avenue and phoenix-like the *Freeman* resumed its functions. "Will it be said that the friends of Liberal Principles here give it a meager and lukewarm aid?" Walt challenged. And the better to win over as many friends as possible he reduced the price of the paper from two cents to a penny. Full of zest he entered the election campaign, wrote his editorials and went with Judge Johnson as a delegate to the Buffalo Free Soil Convention. Alas, in spite of the valiant fight of his supporters Van Buren was defeated; but far from failing with the candidate, the *Freeman* flourished and in the spring of 1849 became a daily.

Dreaming of expansion Walt housed it in ampler quarters. "We are told, moreover," blurted the gossipy *Advertizer*, "that

147

he has lately erected a printing office in Myrtle Avenue . . . to which he intends to add a brick store and dwelling house— the first mentioned in which to traffic in stationery and books, and the other, no doubt, for the accommodation of a family when he becomes a Benedict."

It was his own family, his mother, father, brothers and sisters whom Walt accommodated in the new house, and the hint of the *Advertizer* that he would settle down like other men must have come with irony to the reluctant bachelor. From his larger office he continued bringing out the *Freeman*. Perhaps he also did some small business in books in the brick store. The volumes he had reviewed for the *Eagle* formed the nucleus of a good library. He had the Bible in Harper's illuminated edition, Boswell's *Life of Johnson* and the works of Frederika Bremer whom he esteemed so highly that if he had children, he said, her novels would be the first books he would put into their hands after the New Testament. He owned the poems of Bryant with whom he used to go walking, both with beards in the wind, as the elder poet told the stay-at-home of his travels in Europe. Carlyle he had in a number of volumes—*Past and Present, Heroes and Hero Worship, Sartor Resartus.* "There is a sort of fascination about the man," Walt had written, admitting less influence than he felt. Then there was the *Autobiography* of Goethe which convinced him that a fine book might be written on the materials of life. "What a gain it would be, if we could forego some of the heavy tomes . . . for the simple, easy *truthful* narrative of the existence and experience of a man of genius,—how his mind unfolded in his earliest years—the impressions things made upon him—how and where and when the religious sentiment dawned in him— what he thought of God before he was inoculated with books' ideas—the development of his soul—when he first loved— the way circumstances imbued his nature. . . ." The kind of book, in short, which he would write. He had also the *Journey-*

man Joiner and other novels by George Sand of whom he was
to speak as a genius in the same breath with Emerson and
Victor Hugo, and the *Biographia Literaria* of Coleridge—"that
legitimate child of imagery and true poet," he called him.

Altogether he had reviewed more than two hundred books
on varied subjects. Most of them he must have kept, if not
intact, then in loose pages which he had the habit of tearing
out and hoarding as his own particular treasure. One such
book, with the essay "American Literature" extracted for permanent keeping, was Margaret Fuller's *Papers on Literature
and Art* which had impressed him profoundly, especially on the
topic of the paper he had ripped out. True, the author's repeated call for a purely American literature echoed a need he
had always felt. But he had doubtless heard something fatalis-
tic in her assurance that America would some day foster a
genius "wide and full as our rivers, flowery, luxuriant and
impassioned as our vast prairies, rooted in strength as the
rocks on which the Puritan fathers landed. That such a genius
is to rise and work in this hemisphere we are confident." Did
he, with the humorless acceptance of the dedicated poet-prophet
see himself in her prediction? At any rate he took to heart, if
not the letter of her words, at least the spirit of her prophecy,
and when he came to describe himself did it with an echo of
her terms—"free, fresh, savage, luxuriant. . . ."

He was not too greatly disturbed, therefore, when after the
laudatory well-wishing of Greeley, Bryant and the *Star* which
spoke of him as a vigorous and independent man, party politics once again began to play their part by digging up old
feuds and reviving personalities. From not altogether disinter-
ested motives the *Advertizer* at this juncture saw fit to publish
the reasons for Whitman's break with the *Eagle*: "One was
that he was determined that the paper, while he edited it,
should not be the organ of Old Hunkerism;—on the other,
that on one occasion, when personally insulted by a certain

149

prominent politician, Mr. Whitman kicked the individual down the editorial stairs.—These two solemn facts were the head and front of his 'incompetency.'"

It may be the *Eagle* caught Whitman's accent in the phrase, "the head and front" and suspected collusion; perhaps it resented having its private affairs aired at a time when the editorial success of the man it had dismissed was patent to all. (Did not Whitman boast that the *Freeman* was selling three times more papers than the *Eagle?*) Whatever the cause, the retort it made in the issue of July 19, 1849, showed bad temper, spite and exasperation. The fellow even more than his partisans was proving too much for the *Eagle's* editorial nerves.

"We should suppose that the *Advertizer* had had enough, by this time, of the folly of petting Mr. Whitman," the article began, going on to say that the paper was wreaking its own ruin by making capital of Whitman. "Mr. W. came here from the *Star* office, where he was getting four or five dollars a week; he was connected with the *Eagle* for about two years. . . . Slow, indolent, heavy, discourteous and without steady principles, he was a clog upon our success, and, reluctant as we were to make changes, we still found it absolutely necessary to do so. Mr. W. cried persecution, and by this means interested the *Advertizer*, the *Evening Post*, the *Globe*, etc., in his behalf and through their good offices got a handsome place in New Orleans. How long did he remain there?—Until they could decently get rid of him."

In the same tone the article reviewed the founding of the *Freeman* and closed with a statement contrary to fact: "It is now dragging 'its slow length along' sustained by private contributions and manifesting neither tact, talent or industry.—Mr. W. has no political principles, nor, for that matter, principles of any sort. . . . Whoever knows him will laugh at the idea of his *kicking any body*, much less a prominent politician. He is too indolent to kick a musketo."

An end and a beginning

The *Eagle* did protest too much in its exaggeration of Whitman's indolence. It succeeded, however, in contributing to the myth of his incompetence as a journalist, a myth which it took seventy-five years to explode when his contributions to the *Eagle* were carefully collected by devoted scholars. The articles alone make two substantial volumes. Besides such articles and editorials, he printed numerous short stories and verses, some signed, some not. He commented on the theater and as reviewer he read and criticized books ranging from poetry to the then unnamed science of psychology. With all that, he saw to it that his readers were furnished with what he considered the best of literary fare, and republished poems by Bryant, Longfellow and Whittier and short stories by many contemporary writers. All this besides his selection of foreign and domestic news, his proofreading and other tasks that fall to the lot of the editor. Slow, indolent and heavy indeed! Like others, less prejudiced, the *Eagle* no doubt mistook the manner for the result. Nothing in the world could ever make Walt hurry. With his eye fixed on the assurance of eternity, he laid his foot lovingly on the earth, knowing that as a mortal he had but his allotted term upon it.

As for the *Eagle's* assertion that he had neither political principles nor principles of any other sort, he could make his actions speak for him. Had he not chosen to lose his situation rather than accept the *Eagle's* Old Hunker politics? Had he ever failed to speak boldly in his editorials? Was he not suffering ignominy even now for the very principles the *Eagle* denied him? He could well afford to hold himself above the battle, especially when it was fought on such terms.

From then on he began to lose interest in the *Freeman*, his last attempt at political reform. Soon he allowed himself to be superseded as editor, and on September 10, 1849, took a proud farewell of the embittered arena. "After this present date I withdraw entirely from the Brooklyn *Daily Freeman*. To those who have been my friends, I take occasion to proffer the warmest thanks of a grateful heart. My enemies—and old Hunkers generally—I disdain and defy the same as ever. Walter Whitman."

He knew at last what he was doing and he did it with finality. Henceforth his life was to be given up to the work for which he was born. Too long intimations had been vouchsafed him, whisperings to his soul, as real an entity as the great body which had so lately known the exaltation of love. Now, with the body itself keyed up to mystical apprehensions, everything in him spoke to him of his task. Impelled by the divine afflatus, surging and surging within him, he must break into words. He must make intelligible to his fellow men the magnitude of his meaning. He was great in his own right, for he with all mankind had in him the stuff of godhood. "Not even God," he wrote in his private book in a moment of mystical potency, "is so great to me as Myself is great to me.—Who knows but I too shall in time be a God as pure and prodigious as any of them?" (Under the date of August 15, 1851, Thoreau, with no knowledge of the man in Brooklyn or of the cosmic streams flowing through him, made this entry in his journal: "May I love and revere myself above all the gods that men have ever invented. May I never let the vestal fire go out in my recesses." Who shall speak positively of influences?)

Walt listened to his soul and responded to her wooings. Night and day he communed with her, in the silences of the dark in his room, and out under the sky, in refuges known only to himself, amid childhood scenes which from now on, through the full gestation of his work, he sought for the impulse of creation. It was in some such place that then, or at some unmentioned time, he received the revelation of his soul that loosed the stop from her throat and spoke the ineffable.

152

An end and a beginning

I mind how once we lay such a transparent summer morning,
How you settled your head athwart my hips and gently turn'd
over upon me,
And parted my shirt from my bosom-bone, and plunged your
tongue to my bare-stript heart,
And reached till you felt my beard, and reached till you felt my
feet.

Swiftly arose and spread around me the peace and knowledge
that pass all the argument of the earth,
And I know that the hand of God is the promise of my own,
And I know that the spirit of God is the brother of my own,
And that all men ever born are also my brothers, and the women
my sisters and lovers
And that a kelson of the creation is love. . . .

With the coals of Moses he traced the rapt unutterability.
Wherever it may have occurred, it became a place of miracles.
"I am a look-mystic—in a trance—exaltation." The words
forced themselves out of him as if he were the medium for
some occult force. The Spirit had spoken. What other summons did he need?

Yet there came another, from science, such as it was—and
Walt was too much a man of his time to remain unaffected
by it. He had first become acquainted with phrenology during
his *Eagle* days when among the books for review he had received a copy of J. C. Spurzheim's treatise on the subject. The
far-famed Johann Christoph was no longer among the living.
After a sensational career in England and France, lecturing on
the meaning of cranial bumps, he went to Boston where he
indirectly influenced the Transcendentalists—and died. His
work, however, had been taken up by eager disciples, and his
books went repeatedly into new editions. Whitman was so
fully convinced by what he read in Spurzheim's *Phrenology*
that in his review of November 16, 1846, he communicated his
conviction as a discovery. "Phrenology, it must now be confessed by all men who have open eyes, has at last gained a posi-

153

tion, and a firm one, among the sciences. . . . This large volume of Harpers, well printed, teaches of course from the fountain-head—from the most cautious, skeptical and careful of the Phrenologists, Dr. Spurzheim."

Following close upon the interest roused by the curious science, came the Fowler brothers, Orson Squire Fowler and Lorenzo Niles Fowler, with their associate, Samuel Roberts Wells, who had established a Phrenological Cabinet at 131 Nassau Street, near Beekman. Whitman, of whom none could say that he did not keep his eyes open, discovered it at about the time he read Spurzheim's book. It became as popular a place as Dr. Henry Abbott's Egyptian Collection on Broadway, where Walt would have interminable talks with the proprietor from whom he learned more than from any book about the antiquities of Egypt, its history, religion and the symbolism of the relics exhibited.

However, Dr. Abbott's collection pertained to the dead, whereas the Phrenological Cabinet, in spite of the thousands of skulls, both human and animal from all parts of the world, had everything to do with the living. For it was through the analysis of such skulls, and the application of the knowledge to the crania of the living, that one could discover weaknesses and capabilities, and so make the most of one's life.

Besides specializing in the phrenological science the Fowler brothers branched out to other subjects of interest to the man of emancipated mind. Orson, indeed, was becoming a thorn in the side of respectability for his advocacy of the *recognition* of sex, while Lorenzo was making himself equally suspect for his unorthodox views on marriage. Open of intellect as he was of eye, Whitman saw the value of the Fowlers' crusade, hence, when he received Lorenzo's book, *Marriage*, for criticism in April, 1847, he beheld Arcady come again.

"The verdant prudishness has passed away, which would be offended at any discussion—in the plain, comprehensive, and perfectly decorous style of this book—of the subject which it treats on." The Fowlers had also published books on their specialty. Their *Phrenology Proved, Illustrated and Applied,* done in collaboration, had already gone into many editions. In 1848 Lorenzo alone brought out a *Synopsis of Phrenology,* no doubt to satisfy the demand for a concise handbook. Wells, too, was not behindhand in issuing an *Illustrated Annual of Phrenology and Physiognomy.*

Walt was struck with awe at a science that could literally open the mind of man and read the secrets that nature had there hidden. As he wandered about the Cabinet examining the array of well-polished skulls, he must have had as many thoughts as came to Hamlet at the spectacle of poor Yorick. This large dome, so neatly hinged, the sutures traced with the most delicate art, what mind had dwelt in it? Criminal or genius, whose was the soul that had been its tenant? Was it true as those phrenological charts hanging along the walls demonstrated—was it true that every individual had his destiny charted upon his head? Gargantuan in size, the maps of the mind were there drawn—the two profiles and the back of the cranium. The features of the face were simple lines, as in an anatomical drawing, the eyelid of one profile closed, the other open. In the drawing of the back view a channel, like the Mississippi through the States, flowed down the middle. What was the meaning of the boundary lines, separating one section from another, each section neatly numbered and labeled? "Sublimity, alimentiveness, ideality, marvelousness, amativeness, secretiveness, suavity, benevolence, hope, esteem, cautiousness. . . ." What were these regions of the mind, these tracts of *terra incognita* that held as much mystery as an unexplored continent?

Walt could not leave augury unconsulted. On the same July that had seen him branded by the *Eagle* as "slow, indolent, heavy, discourteous and without steady principles," he sought

155

the phrenological oracle in the person of Lorenzo Niles Fowler, who gave him a reading of the cranial bumps. So flattering were the conclusions, and so much in accord with Walt's concept of himself, that from then on he embarked upon no venture without setting his course by the phrenological chart. In one trait alone did the reading agree with the *Eagle*: it listed indolence among his dangerous faults. What was so small a flaw, however, against the one, great, beautiful, overwhelming fact, the inescapable certainty put into so many words by Lorenzo: "You are a born poet"?

That secret, among others, the phrenologist had uncovered. The big young man who had risen from the "reading," his face beaming with pride, might have in too dangerous a degree the tendencies toward voluptuousness and alimentiveness, a reckless swing of animal will and a large self-esteem: but he was a born poet. The fact had been confirmed by one authority, backed by a still greater authority, that of science. From then on there was no holding Walt from the path nature had traced out for him in the fine intricate lines of his skull, and guided by the polar star of his faith.

"Give me the great trees of the forest!" he cried out to a young typesetter of his acquaintance soon after his visit to the Cabinet. "Give me the roaring cataract—give me the mountains, the ocean, the rushing steam engine, and the monarchs of the storm that plough the seas—give me these for a poem. O Mother Ocean, come to my arms! Great oaks of the forest, abide in my veins!"

Nature who was God had spoken, and Fowler was the prophet.

Chapter XIV: Of many things

A S THE year 1849 drew to a close many were happy to see it go. Just as the previous year had been one of dissidence in Europe with thrones toppling and revolutionists fleeing to exile, 1849 was remarkable in America for violence and catastrophe. The dreaded cholera which had broken out as often before in New Orleans, spread throughout the nation during the spring, blighting the land to all its borders, sparing neither rich nor poor, and turning the burial grounds to plowed fields for the thousands of dead.

At the starting point the epidemic had raged so violently that the vaults could hold no more, and the victims were laid away in the ground once thought fit only for the poor and the slave. Cities streamed with whole families traveling to the suburbs to escape the plague. But there was no safety anywhere. Those who believed that by avoiding contact ·with others they would remain immune, shut themselves up in their houses, afraid to walk the streets. Theaters and libraries, even churches were closed, and people returned to superstition to guard themselves against infection. Tobacco, thought to be an efficient preventive, brought a boom to the growers who saw their weed used not only by men but by small boys and women, unabashed to appear with cigars in their mouths. Others chewed garlic and kept little bags of it somewhere about their persons. Houses reeked with the smell of gunpowder used to fumigate them. Doorsteps, clothes, handkerchiefs were constantly sprinkled with vinegar. The quack and the charlatan had their day, each crying out a cure, an unfailing specific. "Vinegar of the Four Thieves"—appropriately named—be-

157

came so popular that a few new millionaires were made after the epidemic had subsided.

Everybody bought the remedy, and all felt comforted, if not by the smart at their nostrils, assuredly by the plausible tale with which the clever scoundrels adorned their bottles. Long ago, in Marseilles, ran the story, at the height of a fierce visitation of cholera, four thieves were seen to enter and plunder the houses of the victims. Day and night they carried on their nefarious practice without succumbing to the disease. One day the leader fell into the hands of justice, and while being tied to the wheel he pleaded with the executioner, saying that if his life were spared, he would impart the secret of the cure that had warded him and his companions against the plague. Justice stayed its hand, the thief spoke, and the "Vinegar of the Four Thieves" was given to the world.

Nevertheless, people kept on dying, deaths in New York alone reaching fourteen hundred in one week in the middle of July. Cincinnati and St. Louis suffered most of all, each losing over six thousand of the population. That month, from Cincinnati, Harriet Beecher Stowe announced a death to her absent husband: "Our dear little one is gone from us . . . I have just seen him in his death agony, looked on his imploring face when I could not help nor soothe nor do one thing, not one, to mitigate his cruel suffering—do nothing but pray in my anguish that he might die soon. I write as though there were no sorrow like my sorrow, yet there has been in this city, as in the land of Egypt, scarce a house without its dead." For more than four months the cry of the dead-cart drivers rang mournfully through the streets. "Bring out your dead! Bring out your dead!" And the corpses of men, women and children were heaped upon the tumbrils, the living giving them wide berth as they lumbered through the streets. Sometimes when carts were not to be had, the body of a respected citizen might be seen on the shafts of a chair, with only a faithful Negro to drive the horse with the improvised hearse to the cemetery.

By midsummer so general was the mourning that the President appointed the 3rd day of August for fasting and prayer, that God "avert the pestilence that walketh in darkness and the destruction that wasteth at noonday." When the computations of the dead were finally made, it was discovered that though the cholera had spared no class, it had hit hardest the poor of the cities, huddled in their squalid, ill-ventilated houses. Not even rivers of the "Vinegar of the Four Thieves" could have protected them against the combination of disease and poverty.

That spring, before the pestilence had reached its peak in New York, death had stalked the streets in the riots that broke out in front of the Astor Place Opera House, built at an expenditure of many millions by the city's wealthy subscribers. The house had made a triumphal opening in April of 1848, but hardly had the echo of its imported songbirds reached the general ear, when the sponsors had to admit the failure of their undertaking. Without concluding their season, and while the subscribers waited in vain for the scheduled operatic performances, they turned over the theater to Niblo and Hackett for legitimate drama. From the first the public had been against the Opera House for its taint of snobbishness. Matters did not improve under the new management which still catered to the "kid glove" class. Taking as a pretext the rivalry of the American tragedian Edwin Forrest and the British, W. C. Macready, the Knickerbocker *hoi polloi*, on May 10, 1849, staged a demonstration that from a riot assumed the proportions of a battle involving the militia. When the violence was quelled the square about the theater was strewn with the corpses of twenty-six victims. Thirty-six wounded were carried to the hospitals. Nearly twenty thousand people had engaged in the riots. New York never did anything by halves.

159

But, as Mark Twain was to differentiate between the thrill of wholesale slaughter and that of an individual killing next door, the sensation of the Astor Place fracas was as nothing to the shiver that went down the spine of the country at the crime which closed the year. Violence was to be expected from rowdy, conglomerate New York. But from Boston? Who could have dreamed of associating that citadel of the intellect with one of the most macabre murders in the criminal history of the nation? The worst of it all was that not only were the people involved of the Brahmin caste, but the murder was perpetrated in the very halls of learning.

On Friday, November 23, 1849, Dr. George Parkman, a wealthy old gentleman of Boston and one of the founders of the Massachusetts Medical College there, went out as usual to attend to various pieces of business. In his dark frock coat, pantaloons and purple silk vest, with his gray hair topped by a black hat, he was a familiar figure as he walked down the streets. That unlucky Friday was the last in which he exchanged greetings with his neighbors.

When he did not return home as expected, parties went out to search for him throughout the city. For two days they combed the outskirts, and large rewards were posted for information. The only definite clue they turned up was that among his appointments Dr. Parkman had had one with Dr. John W. Webster, Professor of Chemistry at Harvard and lecturer at the Medical College in Boston. Professor Webster was most obliging during the questioning. He owed Dr. Parkman a few hundred dollars, he said. Their meeting, in the presence of Dr. Parkman's brother, had been on a matter of business, during which he and Dr. Parkman had had a slight misunderstanding, soon cleared up. Meanwhile, in the search of the Medical College and the houses nearby, Professor Webster proved most helpful to the police whom he conducted through his own apartments. Not a trace of Dr. Parkman anywhere. The case was one of the most baffling that the Boston police, seldom called on such business, had ever handled.

While the arm of the law was still reaching out for evidence, Littlefield, the janitor of the Medical College, was busy on detective work of his own. Not for nothing had Poe written his mystery stories. Indeed, the setting could not have been more Poesque for a horror tale. There was the lecture room where Professor Webster taught; below, the laboratory with its alembics, its furnace and sink; right behind it, a mysterious closet opening into a vault, through whose brick and lime the sea water had seeped, loosening the masonry. Littlefield had his own theory. In the absence of the professor he prowled about, peering here, knocking there, his suspicions growing as he went deeper into his search. If only he could gain access to the vault! But the professor alone ever went into it. Carried away by his curiosity Littlefield began to remove some of the already loosened bricks, working at night and whenever he was sure of not being watched, as his wife stood guard.

At last he opened a hole large enough for him to look through. There was the *corpus delicti*, rather, a gruesome part of it. Littlefield reported his findings to the police, and Professor Webster was put under arrest. If any doubt remained that the bones in the vault belonged to Dr. Parkman, it was dispelled, as one writer put it, "by the marvelous and beautiful science of anatomy" which set to work upon them and on fragments of the skull found among the ashes of the furnace. Dr. Parkman's set of mineral teeth and a pearl shirt button made the identification absolute.

Through the spring of 1850 the trial of Professor Webster rivaled everything else in the headlines. After pleading *not guilty*, he made a full confession; but public indignation would hear of no mitigation of his punishment. On a high scaffold that gave him a last view of Harvard College to which he had been appointed on the recommendation of no less a personage

161

than Dr. Caspar Wistar, he was hanged by the neck until he died. He was buried in the peaceful dells of Mount Auburn where lay the body of Dr. Spurzheim whose researches had contributed to the "marvelous and beautiful science" which had helped to convict the murderer.

The year that reached the mid-century mark opened and continued full of contrasts. In England and Wales cholera raged after it had been subdued in America. Queen Victoria was presented with the Koh-i-noor, the East India diamond whose eight hundred carats the unskillful European cutters had reduced to the still considerable weight of two-hundred and seventy. Wordsworth died of old age and Sir Robert Peel of a fall from his horse. The first submarine telegraph was stretched across the Channel. Messages passed between England and France amid general rejoicing; then the cable broke. In Canada a movement was set afoot for the annexation of British America by the United States, but Earl Grey, the Colonial Secretary, put a stop to it by threatening trials of high treason. As it was, the Colonial Office had trouble aplenty with the outbreaks of the Afghans in India and of the Kaffirs in South Africa. In China rivalry over the throne of the Manchus, together with the failure of the rice crop and the upheavals of the Taiping rebellion, sent hordes of coolies out of the country. They landed in California, still ringing with the cry of "Gold!" While many were dying to stake their claim in Eldorado, in the Orient the prophet Mirza Ali Mohammed and his followers were suffering martyrdom for the religion of Bab which sought a spiritual way of life through poverty and love.

Spiritual manifestations of a different order, however, were seizing upon the credulity of the populace in America when the "Rochester knockings" first heard in 1847, were given public demonstration in New York. A certain Michael Weekman who was occupying a modest little house in the village of Hydesville, used to complain that he heard rappings at his door yet when he opened it, there was no one to be found. From the door the knockings spread to other parts of the house, and finally became such a nuisance that Weekman left the place for a quieter dwelling. Soon afterward, to the bedeviled cottage, came John Fox and his family. At first nothing untoward disturbed the peace of the household. But from March 1848 the family had not a moment's rest from the unseen tenant whose chief amusement seemed to be to keep their nerves on edge, day and night. After a while the rappings took on a more purposeful sound, concentrated near the bed of two of the Fox girls, Margaret, twelve years old, and Kate, three years younger. One night Margaret, unable to sleep, hit upon the idea of making a pastime of the noise. With her fingers she rapped out sounds approximating those she heard; immediately the unseen agency answered. Little by little, with the help of Kate, she made up a language with which she communicated with the "spirit"—for a spirit it must be, judging by the definite "yes" it gave to the question.

Mrs. Fox was let into the secret and she in turn took counsel of the Rev. Mr. Fishborough, before whom the girls gave an exhibition of the phenomenon. There could be no mistake about it. Kate and Margaret had the power to make the spirits speak. From Hydesville the now celebrated family went on to Rochester, where the knockings, far from ceasing in the unfamiliar neighborhood, not only increased before the paid audiences, but assumed a wonderful virtuosity. It required only the presence of the two girls to make the spirits almost deafening in their garrulity. There was no question they could not answer, no information they could not obtain from the other world. When sufficiently in the vein, they playfully tipped tables and moved furniture from one end of the room to the other, tickled women with their invisible fingers, and played pranks on old gentlemen. So accurately did they answer questions on the most private matters that one believer converted

163

a dozen skeptics. Soon even Rochester became too small for the Fox sisters.

In May, 1850, they were invited to give a public demonstration in New York before a gathering of big-wigs, journalists, the gullible and the unbelieving. Other invitations followed at a hundred dollars a night. It was a profitable business to be a "medium"—a word coined to meet the new profession. A married sister of the girls found that she also possessed the power to bait the spirits, and with the others she too made New Yorkers gape. N. P. Willis, invited to one of the séances, was astonished at the company he found. There was the Rev. Rufus Griswold, the indefatigable maker of annuals and the enemy of Poe; there were the Rev. Dr. Hawks, Dr. Francis, Dr. Marcy, Mr. Bigelow of the *Evening Post*, Dr. Ripley who had descended from Utopia to journalism on the *Tribune*, General Lyman, Tuckerman the essayist, and two writers of the first rank, Cooper and Bryant. On the way to Griswold's home, for it was there that the séance was being held, Willis saw four women, whom he took to be the "knockers," looking for the house number. Mrs. Fox was a stout youngish matron; her daughters, also plump, were very pretty. Willis was at once predisposed in their favor, reasoning that since they had not yet been in the premises they could not have crammed the rooms with accomplices and hammers.

Grouping themselves about a large table, the audience waited for the spirits, responsive to the influence of the Fox sisters, to announce themselves. At first they refused to give any sign, which made the skeptics smile as the word "impostors" hovered on their lips. But suddenly a faint knocking came from somewhere in the room. The spirits were ready to answer questions. One by one the names of the people in the party were called out to them, with the invitation that the visitors from the other world communicate with them. But the spirits were obdurate. Being of an unliterary cast they refused to have anything to do with the one poet there, but finally answered the questions that others put to them. It was a slow, roundabout procedure. In the end, however, those who had come to mock remained, if not to pray, at least to wonder whether there might not be things in the world undreamed of in their philosophy. As Willis summed it up, the demonstration was "of sufficient extent and respectability to warrant grave attention." Knockers and mediums sprang up in every part of the country, till there was a veritable epidemic of spiritual manifestations.

Men like Horace Greeley had their doubts sufficiently shaken to harbor a shamefaced belief in the phenomena, especially after Kate Fox came to live for a while in his household. On the other hand Professor Agassiz pronounced them pure delusion. From a historic perspective there was much encouragement to be taken from the fact that Spiritualism, as the cult was called, did no one any harm. A similar outbreak in Salem, in 1692, engineered also by a number of young girls, had brought nineteen to the gallows on the charge of witchcraft. Humanity was learning to grope out of blind alleys.

Whitman, to whom nothing was alien, felt himself part of everything that happened. Together with the poet-prophet he was also the average man, the democrat, the eyes, ears and tongue of that immense entity which he was to express in the keyword for which he found no equivalent in English.

> One's self I sing, a simple separate person,
> Yet utter the word Democratic, the word En-Masse.

He was one with that En-Masse. If a murder occurred, he was the doer and the victim. If the body of an outcast was brought into the dead-house, he was there to mourn over that other house, abandoned, shunned, once the tenement of a soul. High and low, according to the accidents of birth, all formed part of that En-Masse, and the kinship made him love them all,

165

tolerate them all. "The poets are the divine mediums," he held. "Through them come spirits and materials to all the people, men and women."

After his leavetaking of the *Freeman* he changed his mode of living. He had had enough of factional politics, enough, for the time, of the so-called intellectual life. He was working on his poems. The jottings in his notebooks filled many pages; the notebooks increased in number. He made the books himself of a few sheets of paper folded and fastened with a pin or two. Invariably he carried one such book in his breast pocket. He had tried all others, but he liked his kind best. They were of a size he could always have with him; they were simple and easily duplicated. Besides, they could be kept out of sight, among heaps of papers, when he had filled them.

He did not stay in his room at home to work. If he was walking in the street and an idea, or even a phrase, occurred to him, he would step aside from the crowd and write it down. If he saw something from the top of a bus that suggested a theme, he steadied the book on his knee and scrawled with his pencil. As in his childhood, he walked alone. Solitude was essential to him, the lover of the masses, when he was inviting his soul. The good companion, the greeter of the stranger, the comrade of pilots and bus drivers was his other self, the Walt of the En-Masse, plunging into the stream of humanity, and rising out of it revitalized for the raptures he could know only from contact with that other, his spiritual ego. The friendly optimist seemed, at times, to have but little in common with the solitary. For like all those who walk alone he had his moments of gloom, the brooding of the soul over the gulfs of self. "I am not glad to-night," reads one of his self confessions. "Gloom has gathered round me like a mantle, tightly folded. The oppression of my heart is not fitful and has no pangs; but a torpor like that of some stagnant pool. Yet I know not why I should be sad."

Of many things

There might have been reasons, had he not feared to avow them even to his private books wherein he put down only that part of his personal experience which remained enigmatic to the careless eye, or else of such objective interest that scarcely any reading would have been possible between the lines. Even there his caution, later in life, exercised its censorship in the destruction of many pages. Despite his attempts at mystification, it is known that Walt made more than one voyage to the South that drew him with the magnet of his one intense passion. One proof remained hidden till after his death when the Cincinnati *Post*, on April 20, 1892, published the poem known as "Isle of La Belle Rivière." Whitman, an accompanying note explained, had written the poem at Blennerhasset Island, and had given it to his host, Farmer Johnson, who laid it between the leaves of his Bible where it was discovered after his death.

In the diary notes of his voyage to New Orleans in 1848 Walt had made no mention of Blennerhasset Island. Had he stopped there at the time there could have been no reason for concealment, unless he broke off the journey home—which is hardly likely since the voyage was accomplished with the utmost expedition. Furthermore, at the close of the poem appear the words, "At Blennerhasset—aged 30." From internal evidence, the imagery, the mood, the dwelling on sexual union and fertility—with Walt the inevitable concomitant—the poem must have been written after another meeting with the loved one and a final leavetaking. Had a child been born of their passion? And had he had to relinquish woman and child forever to one who had prior rights? Like all else of biographical interest that Whitman left behind, the poem raises more doubts than it clears.

> Bride of the swart Ohio
> Nude, yet fair to look upon,
> Clothed only with the leaf,
> As was innocent Eve of Eden,

The son of grim old Allegheny,
And white-breasted Monongahela
Is wedded to thee, and it is well.
His tawny thighs cover thee
In the vernal time of spring,
And lo! in the autumn is the fruitage.
Virgin of Nature, the holy spirit of the waters enshrouds thee
And thou art pregnant with the fruits
Of the field and the vine.
But like the Sabine maid of old,
The lust of man hath ravished thee
And compelled thee to pay tribute to the
Carnal wants of earth.
Truth and romance make up thy
Strange, eventful history,
From the cycle of the red man,
Who bowed at thy shrine and worshipped thee,
To the dark days of that traitor
Who linked thy beautiful name to infamy.
Farewell, Queen of the Waters,
I have slept upon thy breast in the innocence of a babe,
And now I leave thee
To the embraces of thine acknowledged lord.

It is notable that Whitman wrote the poem in the unrhymed chant which was so much his personal voice.

Neither this second meeting, if there was one, nor the second parting, had been necessary to confirm Walt in the career from which, in its essential lines, he was no more to deviate. As early as the spring of 1849 the *Advertizer* had seen the change in him and interpreted it as a desire to settle down. Walt had begun housebuilding with his father. From then on, till 1855, he pursued the building trade more or less regularly, as he did everything but his writing. His book now became the fixed purpose of his life. Disorganized though he might appear in his habits, that very disorganization provided the freedom he needed to fulfill his manifest destiny. Anyone could write a book. But only one in an age could be a poet-prophet. Literary

ambition alone meant nothing to Walt who had always been
ridden by a moral purpose. Moreover, he had seen his name too
often in print for him to take pleasure in it. Who knows but
that when his work was ready for America he might not give
it without his name, like the words of revelation? When his soul
had plunged her tongue to his bare-stripped heart and reached
till she possessed him wholly, she had made him of the company of the chosen whose words had changed civilizations. That
certainty he knew, as he had known there had been that in him
to invite revelation.

Since he must do everything consistently he adopted a laborer's costume to take the place of the frock coat and top hat
of the dandy. Whether working with his father or going to
the theater, he now appeared in the denim or stripes of the
carpenter, his shirt open at the throat, his head covered by the
wide-brimmed hat which he wore like a Quaker. People who
had known him before the transformation were scandalized by
the new costume. After all, what could the world see in it but
affectation? How were his former acquaintances to realize that
his laborer's suit was the vestment of dedication, the robe of
humility he put on to serve poetry?* How were they to know
that perhaps the manual work he chose to do at this time was
not undertaken as part of his conscious desire to make himself
in all things like the heroes Carlyle had selected for his worship? Mahomet had been only a wild man of the desert; Luther
a son of mine-laborers; Shakespeare a Stratford peasant. Yet
all of them had changed the world and the spirit. Had not
Christ been a carpenter's son? He saw no irreverence in such
a comparison. The messianic urge strong within him, he must
live, as far as the nineteenth century allowed, like a messiah,
chaste, poor, unrecognized as an individual, yet of the immor-
tals for the largeness of his vision. To the outside world the

* See Esther Shephard's *Walt Whitman's Pose* for the influence on Whitman
of a character in George Sand's *The Countess of Rudolstadt.*

changed Walt held an element of the ridiculous. His own brother George often asked him, genuinely puzzled: "I say, Walt, what's the game you're up to, anyway?" Assured of the call of which he must deliver himself, Walt did not allow his spirit to be ruffled.

He continued writing occasionally for the papers and now and then interrupted his housebuilding by undertaking a small printing job on his own press. On the whole, however, he strove to see contemporary events *sub specie aeternitatis* except where his patriotism was touched. Then he awoke from his creative trance and lashed right and left at those he despised as enemies of the nation.

Problems of more than usual gravity weighed upon the country in 1850. During the rush westward following the discovery of gold in Sutter's mill in 1848 which was still transplanting families by the thousands, California had attained such importance that Congress was debating whether it should be admitted into the Union. At once the question of slavery or anti-slavery reared its head. In the Senate, Henry Clay introduced a proposal for a compromise, favoring the admission of California as a free state. Pro and con, the press seethed and boiled over in editorials, polemics and verse. Walt, to whom the issue had been clear since his last editorials in the *Eagle*, was so angered by the Northerners who could even debate the question, that he wrote a "dough-face song" for their despicable ranks. He sent it to Bryant who found it acceptable for the *Evening Post* where it appeared as a "Song for Certain Congressmen."

> We are all docile dough-faces,
>   They knead us with the fist,
> They the dashing southern lords,
>   We labor as they list;
> For them we speak—or hold our tongues,
>   For them we turn and twist . . .

> Principle!—freedom!—fiddlesticks!
> We know not where they're found.
> Rights of the masses—progress!—bah!
> Words that tickle and sound;
> But claiming the rule o'er "practical men"
> Is very different ground. . . .

Twelve stanzas of bitterness and name-calling, for Whitman was unsparing in a just cause. How could it not be just when the principled men of the nation were on the same side?

Shortly after Walt's outburst, Daniel Webster from whom the North had expected support, made his Seventh of March speech which his followers could not interpret as anything other than betrayal. The Fugitive Slave Law adopted soon afterward by Congress proved only too conclusively what side Webster's speech had advantaged. Now, in the land of the free, a fine of a thousand dollars and six months' imprisonment could be imposed upon anyone who harbored a fugitive slave or helped him to escape. Not only Abolitionists, but every right-thinking person was horrified. "This filthy enactment," Emerson, the placid, wrote in his journal, "was made in the nineteenth century, by people who could read and write, I will not obey it, by God." Again and again he returned to the subject, seeing in it a painful augury for the nation. "All I have and all I can do," he pledged, "shall be given and done in opposition to the execution of the law . . . The word *liberty* in the mouth of Mr. Webster sounds like the word *love* in the mouth of a courtezan." Words were not spared in condemnation of the lost leader, whom Whittier addressed in his "Ichabod":

> So fallen! so lost! the light withdrawn
> Which once he wore!
> The glory from his gray hairs gone
> For evermore!

Freedom wore mourning. The people knew that if ever Web-

171

ster had harbored hopes for the presidency, he had wrecked them forever.

Incensed as much as Emerson had been, Walt wrote another poem in which he compared the betrayal to that of Judas, and sent it to the *Tribune*. "Blood-Money" he called it. The *Tribune* published it, overlooking the fact that it was written in the strangest prose-like verse its readers had ever had to read. But Walt had not yet had his say. A few months later he delivered himself with angry vehemence of still another poem carrying the biblical title, "Wounded in the House of his Friends." He was doing his messianic duty, scourging the barterers of Freedom in the temple of Democracy.

> Virginia, mother of greatness,

he apostrophized,

> Blush not for being also mother of slaves;
> You might have borne deeper slaves—
> Doughfaces, crawlers, lice of humanity . . .
>
> Arise, young North!
> Our elder blood flows in the veins of cowards!

Walt's poem was published on the 14th of June, at the peak of the agitation. On the 9th of July President Taylor died and Fillmore, the Vice-President, succeeded him, his Cabinet headed by Webster as Secretary of State. Under them the new fugitive slave bill was passed. From then on they were looked upon as traitors to the anti-slavery cause and Fillmore forfeited his chance of re-election, two years later, when the protest votes went to Pierce. Death providentially put Webster out of the running.

Before the 'forties turned into the 'fifties, and the whole continent was webbed by the caravans of migrants in search of Eldorado, another death occurred, scarcely noticed except by the literary. Edgar Allan Poe had always been a bosom friend of death. He saw its shadow on the face of beauty, its sorrow in the bliss of love. When all about him were rejoicing at the discovery of an actual Eldorado that sent its streams of gold pouring into the country, he sought it

> Over the Mountains
> Of the Moon,
> Down the Valley of the Shadow.

While passing through Baltimore during a local election, he fell into the hands of repeaters who drugged him for his vote and then left him unconscious in the street. He was found the following morning and taken to the hospital to die.

More spectacularly tragic was the end of Margaret Fuller in 1850, in the wreck-filled waters off the Hamptons in Long Island. Often had Whitman gazed from the shores into those treacherous depths, remembering stories of fatal losses, witnessing one himself when the ship *Mexico* was wrecked in 1840.

> I look where the ship helplessly heads end on, I hear the burst as she strikes, I hear the howls of dismay, they grow fainter and fainter.
> I cannot aid with my wringing fingers,
> I can but rush to the surf and let it drench me and freeze upon me.
>
> I search with the crowd, not one of the company is wash'd to us alive,
> In the morning I help pick up the dead and lay them in rows in a barn.

It was the same story, ruthlessly repeated, when the brig *Elizabeth* went down in a gale. Margaret Fuller, returning to America from Europe as the Baroness Ossoli with her young husband and infant son, perished with the rest. Later, when the bodies were washed ashore, Thoreau, come down from Concord, leaned over the corpse of Margaret Fuller's husband and ripped a button off his coat to take back home with him. "To the last," wrote Emerson in his journal, "her country proves inhospitable to her; brave, eloquent, subtle, accomplished, devoted, constant soul!" Margaret Fuller needed no other epitaph.

But the world went on. Emerson returned to his lectures and Thoreau to the practice of his master's preaching of non-conformity by rejecting everything in life, government and man, that did not coincide with his principles. Whitman continued, for he had never left it, the elaboration of his Idea, working most when he seemed most idle. He heard Jenny Lind at Castle Garden when the Swedish Nightingale captured not only New York but the rest of America. Again, he must have stood by, in 1851 when Louis Kossuth, the champion of Hungary, made his patriotic speeches as the lights flashed from his medals and gold lace. When the yacht *America* bore away the trophy at the international regatta, his heart must have beat high with pride—and chilled with horror when nearly fifty children, "in their beauty and innocence" as an account put it, perished in a panic at the cry of "Fire!" that had broken out in a New York public school.

The following year, 1852, saw Harriet Beecher Stowe's *Uncle Tom's Cabin* not only fulfill Henry Ward Beecher's promise that he would scatter it "thick as the leaves of Vallombrosa," but better it by selling in the millions at home and abroad. Yet when it had appeared serially in the *National Era* two years earlier it had brought the author a mere three hundred dollars and had gone almost unnoticed but for the Abolitionists. Then, in 1853, came the World's Fair in New York, modeled after the First International Exposition of 1851, sponsored by the Prince Consort in London.

A colossal edifice of glass and iron sprang up as if by magic on the acres of Reservoir Square* where the city's Egyptian water works had been. Arched, columned, with turrets at the corners of the buildings that formed a Greek cross, it was surmounted by the largest dome America had ever seen. From

* Now Bryant Park, behind the New York Public Library.

August, 1852, when the plans of Messrs. Carstensen and Gilde-meister had been approved, until the day of the opening, crowds had watched the wonder come to pass, but none more proudly than Walt Whitman, "of Mannahatta the son." For the World's Fair was no mere international event, soldering friend-ship among nations by the industries of peace, but the achieve-ment of America, the young giant welcoming the world.

It required but a minor transition in the mind of Walt for the Fair to become his creation as well as America's. Was he not a representative of his country's largeness and aspiration? From the day the gates of the Fair opened amid a general jubilee, with the cannons roaring, the bells pealing and President Pierce himself leading the procession on his steed Black Warrior, Walt visited and revisited the grounds. "Here where all climes their offering send," as the inaugural chorus sang, Walt found room for his soul to expand. He rejoiced in the plenty of America and her wonderful industry, and compared her exhibits with the goods of the transatlantic bazaars. Iron ore, steel, geological specimens, intricate machinery, wood carvings, a musical instru-ment called a psalmodicon, paintings by European masters, sculptures, everything that the mind of man could conceive and execute from the gifts of nature, filled the exhibition halls. Here was a painting, contributed by Queen Victoria, showing the Duke of Wellington presenting a birthday gift to her youngest son, Prince Arthur. From Italy had come a statue of Columbus in purest marble, his right hand pointing to the globe on which his left hand rested. Thorwaldsen showed his masterpiece in sculpture, the large group of Christ and his dis-ciples. Delicate where the other had power, a cage of captive winged cupids, all in marble, drew the admiring cries of the ladies.

Walt allowed nothing to escape him, not even the embarrass-ing fact that the Fair policemen followed him suspiciously until he reassured them that he was harmless. Indeed, what could the

175

officers of the law have made of the unconventionally attired man who day in and day out would stand in a trance before the Thorwaldsen group and stare upward at the central dome with its radiant golden sun? How could they have known that he was in those very moments unfolding his creative soul to the promptings of God and man?

Chapter XV: Leaves of Grass

HARDLY had the trees along Brooklyn's broad avenue put forth their leaves in the spring of 1855 when the printing shop of the Rome brothers in the little red brick building on the corner of Cranberry and Fulton Streets awakened to remarkable activity with the unheralded incursions of Walt Whitman. He had brought them a book to print, his own, and he hung over it with such solicitude that the routine of the shop was disrupted. Other people left their manuscript in the hands of the printers who set it and submitted proofs for correction. Not Walt. He insisted on selecting his own type, he gave explicit directions on how the lines of the text should be disposed, and the better to show what he wanted, settled himself at the case and ran off a couple of pages. Not for nothing had he served his apprenticeship.

James and Andrew Rome let their friend have his way. They knew authors to be an exacting lot, and were therefore not surprised when even the free and easy Walt proved no exception the moment the mantle of the poet covered his open shirt. At the *Eagle* he had exasperated the printers by checking the least paragraph of his work. Woe to the bold one who dared change a single comma! If he had been particular about his pedestrian writing, he was meticulous to eccentricity with the labor of his spirit. For it had been labor, as a glance at the writing on the scattered pages showed. Indeed, the printers must have sighed with relief when he offered to take over the task of deciphering his manuscript.

Like a palimpsest, a poem would be written over and over, in ink, in pencil, red and blue, the original words crossed out and substituted, the first skeleton version covered with the flesh

177

of poetic suggestion, as ideas and images came to him. There was something in the appearance of his pages that spoke of hard, painful growth, as if each poem, like the germ of an oak, began as the tiny two-leaved plant which after long seasons unfolded branch and leaf, towering at length, the finished creation. In him inspiration did not work at white heat, shaping the idea with quick, directed strokes till the final cooling plunge when it issued complete. In the laboratory of his mind there was no forge. Rather he matured his poems with the slow sureness of the earth, allowing the seasons of rain and sun in their good time to bring forth the hidden life.

From his first knowledge of himself as the *vates*, Walt was convinced that every impulse of utterance came to him from a reservoir outside himself, a consciousness that might be called that of God in the universe. Again and again he laid the birth of his poems at the door of divinity. "The Book," he wrote, using capital letters as if he were writing of the Scriptures, "the book is a product, not of literature merely, but of the largest universal law and play of things, and of Kosmical beauty, of which literature, however important, is but a fraction." "Walt Whitman, an American, one of the roughs, a kosmos," —with this description that he was running off himself on the Cranberry Street press, he was linking the accidental Walt Whitman, by the indicative word kosmos, with the divine power that moved him. Again, he affirmed later, "One deep purpose underlay the others—and that has been the religious purpose,"—an assertion that might have made the simple printers open their eyes in amazement had they known, as they finished setting those spiritual convulsions which Walt called by the name of *Leaves of Grass*.

Whatever anyone else might think, the half-Quaker Walt had not the smallest doubt that the voice of God spoke through him. "My greatest call," he designated his poetic mission. "The Spirit commanding," he noted of a plan that had suggested itself for spreading his message through a series of lectures. And he awaited the command, receptive as the newly made Adam for the breath to give him life and voice. Mistrusting the intellect, he never went out to seek the idea, but waited rather for the idea to come to him. It was in the quiescence of loafing, when he retired within himself to muse, that he invited the Spirit.

His family, during the unfolding of *Leaves of Grass*, must sometimes have caught him in the trance-like state which literate friends who knew him in later years, were to try to explain. But his family left no impression except to account for him as different from the rest. Walt, however, not infrequently recorded the genesis of his poems. Once in a notebook he wrote an account of the state of mystical exaltation that preceded the annunciation,—"a trance, yet with all the senses alert—only a state of high exalted musing—the tangible and material with all its shows, the objective world suspended or surmounted for a while. . . ." It was such a state as religious mystics like George Fox and Elias Hicks had been known to fall into as they waited for the Voice to speak through them. Walt never thought of comparing himself with them. Against their authentically divine utterance he knew his poems to be mere whisperings.

Nevertheless his faith in them had the power to make him give up everything and cling to them. Five times he wrought and destroyed and wrought again the twelve poems that he finally decided to publish at his own expense. While working with his father who was now old and failing, it was his book he had been building, letting his subliminal processes function undisturbed as the other Walt Whitman, carpenter of the people, hammered the shingles on the houses that sold readily at a profit. In the noon hours when he would disappear with his dinner pail and a few pages torn out of a favorite book, he was not only feeding his body, but nourishing his dream.

The ocean with its rhythmic ebb and flow mingled with the

internal cadences of his songs, giving them the pulsation of living things, as if the heart of nature beat in them. It was the sound he had heard as a child, the pulsing to which his nature never ceased to respond. At other times when he would trudge back and forth on the hard wet sand, alone with the elements, declaiming with his lusty voice the plays of Shakespeare, it was a comparison he was making between those mighty lines and his novel music which borrowed the inspired incoherence of the mystic together with the newspaperman's prose and the lecturer's hortative style.

He had always looked longingly toward the lecturer's platform, the more directly to reach the men and women of America for whose good he felt he had been born. In 1851, after praising in the *Evening Post* the exhibition of paintings held at the Brooklyn Art Union by the young artists of the town, he had been invited to address them. Two of the exhibiting painters, Walter Libby and William Mount, had struck the right chord with their pictures of American country boys, Negroes, the landscapes Walt knew so well, and homely scenes. Their art was free, he remarked joyfully, of the "stamp of class" which marred that of Europe. "A sunny blessing, then, say I, on the young artist race!" he exclaimed in the friendly *Post*. "For the thrift and shrewdness that make dollars, are not every thing that we should bow to, or yearn for, or put before our children as the be all and the end all of human ambition." The same message he echoed in his speech at the Art Union where he spoke before the assembled youths on the theme of "Art and Artists." "In the life we live upon this beautiful earth, there may, after all, be something vaster and better than dress and the table, and business and politics." That something vaster and better he strove to make them, the creators see, before he gave it to the world.

So enthusiastically had he been cheered by the young artists, glad to have a spokesman for their side, that Walt proceeded to write what his mother called "barrels" of lectures. The era was favorable to lecturers. With the growth of the West in scattered towns and cities, the demand increased for culture to fill prosperous leisure. The lecture lyceum was born. Emerson, indeed, had been a pioneer in the field, making the transition from the pulpit to the platform with such success that, as someone said, he created a new profession. For him the lecture platform was really the testing ground for the ideas which he later published in his essays.

Following close upon him came a line of golden-tongued orators, eagerly awaited by the distant towns between November and April, for light on the questions of the times. Wendell Phillips, Beecher, Horace Greeley, Theodore Parker, each had his circuit and each his audience, gathered from the ladies' clubs that had begun to spring up from New England to far west of the Mississippi. Nor were women, or *female* lecturers, as they were ungallantly called, wanting to disseminate their views on subjects ranging from the practicability of the bifurcated costume, to the fight of the moment, the agitation for women's rights. Mrs. Amelia J. Bloomer, indeed, succeeded in pleading for the two reforms at once by appearing in the much-reviled pantaloon while lecturing on the superiority of woman to man. By 1855, however, the fight for dress reform had ended in defeat. Women's rights, on the other hand, gained so much in scope that colonies were being founded for the testing of "free love."

Walt kept above the temporal in his lecture themes, preferring the universal in such subjects as Democracy and Religion, always with capital letters. "Walt," George remembered, "would go to hear fellows like Father Taylor and Hicks, whom he considered geniuses, but men like Spurgeon and Beecher and Brooks he would not go to hear." If the shrieks of the campaigners for women's rights reached his ears, it was only that he might shout them down impatiently with his ideal—a true

181

woman, first of all, capable of raising a vigorous brood, strong, loving, wise though uneducated, the sharer with her mate in pleasure and responsibility. On every matter that engaged his contemporaries, he had his own point of view, always from the perspective of his poems. Indeed, the main themes of his book might have been found, in slightly different words, in his lecture notes which he was still making even though his first address had not led to another. With a seriousness that bordered on the ludicrous, he would put down admonitions to himself, the would-be lecturer. What was there, after all, to prevent his adopting a career that would enable him to be, like Emerson, a great teacher as well as a poet?

Undaunted by his lack of opportunity he not only elaborated the subjects close to his heart in endless observations, but also taught himself the use of the voice and effective gesture, reenforcing his self-advice with the drawing of a crude hand, forefinger extended, admonitory. "Besides direct addressing *to You*, another leading trait of Lectures may well be—strong assertion . . . launched out with fire, or enthusiasm, or anger . . . Each of the above emotions may come in well in the elocution of lectures." One pointer on the delivery of a certain passage read with unintended humor, "With energy and as a fruit or crowning flowerage."

In the excitement of the printing of *Leaves of Grass* all else took second place. Besides, the book contained everything, even a lecture introducing the poems and in itself a poem, albeit printed in small type in double columns of running prose. Everything Walt had thought and felt in the course of his thirty-six years found expression in those pages that looked, as they ran off the press, like the pages of no other volume ever printed, with their wide margins and generous sprinklings of dots. He designed the book as a quarto. No miniature size for him, who contained multitudes! The Book was his Bible, and must look like one.

182

Some time before July, *Leaves of Grass* was ready for distribution. Incongruous in its thinness, the ninety-five pages of its text running across the sheet in unequal broken lines bolstered up by capitals, the quarto was held together by a binding so feminine that at first glance it might have been mistaken for one of the effusions of the female writers who had been descending like locusts on the literary field. The cover of dark green cloth, tooled in designs of flowers and leaves, was framed with a triple line in gold on both the front and the back. In the middle the title, also in gold, was stamped in the homely ornate letters which the women of the day employed in embroidering the mottoes that bade the Lord bless the home. Strange rootlets reached downward from the letters, and minute triple leaves sprouted upward from the capital G of Grass and the rest of the title. Along the back strip the name was again stamped in gold, this time in simple letters, and decorated above and below with flowers and leaves and even a fern. Nowhere could one discern the least suggestion of a leaf of grass. Grace Greenwood's *Greenwood Leaves* and Fanny Fern's *Fern Leaves from Fanny Fern's Portfolio* might have lain side by side with *Leaves of Grass* on the same boudoir table but for its incongruous size. The resemblance, however, ended in the binding, as the incautious were to discover with a gasp.

Whitman knew both Fanny Fern, the sister of Nathaniel Parker Willis who edited the *Home Journal*, and her book which had caused the plunder of the cracked china pot in at least eighty thousand homes when it appeared in 1853. A plump, fair, arch woman of forty, with a large mouth and nose and cornflower blue eyes, Sara Payson Willis had been widowed at an early age, divorced at a slightly later day and thrown upon the literary world with her children. Now, in 1855, she was about to acquire her third husband, James Parton, eleven years younger than herself. It was Parton, assistant editor of the *Home Journal* who had first responded to the heart throbs of

Fanny Fern, and who, when her brother refused to print them in the magazine withdrew in a huff. Her success in a rival paper, however, and the timely publication of her book which set the whole generation weeping and calling for more *Fern Leaves* to renew the flood, vindicated him completely.

Fanny, who had always had an eye for men, was very much attracted to the bearded laborer, a friend of James Parton's. Whether Walt reciprocated her interest is uncertain, but he gave her cause for feeling flattered when he bound his book in a style so similar to hers. It is more than likely, however, that Walt, a believer in mysterious forces, may have sought to obtain by the magic of imitation as much success for his own *Leaves* as Fanny's were still enjoying. Had there been anything of a sentimental nature between the two, Whitman's ideals of friendship would not have encouraged it beyond the limits of honor. Money matters, unfortunately, entered into the affair after Walt found himself obliged to borrow from Parton. Eventually the case was brought to court, perhaps through the fury of the woman scorned. At least so much Walt intimated when he told of his rupture with Parton. "There were other elements in the story—venom, jealousies, opacities; they played a big part; and if I may say it, women: a woman certainly . . . they kept alive what I felt James Parton would have let die."

Whatever the complexity of the emotional tangle of 1855, it had not reached the revulsion to hatred, a formidable passion in Fanny Fern who, that very year, had published her autobiographic *Ruth Hall*, in which she told off old scores against everyone by whom she fancied herself injured, her brother included. Although her novel did not have the reception of *Fern Leaves*, it was still a best seller. But then she could not have had any monetary worries, for that June she signed a contract with the astute Robert Bonner of the New York *Ledger* who knew a good piece of literary property when he saw one. After months of coyness on the part of Fanny, and tempting lures on Bonner's, she agreed to write regularly for the *Ledger* at the

WALT WHITMAN'S FATHER
From a painting

WALT WHITMAN'S MOTHER
From a painting

unheard-of rate of a hundred dollars a column. Somehow or other, either Walt or his distributors saw to it that Fanny received a copy of *Leaves of Grass* for comment. She would know by the portrait frontispiece who the author was.

Walt had trouble in finding an agent to handle his book, for the Rome brothers, once *Leaves of Grass* was printed, considered their work finished. They had prepared between eight hundred and a thousand copies, some bound and some left in sheets to be covered later by green or pink paper wrappers. On beholding the labor by which he justified his existence, Walt's heart leaped for joy. But how was he to sow his book among the people? He had no publisher, no one to take care of the mechanics of distribution. But he knew many of the booksellers of Brooklyn. Taking a few copies of *Leaves of Grass* in a bag, he made the rounds. None of the shops would accept it. At last he found a bookseller in Nassau Street who took some copies on consignment. Walt thrilled with gratitude. His book at last was launched. But his hopes that had risen so high collapsed the following day. Invited by the flowery gilt binding and the title that contained the word so popular among the lady writers, the respectable book dealer had taken it home to read overnight. He did not have to go farther than the first page to be startled by a "barbaric yawp."

The smoke of my own breath,
Echos, ripples and buzzed whispers . . . loveroot, silkthread, crotch and vine,
My respiration and inspiration . . . the beating of my heart . . . the passing of blood and air through my lungs,
The sniff of green leaves and dry leaves, and of the shore and dark-colored searocks, and of hay in the barn,
The sound of the belched words of my voice . . . words loosed to the eddies of the wind,
A few light kisses . . . a few embraces . . . a reaching around of arms.*

* Quotations in this chapter, except where otherwise indicated, are taken from the first edition of *Leaves of Grass*. The suspension points are Walt's favorite punctuation and do not imply omissions.

If he read more in the book to recover from the first shock he was doomed to disappointment. As a citizen of exacting standards he had no choice but to tell Walt that he would have none of the *Leaves*.

By this time Walt was used to the prudence of shopkeepers. Putting the rejected copies back in his bag, with more of the edition, he lugged them to the phrenological depot of Fowler and Wells. Had they not told him he was a poet? They might be willing to sell the *Leaves* among their own books. Surely they must note with gratification his use of phrenological terms in his poetry, and the tribute he paid the phrenologist when he included him in his preface among the "lawgivers of poets" saying that "their construction underlies the structure of every perfect poem." Fowler and Wells took over *Leaves of Grass* and, doubtless at Whitman's instance, brought it out on the Fourth of July. The book had been written for the great Democracy. It was fitting that it should reach the people on Independence Day.

That day Fowler and Wells offered special attractions to the public in exhibitions, readings and instructive entertainment. No doubt *Leaves of Grass* was prominently displayed, with Walt, looking like his portrait, lingering near,

Sure as the most certain sure . . . plumb in the uprights, well
  entretied, braced in the beams,
Stout as a horse, affectionate, haughty, electrical.

He and his mystery, there they stood.

They stood and waited in vain. In spite of the advertisements that Fowler and Wells put into the papers, offering the bound copies of *Leaves of Grass* for sale at a dollar, and seventy-five cents for those in cheap wrappers, notwithstanding their efforts to entice buyers both in their Broadway depot and their Washington Street shop in Boston, they failed to sell the book. It was a discouraging beginning for one who asserted in his preface: "The proof of a poet is that his country absorbs him as affectionately as he has absorbed it." Nevertheless, the firm continued sending complimentary copies to the newspapers and magazines and to distinguished literary persons.

At home Walt's family had no balm to offer. Walter Whitman was dying. With the head of the family gone who was to take his place? Jesse had never been too strong in the intellect. Walt, as the next in line, should succeed. But he wasn't turning out to be what the family considered a good provider. During the building boom he could have made money had he stuck to business. Instead he became involved in what George referred to as "the *Leaves of Grass* affair," neglecting his opportunities and even turning down good offers of literary work. Fortunately Jeff was well on his way to a comfortable career in the water works.

Sometimes George took Walt to task for his indifference to money matters, but Walt would cut short discussion by saying, "We won't talk about that." George was then wise enough to stop battering his head against an immovable force. Perhaps Walt knew what he was doing, though George had his doubts. When Walt brought home *Leaves of Grass*, George picked it up, fingered it a little. "I . . . didn't read it at all—didn't think it worth reading." Neither did Louisa, until later, after Longfellow's *Hiawatha* had proved so popular that a copy found its way to the Whitman household. Longfellow, Louisa knew, was a proper poet. She read him, and then she read Walt. But, she confided to George, the one seemed to her "pretty much the same muddle as the other." "If *Hiawatha* is poetry," she said, "perhaps Walt's is."

Walter Whitman probably never looked into the book at all. Hardly a week after it appeared, the sixty-six-year-old housebuilder, worn out with work, was dead. He had never understood Walt, nor had Walt ever understood the dour, silent man whose body, laid in Evergreen Cemetery, was still alive in his.

His own parents . . . they and of them became part of him . . .
The mother with mild words . . .
The father, strong, selfsufficient, manly, mean, angered, unjust,
The blow, the quick loud word, the tight bargain, the crafty
 lure. . . .

Leaves of Grass contained Walt's last words on the dead.

Anxiously Walt waited for the reviews. He had begun with soaring hopes. Like a nourishing rain after a drought, his words were to descend upon the soil of America, to be absorbed by it and returned in wonderful fruitage. So long had he dwelt alone with his vision, and so intensely had he lived in it, that he who assimilated every aspect of the life about him had nonetheless lost all sense of reality. He had been wounded by the reactions of the booksellers who found his book indecent and immoral, but he had not been discouraged. He knew that indecency and immorality dwelt in the minds that saw them. It was the indifference of the people whom he tried to reach that fell like a blight on his spirit. One can fight opposition. There is no power that can forge a weapon mighty enough to destroy indifference.

Then suddenly, probably on the very day that Walt read the first review of *Leaves of Grass*, he received a letter which was to counterbalance unfavorable criticism by its magnificent assertion. The notice in the *Tribune* for July 23, with its qualified praise, had no doubt been writen by Charles A. Dana whose pen had tempered criticism with friendship. The letter, however, came from a man personally unknown to Walt, although his name had long been a household word.

"Concord, Mass'tts, 21 July, 1855.

"Dear Sir, I am not blind to the worth of the wonderful gift of 'Leaves of Grass.' I find it the most extraordinary piece of wit and wisdom that America has yet contributed. I am very happy in reading it, as great power makes us happy. It meets the demand I am always making of what seemed the sterile and stingy nature, as if too much handiwork, or too much lymph in the temperament, were making our western wits fat and mean.

"I give you joy of your free and brave thought. I have great joy in it. I find incomparable things said incomparably well, as they must be. I find the courage of treatment which so delights us, and which large perception only can inspire.

"I greet you at the beginning of a great career, which yet must have had a long foreground somewhere, for such a start. I rubbed my eyes a little, to see if this sunbeam were no illusion; but the solid sense of the book is a sober certainty. It has the best merits, namely, of fortifying and encouraging.

"I did not know until I last night saw the book advertised in a newspaper that I could trust the name as real and available for a post-office. I wish to see my benefactor, and have felt much like striking my tasks and visiting New-York to pay you my respects.

"R. W. Emerson."

Walt was "set up," George said, on receiving Emerson's letter, and well he might be. Not in his wildest dreams could he have hoped for a letter, and such a letter, from the one man in America whose praise gave the seal of the highest approval. It was as if God had spoken, for was not Concord the literary Olympus, and Emerson its Jove? Emerson, happily, was no jealous god. Conscious of his enduring worth, he could afford to be generous, though indeed, in the light of literary history which abounds in more examples of rivalry than of encouragement, Emerson's generosity might appear to be rather godlike than human.

He did not himself go to see his "benefactor." Instead he sent as his emissary Moncure Conway, a young Virginian who had come to worship at the Concord shrine before setting out on his own literary career. With *Leaves of Grass* to read to sea and sky on his way to New York, Conway found himself in the right frame of mind when on a broiling summer's day he discovered Emerson's portent stretched out on the unshaded grass near his house, staring at the noonday sun with blue, unblinking eyes.

Considerately Walt took his guest indoors and showed him up to his room to be out of the way of the busy womenfolk at that inconvenient hour. Conway looked about him. The hermit Thoreau did not live so simply. Almost too small for him Walt's room dispensed with all but the most necessary furnishings— a cot, a pine table, a washstand and mirror, and two line drawings on the wall. The people's poet had no need of more.

Fascinated by the man, Conway joined Walt day after day in his perambulations. They went swimming round Staten Island and took sun baths in secluded coves. Conway admired the perfection of that body, large yet graceful and harmoniously formed. The coarse clothes only enhanced its superb manliness. Everywhere they went simple men, laborers, gave Walt hearty greetings and heartier handclasps. "Nearly everybody knows him and loves him," one of them told the aristocratic Virginian. But did those men know anything of Walt's book? Had they seen it? What had they made of the voice that had caused Emerson to declare: "Americans abroad may now come home: unto us a man is born"?

It may be that in accepting Walt Whitman Emerson was acknowledging the Transcendental succession, seeing in the Brooklyn rough whose effigy stood so jauntily on the threshold of his book, his own true literary son. For Transcendentalism, planted so lovingly in New England, had borne no issue through procreant literary men. Thoreau, Emerson's beloved disciple—if that independent spirit could be said to have followed leading strings held by even such a hand—lived his Transcendentalism, rather than wrote it. His energetic naysaying to all forms of tyranny exerted itself also against the tyranny of intellect. When Brook Farm, created to put Transcendentalism to the test, invited him to the experiment, he replied with an emphatic *No*, giving as the reason in his private journal that he thought it better to keep bachelor's hall in hell than to live in a boarding house in heaven. He sought no companionship in his spiritual explorations. There, as in the woods round Walden Pond, he preferred to roam alone. "I would rather sit on a pumpkin," he said, "and have it all to myself than be crowded on a velvet cushion." Rugged, blunt, simple, he had more in common with the wild life he studied with such delight, than with humanity to which, but for a few cherished individuals, he might have been a stranger. He was no stone on which Transcendentalism could build its temple.

Oddly, the seed had found roothold far from home. The Concord seer had never heard of Walt Whitman. Even the name in the copyright notice and tucked away in a verse of *Leaves of Grass* he believed might have been fictitious. And yet, behold a book that with much else besides, incorporated the wide, great, comprehensive view of life which, like a mass revelation, had come to New England.

But *Leaves of Grass* was too large a book to fit into any category, even the Transcendental. More than the book of an idea, it was the book of a man. Here and there among its pages Walt hinted at the keyword. In the edition of 1860, his best, he gave the clue in a short poem.

As Adam early in the morning,
Walking forth from the bower refresh'd with sleep,
Behold me where I pass, hear my voice, approach,
Touch me, touch the palm of your hand to my body as I pass,
Be not afraid of my body.

Thus Walt Whitman, the New Adam, awakened, not in the bower of Eden but in the nineteenth century world of wonder, his hale body large-lunged for the vital air, his senses sharpened for enjoyment, his roused imagination receptive to the miracle of everyday living. He is no primitive. Though his eyes are fresh as the dawn, they are wise with the wisdom of ages. A son of the green countryside, neighbor of the waters, he is equally at home in the cities of man. Past, present and future are fused in him, as in every being that lives.

I am an acme of things accomplish'd, and I an encloser of things
    to be.

He is as enduring as the earth, as immortal as the stars.

And I know I am deathless,
I know this orbit of mine cannot be swept by a carpenter's compass,
I know I shall not pass like a child's carlacue cut with a burnt stick
    at night. . . .
My foothold is tenoned and mortised in granite,
I laugh at what you call dissolution,
And I know the amplitude of time.

Man and woman are his equals, the races are equal, rich and poor, high and low, the president and the slave share alike his wide humanity. He reveres the body and he reveres the soul, for

Lack one lacks both . . . and the unseen is proved by the seen,
Till that becomes unseen and receives proof in its turn.

And because soul and body are equally noble,

Welcome is every organ and attribute of me, and of every man
    hearty and clean.
Not an inch nor a particle of an inch is vile, and none shall be less
    familiar than the rest.

For as the vessel of the spirit, the lamp of the inner light, the body partakes of divinity.

    And so, "bearded, sun-burnt, gray-neck'd, forbidding," Walt Whitman goes forth into the great world that is his land. He leans and loafs at his ease, observing a spear of summer grass.

A child said, What is the grass? fetching it to me with full hands;
How could I answer the child? . . . I do not know what it is any
    more than he.

192

I guess it must be the flag of my disposition, out of hopeful green
stuff woven.

Or I guess it is the handkerchief of the Lord,
A scented gift and remembrancer designedly dropped,
Bearing the owner's name someway in the corners, that we may see
and remark, and say Whose?

Or I guess the grass is itself a child . . . the produced babe of the
vegetation.

Or I guess it is a uniform hieroglyphic,
And it means, Sprouting alike in broad zones and narrow zones,
Growing among black folks as among white,
Kanuck, Tuckahoe, Congressman, Cuff, I give them the same, I re-
receive them the same.

And now it seems to me the beautiful uncut hair of graves. . . .

The smallest sprout shows there is really no death,
And if ever there was it led forward life, and one does not wait at
the end to arrest it,
And ceased the moment life appeared.

He comes stretched atop of the load into the country barn,
and watches the dried grass of harvest time being heaped by the
armful on the sagging mow.

I am there. . . . I help. . . .
I jump from the crossbeams, and seize the clover and timothy,
And roll head over heels, and tangle my hair full of wisps.

Across the breadth of the prairie his mighty limbs carry him.
He sees the huge beasts wallowing among the reeds. He watches
the wild gander leading his flock through the night.

Ya-honk! he says, and sounds it down to me like an invitation.

In the open air, in the far West, he sees the marriage of the
trapper to the Indian girl, he dressed in skins, his beard and
curls protecting his neck, and she with her head bare and the
long locks descending to her feet. He stands looking at the

193

naked youths bathing by the shore, and he sees the woman, frustrate, spying upon them, and desiring them, from behind the blinds of her window. He is everywhere, and there is no secret from him in his loving identification with all things that breathe.

The wilds and the city pavement know the step of the wanderer. All experience he makes his own. The runaway slave who stops at his house he hides in a room that enters from his; he nurses the galls of his neck and ankles, and then passes him North to safety. In the city he enjoys watching the men that labor, and joyously labors with them.

The carpenter dresses his plank . . . the tongue of his foreplane
    whistles its wild ascending lisp . . .
The pilot seizes the king-pin, he heaves down with a strong arm . . .
The deacons are ordained with crossed hands at the altar . . .
The jour printer with gray head and gaunt jaws works at his case,
He turns his quid of tobacco, his eyes blurred with the manu-
    script. . . .

Happiness and tragedy, domestic peace and turmoil, good and evil, all pass before him and all become part of him who understands and therefore cannot condemn.

The lunatic is carried at last to the asylum a confirmed case,
He will never sleep any more as he did in the cot in his mother's
    bedroom. . . .
The quadroon girl is sold at the stand . . . the drunkard nods by
    the barroom stove. . . .
The young fellow drives the express wagon. . . . I love him though
    I do not know him. . . .
The young sister holds out the skein, the elder sister winds it off in
    a ball and stops now and then for the knots,
The one-year wife is recovering and happy, a week ago she bore her
    first child. . . .
The prostitute draggles her shawl, her bonnet bobs on her tipsy and
    pimpled neck,
The crowd laugh at her blackguard oaths, the men jeer and wink to
    each other,

194

(Miserable! I do not laugh at your oaths nor jeer you)
The President holds a cabinet council, he is surrounded by the
    great secretaries. . . .
Seasons pursuing each other the indescribable crowd is gathered . . .
    it is the Fourth of July . . . what salutes of cannon and small
    arms!

Throughout, in a deep and solemn bass, sounding above the chants of discovered life and giving them coherence, roared his hymn of democracy.

For democracy, as he said in his preface, was the strength of the nation. "The United States themselves are essentially the greatest poem . . . Other states indicate themselves in their deputies . . . but the genius of the United States is not best or most in its executives or legislatures, nor in its ambassadors or authors or colleges or churches or parlors, nor even in its newspapers or inventors . . . but always most in the common people . . . The terrible significance of their elections—the President's taking off his hat to them not they to him—these too are unrhymed poetry. It awaits the gigantic and generous treatment worthy of it."

Humbly, the man who was even then being branded a shameless egoist, spoke of the poetry worthy of America as still unachieved although his mighty words drowned with their thunder the pipings of those who called themselves poets. For it was democracy that gave him the breath to utter. Rising from the sphere of a government wherein the individual was independent yet correlative to the mass, indeed, formed the strength of that union of free men and women, democracy became the password to a perfect society attainable for the fulfillment of all. The poet might be among the first to envision that era of the soul, but he offered the reality to everyone saying, "Come to us on equal terms, Only then can you understand us, We are no better than you, What we enclose you enclose, What we enjoy you may enjoy. Did you suppose there could be only one Supreme? We affirm there can be unnumbered Supremes, and that one does not countervail another any more than one eyesight countervails another . . . and that men can be good or grand only of the consciousness of their supremacy within them."

Chapter XVI: The poet speaks for himself

NEITHER the common people nor the critics accepted the invitation that Walt magnanimously extended. On the contrary the proffered hand was struck angrily, while the virtuous looked the other way when the new Adam came by with his gift. The female writers of both sexes threw up their hands on finding this interloper in their prim garden and shooed him off with pen pricks. Of the fifty copies of *Leaves of Grass* which Fowler and Wells managed to dispose of, some in sales, but most of them in gifts, many fed the fire, while others came hurtling through parlor windows on the innocent passerby.

Walt had no joy of the reviews that came to his notice. Although the first one had been friendly, it hardly touched upon the true spirit of his poems. The New York *Criterion* was decidedly inimical. After reviling the poet and the poems, it closed with a threat: "Thus, then, we leave this gathering of muck to the laws which, certainly . . . must have power to suppress such obscenity." The Boston *Intelligencer* played upon the theme, adding suggestions of its own for the treatment of the Brooklyn rough who offended public decency. "We were attracted by the very singular title of the work to seek the work itself, and what we thought ridiculous in the title is eclipsed in this heterogeneous mass of bombast, egotism, vulgarity and nonsense. The beastliness of the author is set forth in his own description of himself, and we can conceive no better reward than the lash for such a violation of decency as we have before us . . . This book should find no place where humanity urges any claim to respect, and the author should be kicked from all decent society as below the level of a brute." And this in spite of the approval of the Concord sage, whose letter Dana, as an act of friendliness to Walt, made public in the *Tribune* of October 10.

But thought, unfortunately, travels on slow wings, and tolerance barely crawls. How was the Boston critic to understand that in the poem of himself Walt was singing the praise of man, indeed, of the very one who reviled him?

I celebrate myself,
And what I assume you shall assume,
For every atom belonging to me as good belongs to you.

Missing the essential spirit the puny mind, unable to rise, wallowed in its own element, finding its image in the stagnant holes when Walt beckoned it upward. How else could it have failed to perceive the divinity conferred in the poet's fervid reiterations?

I am the mate and companion of people, all just as immortal and
    fathomless as myself;
They do not know how immortal, but I know. . . .

I know I am august,
I do not trouble my spirit to vindicate itself or be understood,
I see that the elementary laws never apologize.

In the older culture of England *Leaves of Grass* found no better reception. "Is it possible," asked the London *Critic*, "that the most prudish nation in the world will adopt a poet whose indecencies stink in the nostrils? . . . We grant freely enough that he has a strong relish for Nature and freedom, just as an animal has; nay, further, that his crude mind is capable of appreciating some of Nature's beauties . . . Walt Whitman is as unacquainted with art, as a hog is with mathematics. His poems . . . are innocent of rhythm, and resemble nothing so much as the war-cry of the Red Indians." Echoing his Boston cousin the British critic suggests the public executioner's whip for the man who, as he modestly puts it, "wrote page 79 of *Leaves of Grass.*"

Needless to say, those of his readers who could obtain a copy of the book made it their business to read that page if they read nothing else. What was it that so roiled the virtuous censor? A pæan of praise for the body of woman.

This is the female form,
A divine nimbus exhales from it from head to foot,
It attracts with fierce undeniable attraction,
I am drawn by its breath as if I were no more than a helpless vapor
   . . . all falls aside but myself and it,
Books, art, religion, time . . . the visible solid earth . . . the atmosphere and the fringed clouds . . . what was expected of heaven or feared of hell are now consumed,
Mad filaments, ungovernable shoots play out of it . . . the response likewise ungovernable.
Hair, bosom, hips, bend of legs, negligent falling hands—all diffused
   . . . mine too diffused,
Ebb stung by the flow, and flow stung by the ebb . . . loveflesh swelling and deliciously aching. . . .

From the beginning Whitman had made it clear that shame had no place in the viewing of God's handiwork, the body, the enfolder of the past and the gates of the future. As Eve was created for Adam that life endure upon the earth, so woman was the encloser of things to be, awaiting only "the limpid jets of love hot and enormous" that her mate brought to the fruitful consummation. It was as simple as that, and as holy. With a concreteness that while robbing mysticism enriched poetry, Whitman described the rapt union of male and female.

Earlier in his book, however, he had already given expression to the omnipotent fact, making it cosmic where the other remained isolated. But the blind critic had not seen the grandeur of Whitman's conception; his ears, too deaf to hear anything but the "war-cry of the Red Indians," remained closed to the music which the poet had learned in his solitary night walks when earth and sea and sky taught him the elementary yet universal rhythms of creation, himself part of the eternal mystery.

I am he that walks with the tender and growing night;
I call to the earth and sea half-held by the night.

Press close barebosomed night! Press close magnetic nourishing
   night!
Night of south winds! Night of the large few stars!
Still nodding night! Mad naked summer night!

Smile O voluptuous coolbreathed earth!
Earth of the slumbering and liquid trees!
Earth of departed sunset! Earth of the mountains misty-topt!
Earth of the vitreous pour of the full moon just tinged with blue!
Earth of shine and dark mottling the tide of the river!
Earth of the limpid gray of clouds brighter and clearer for my sake!
Far-swooping elbowed earth! Rich apple-blossomed earth!
Smile, for your lover comes!

Prodigal! you have given me love! . . . therefore I to you give love!
O unspeakable passionate love!

Thruster holding me tight and that I hold tight!
We hurt each other as the bridegroom and the bride hurt each other.

Notwithstanding, Whitman's treatment of sex leaves a problem for the psychologist. From the first he insisted on the element of sexuality in his work; otherwise, he said, "We are all lost without redemption." A deep religious inwardness dwelt in his most exuberant expression, an exaltation that found release through the physical being only because God had ordained it the medium for the mystery to declare itself. He could never get over the wonder of procreation whose force he saw explicit in every fact of nature, from the silently growing leaf of grass to the multiple stars. His first complete experience of the miracle had changed his life. Therefore he must write about

WALT WHITMAN'S TOMB
Photograph by Arnold Genthe. Courtesy Haddon Craftsmen
"There, built into the hillside, stood a rough, druidical hut . . . ."

WALT WHITMAN'S BIRTHPLACE
Photograph by Tet Borsig
"A plain, story-and-a-half house of shingles, weathered a soft gray by the years . . . solid and unpretentious."

it, perhaps because he could never again re-live it completely.

Guilt-consciousness, however, rising as much from his ethical sense as from a shirking of responsibility, compelled him to transvalue what a free and pagan nature would have accepted for what it was, a force working itself out toward unquestioned completion. Whitman must give it purpose, and that purpose he makes the foundation of his building of democracy. Romantic love has little room in his social order, just as there is no place for the weakling. In his scheme, humanity has come to perfection of health and vigor. His women are an athletic breed, capable of mothering a race of heroes; his youths arise, Adams of the dawn, before sin has come to trouble the flesh or mar with repentance the face of the spirit. They belong to the achieved democracy, where the lame and the blind have perished in an as yet unpromulgated theory of the survival of the fittest.

Completely unprepared for so robust a gospel, America was shocked, more, perhaps, by the letter than by the spirit. Even New England that had sent the first word of encouragement to the poet, found itself agreeing heartily with Wendell Phillips who said of *Leaves of Grass* that it contained every leaf except the fig leaf. Chaste Brahmin virgins found their faces suffused with blushes at the poet's bold summons. Shy bachelors like John Greenleaf Whittier promptly threw the book into the fire. Not yet, not yet. Too harsh were the words of this Mercury after the songs of the would-be Apollos.

Still the reviews kept coming in, each discovering some fault, if not in manner, then in content. Even Whitman's originality was attacked. *Putnam's Monthly* found his work "a compound of New England Transcendentalism and New York rowdy." The *Crayon* attacked his idealistic optimism, countering that since "to Walt Whitman all things are good,—nothing is better than another, and hence there is no ideal, no aspiration, no progress to things better." The Brooklyn *Eagle* which temporarily buried the hatchet in its pride at the achievement of an ex-employee, felt obliged to make some strictures after saying that all who read *Leaves of Grass* "will agree that it is an extraordinary book, full of beauties." To the sensitive author, more than kind words it was the adverse criticism that counted, for who likes to be told that the book on which he had hoped to build the future was a mixture of "bombast, philosophy, wit and dullness which it ever entered the heart of man to conceive"? There was little balm for his wounds in the praise that began to filter in as timid critics, taking heart from Emerson's published encomium, reasoned that where such a man led they could afford to follow.

Fanny Fern, when she finally published her review in the *Ledger* in May of the following year, made the point. But she had no need of Emerson's example to give wings to her pen in praise of the man with whom she was still infatuated. Her thumbnail sketch of him in her series, "Peeps from under a Parasol" three weeks earlier, had betrayed something more personal than literary appreciation.

"Here comes Walt Whitman . . . His shirt collar is turned off from his muscular throat, and his shoulders are thrown back as if even in that fine, ample chest of his, his lungs had not sufficient play room. Mark his voice, rich, deep and clear . . . A fig for phrenology! Let me but hear the *voice* of a man or woman and I will tell you what stuff its owners are made of."

Her review was a rhapsodic address to the book, the author and the people of America. Unrestrained because her heart prompted her words, she was sufficiently discerning to know that with all its flaws *Leaves of Grass* had merits which it did not take a woman in love to discover. She could write with authority not only because she knew the man but because she understood him. Indeed, some parts of her article reveal so deep a sympathy with his aims that she unconsciously falls into Whitman's style.

"Well baptized: fresh, hardy and grown for the masses . . . *Leaves of Grass:* thou art unspeakably delicious after the forced, stiff, Parnassian exotics . . . Walt Whitman, the effeminate world needed thee . . . Walt Whitman, the world needed a 'Native American' of thorough out-and-out breed—enamored of *women*, not *ladies—men*, not *gentlemen*. It needed a man who dared speak out his strong, honest thoughts in the face of pusillanimous, toadying, republican aristocracy; dictionary men, hypocrites, cliques and creeds; it needed a large-hearted, untainted, self-reliant, fearless son of the Stars and Stripes . . . It were a spectacle worth seeing, this glorious Native American, who, when the daily labor of chisel and plane was over, himself with toil-hardened fingers, handled the types to print the pages which wise and good men have since delighted to indorse and honor. . . ." Then, with a boldness astonishing in a woman of the day, she defended him with impassioned arguments against the charges of sensuality that had colored nearly all the criticisms of the book.

Whitman, however, had already spoken for himself, albeit in the sly disguise of the third person. Whichever way he looked at the welcome accorded his poems, it fell far short of his expectations. Other "Leaves," not only Fanny Fern's, had sold in the hundreds of thousands during the past five years; his own were not selling at all. Yet he knew that whereas the others were already fading with the season that gave them birth, his, deep in human experience, would endure as long as there were men and women to identify themselves with them. Had not the mightiest intellect of America confirmed his trust in his work? He must bring it before the people, no matter how.

There was no longer in his mind any question of ethics. And so, the man who had written in no uncertain terms in the *Eagle* against the practice of "puffery" composed article after article on the poems and on himself. Fowler and Wells connived in Walt's trickery when, in their *American Phrenological Journal* for October, 1855, they printed what was ostensibly an objective estimate of Tennyson and Whitman, "An English and an American Poet."

"It is always reserved for second-rate poems immediately to gratify," the nameless author begins fox-like before the coveted grapes that Tennyson was enjoying. After a few clumsy improvisations on the pet theme that foreign allegiance means death to American writing, and that Tennyson is no exception in the menace by being the "bard of ennui and of aristocracy and their combination into love," he bursts forth: "Meanwhile a strange voice parts others aside and demands for its owner the position that is only allowed after the seal of many returning years has stamped with approving stamp the claims of the loftiest leading genius. Do you think the best honors of the earth are won so easily?" he asks Walt Whitman with disingenuous reproof. "Do you think city and country are to fall before the vehement egotism of your recitative of yourself?" Quoting a passage from *Leaves of Grass*, he then expatiates upon the qualities of its poetry as against the poetry of the past and inquires, not altogether rhetorically: "And what is at once to become of the ranks of rhymesters, melancholy and swallow-tailed, and of all the confectioners and upholsterers of verse, if the tan-faced man here advancing . . . typifies indeed the natural and proper bard?"

A more bungling effort at concealment would be hard to find. Here was not only the hand of Esau, but his voice, too. Luckily for the anonymous writer the prose preface of *Leaves of Grass* had been seen by few, and not too perspicacious readers, or the critical hatchet-men would have fallen at once upon so awkward a masquerading wolf. If anything, Whitman's disguise left wider chinks in the article he published in the

The poet speaks for himself

Democratic Review. He sought no point of departure here but boldly plunged into a sea of praise.

"An American bard at last! One of the roughs, large, proud, affectionate, eating, drinking and breeding, his costume manly and free, his face sunburnt and bearded, his postures strong and erect, his voice bringing hope and prophecy to the generous races of young and old. We shall cease shamming and be what we really are. We shall start an athletic and defiant literature . . . The interior American republic shall also be declared free and independent . . . Self-reliant, with haughty eyes, assuming to himself all the attributes of his country, steps Walt Whitman into literature, talking like a man unaware that there was ever hitherto such a production as a book, or such a being as a writer. Every move of him has the free play of the muscle of one who never knew what it was to feel that he stood in the presence of a superior. Every word that falls from his mouth shows silent disclaim and defiance of the old theories and forms. Every phrase announces new laws . . . He makes audacious and native use of his own body and soul . . . Walt Whitman himself disclaims singularity in his work, and announces the coming after him of great successions of poets, and that he but lifts his finger to give the signal . . . You are come in good time, Walt Whitman!"

It took a man of either extreme egotism or utter unself-consciousness to write of himself in the strain of such an article and of a third which purported to be a review of *Leaves of Grass.* Even pretense was now stripped away as Whitman, naked as in his preface, stalked through the timid crowd, thumping his chest and filling the air with the newness, the genuineness, the importance of himself.

Nonetheless there was a world of difference between Whitman's shouted egotism and the self-esteem of a Margaret Fuller who had written in no doubtful terms: "I now know all the people worth knowing in America and I find no intellect comparable to my own." In her, egomania removed the individual from level ground to the pinnacle of self; in Whitman glorification of self had the ulterior aim of bringing before the average an attainable ideal. Here was no withdrawing but a merging. Had Whitman, the prophet, not been deficient in a sense of humor, he would have seen the absurdity of his posturing, however necessary to his purpose. But even in this he had to accept defeat. The more he shouted to call attention to his originality, the farther away people ran from the madman. In his absorption in his mission Walt forgot that people always shrink from the prophet's uncouthness, when they do not throw stones. He was aware of his own weakness, however. On an article on egotism clipped from a magazine, he wrote, in large letters: "See above and BEWARE."

Fowler and Wells, at least, had enough confidence in him to retain his book and try to coax buyers by reprinting laudatory comments in their magazines. *Life Illustrated,* one of their most popular, carried Fanny Fern's review in a prominent place, and to show that Whitman was not wholly without friends abroad, published also the London *Leader's* favorable estimate of *Leaves of Grass.* Articles on general topics by Whitman himself, though not signed, found room in the hospitable magazine, and became more frequent after the benison of Fanny Fern, much admired by the editors.

Meanwhile Whitman was taking stock of himself and preparing poems for a second edition which Fowler and Wells considered issuing. Emerson was much on his mind. Now, with other reading matter for his habitual excursions to Coney Island, he included a volume of Emerson's essays in the little basket that contained his dinner and towel. He had not answered Emerson's letter. He could not have answered it adequately within the limits of ordinary correspondence. He wanted to do much more than send the conventional note of thanks, yet he wished to do it in a way that would not make

Emerson feel that he, Walt, was too much beholden to him. He admitted having "a touch of Emerson-on-the-brain." But let none make the mistake of thinking that he owed Emerson anything as a source of inspiration of *Leaves of Grass*! For a long time, as he put it to John Townsend Trowbridge, "I was simmering, simmering, simmering; Emerson brought me to a boil." That was all. Emerson had simply stimulated the fire that was already burning, bringing the seething thoughts to the point. The Adamic Whitman could not bear to admit that there might have been another before him.

And so, while testing his new poems in the open air, by the trees, the stars and the ocean, he was also building the myth that, like another Minerva, he had burst full grown from the mind of God. But there was still that letter which had to be answered. He had qualms of conscience about it. After Dana published it without asking Emerson's permission, it was brought home to Walt that it had not been the thing to do. Guiltily he blamed his friend, but he knew that had he not wished the letter made public he would not have left it with Dana; or, if he had, he might have said explicitly that it was not for publication. Honest in his work, he possessed a devious streak in his anxiety to further it.

He hit upon the idea of answering Emerson publicly in the next edition. It came out in the summer of 1856, a small compact book, without the original preface, but containing twenty new pieces. A careful husbandman, Whitman had used the material of the discarded foreword in the long poem, "As I Sat Alone by Blue Ontario's Shore," and in several of the shorter ones. Again copies were sent out for review, inciting more violent reactions than before. Not only was the new edition virulently attacked despite the obvious development of the poet both in discipline and conception, but public feeling rose to such a pitch that the threat of prosecution looked for a time as if it might be carried out. No wonder the publishers had not put their imprint on the title page!

Now at last Walt paid his debt to Emerson, a debt with difficulty acknowledged and only after long struggle with a self that grudged admitting any influence from another. "Here are thirty-two poems," he began in an open letter to Emerson, "which I send you, dear Friend and Master . . ." He had written the word, no doubt with the relief of soul that accompanies confession. But having written, he felt he had done his duty in the indebtedness the word implied. All else was to his credit alone, as it would be to the credit of future poets who, with his own work as a springboard, would leap to greater heights.

I am the teacher of athletes;
He that by me spreads a wider breast than my own proves the width
    of my own,
He most honors my style who learns under it to destroy the teacher.

At the most, Emerson had been his springboard. He had not the least shadow of a doubt that he had outleaped the master.

But how explain the still unsold copies of the original *Leaves of Grass?* It was not in Walt's nature to confess himself defeated. In his faith-bolstered optimism he took a long view of his present failure. The time would come, hence the time was now. With self-deceiving perversion of fact, he sought to deceive Emerson. "The first edition . . . was twelve poems. I printed a thousand copies, and they readily sold; these thirty-two poems I stereotype, to print several thousand copies of. I much enjoy making poems. Other work I have set for myself to do, to meet people and The States face to face, to confront them with an American rude tongue; but the work of my life is making poems . . . A few years and the average annual call for my poems is ten or twenty thousand copies—more, quite likely. Why should I hurry or compromise?"

Did Emerson, reading the braggart words, guess at the tragic

208

pathos that lay beneath? And reading, did he forgive as he had forgiven the shocking violation of confidence in the publication of his letter—followed by a quotation from it in gold on the spine of the book, "I greet you at the beginning of a great career," and his name in print?

"Dear, dear!" he exclaimed when a friend informed him of the indelicacy. "That was very wrong, very wrong indeed. That was merely a private letter of congratulation. Had I intended it for publication I should have enlarged the *but* very much— enlarged the *but*—" And then he was speechless, as he gazed out of the window at nature which bars none, rather, makes room for all in its indiscriminate acceptance. Whitman was a force of nature. There must be room for him also, even if on closer acquaintance he might prove too elemental for comfort.

Somewhat shamefaced Emerson still took a certain grand-fatherly pride in Whitman's uncouth offspring, and pushed it forward wherever it had a chance of being welcomed. Now, however, he took care to "enlarge the *but*" to spare himself possible embarrassment. When the second edition appeared, he wrote to Thomas Carlyle: "One book, last summer, came out in New York, a nondescript monster, which yet had terrible eyes and buffalo strength, and was indisputably American— which I thought to send you; but the book throve so badly with the few to whom I showed it, and wanted good morals so much, that I never did. Yet I believe now again, I shall. It is called *Leaves of Grass* . . . After you have looked into it, if you think, as you may, that it is only an auctioneer's inventory of a warehouse, you can light your pipe with it."

None knows what use the sublime dyspeptic made of the "nondescript monster" at that time. Did he, like Emerson, discern in it a resemblance to himself, whose gospel, now twice removed, came back to him, large and more powerful, as from the thunder of the ocean between? He did not write to Whitman. For that matter, no letter was expected. It would have been unreasonable even for one of such resilient hope as Whitman to look for another "letter from God dropt in the street." One knows, however, that Carlyle read the book, but was not altogether pleased, chiefly for its stress on largeness. "I cannot like him. It all seems to be—'I'm a big man myself because I live in such a big country.' But I have heard of great men living in very small corners of the earth." Was he thinking of Craigenputtock—and of himself?

Notwithstanding the bravado of his lies to Emerson, Walt suffered pangs of bitter discouragement. He knew that his book was great enough to look after itself, yet he could not leave it alone to make its own way. Emerson's word was much, but it was not all. He wanted a sign from the common man. No sign came. In agony of spirit after the first savage reviews, he went off by himself to wrestle with a doubt, for the first time looming forbidding against the radiance on which he had stubbornly set his gaze. Was he wrong to hope, or was the world wrong to condemn?

Through the late summer and the fall, he stood face to face with himself, in the solitude of Peconic Bay, questioning, irresolute, yet strangely happy amidst those healing scenes. Then the answer came, confirmed by the voice of nature which above all he trusted. To New York he returned, strong in the resolve to go on, as he had begun, in his own way. A birthday came and went, spent as he always spent it, in meditation and self-analysis. For the Quaker that day never failed to bring stern resolutions, promises for improvement, schemes for the furthering of his "poetic enterprise" against the shattering negations that continued to come from the hostile world.

By the 21st of June, 1856, he had no shred of doubt left of the importance of his work. "It seems to me quite clear and determined that I should concentrate my powers on *Leaves of Grass*," he noted in his pocketbook, "—not diverting any of my means, strength, interest, to the construction of anything

210

else—of any other book." With mythical thoroughness he welded himself to his creation, at once his offspring and his mate.

The poet had strength of purpose too great, almost, for the man. People never ceased wondering why he did not marry. He could, if he wished, earn enough to support a family as journalist, printer, certainly as carpenter. Mrs. Abby Price, a woman whose friendship he treasured, asked him point-blank one day, "Walt, have you ever been really in love?"

Taken by surprise, Walt hesitated a long time before replying and then said, "Your question, Abby, stirs a fellow up."

Nothing more. But seeing there must be an answer to so direct a question, he reluctantly took something out of his pocket and showed it to Mrs. Price and her daughter Helen who was standing by. It was the photograph of a young woman.

The man had not forgotten—nor had the poet. But he had made of his remembered passion a universal theme, preluded in his treatment of sex in his first edition, and now developed with no withholding of word or fact. "The Poem of Procreation"* shocked by its outspokenness on a subject always treated with evasion. It was the one poem, among others, that raised the loudest outcry, despite its ingenuous truism, "All were lacking if sex were lacking." In bold print the objectionable word *sex* alone sent shivers of horror through the people who spoke of *limbs* and *bosoms*, and draped piano legs in chaste pantalettes. To have the act of procreation written of boldly in a book that women might read, was to commit the unforgivable sin. For a mere figure of speech Charles Sumner was severely censored when in his debate on Louisiana he spoke of the state as "a seven months' child, begotten by the bayonet, in criminal conjunction with the spirit of caste." What should be the punishment of a man who presented himself as the eligible

* Later called "A Woman Waits For Me."

211

husband of warm-blooded women ("I will dismiss myself from impassive women") to beget children for America?

Ignoring Whitman's purpose, to unfold a complete man in the dawning spiritual order he foresaw for the States, the reader could find only a mystery desecrated, and womanhood placed on a level with those outcasts who walked the streets. Even minds as open as Emerson's could not admit such a passage as:

It is I, you women, I make my way,
I am stern, acrid, large, undissuadable but I love you,
I do not hurt you any more than is necessary for you,
I pour the stuff to start sons and daughters fit for these States, I press
    with slow rude muscle,
I brace myself effectually, I listen to no entreaties,
I dare not withdraw till I deposit what has so long accumulated
    within me . . .

or from "Spontaneous Me" such anatomical listings as

Love-thoughts, love-juice, love-odor, love-yielding, love-climbers and
    the climbing sap,
Arms and hands of love, lips of love, phallic thumb of love, breasts
    of love, bellies press'd and glued together with love.

Whitman the poet was nothing if not honest, no matter what deceptions the man might perpetrate. There could be no question of his incredible sincerity in the plain speaking which even today, in some quarters, stands in the way of the full acceptance of *Leaves of Grass*. But the individual is a complex world, full of inner tumults belying the peaceful aspects on the surface. True, Walt wrote of himself with painful shamelessness, exposing what others concealed, so that by the shock people's eyes might be forced open. Nevertheless he betrayed something of the tormented imagination of the ascetic in his preoccupation with the body, as if like Anthony in the desert, the poet saw unrolling repeatedly before him the pageant of temptation. He was no worse and no better than anyone else, he confessed,—

212

The poet speaks for himself

> I too knitted the old knot of contrariety,
> Blabb'd, blush'd, resented, lied, stole, grudg'd,
> Had guile, anger, lust, hot wishes I dared not speak . . .
> The wolf, the snake, the hog, not wanting in me. . . .

But the public credited only the worse half of the confession, losing sight of the motive of oneness with mankind that forced him to his admissions.

Fowler and Wells saw no diminution in their stock of *Leaves of Grass*, whereas on the other hand menacing voices increased in volume. Afraid that the book might seriously injure their reputation as well as their business, they let it drop. The poet of America found himself without a publisher.

Chapter XVII: The love of comrades

FOR the next four years, as far as the general public was concerned, *Leaves of Grass* might never have been written. Little by little the hounds of the press also ceased their baying, and feminine virtue, guarded by Godey's *Lady's Book*, sat serene in her boudoir. The first edition had disappeared, no one could tell where, except for a few copies that found their way to England in the sack of an itinerant bookseller. The second accumulated dust. At the press of the Rome brothers the original manuscript lay about for several years, then vanished, probably to kindle the fire or to feed the rag man. The publication of the book had been a loss in every way.

Stubbornly and in secret Whitman kept on working. Everything that touched the nation affected his book, hence although he had ceased to be an active participant in politics, he took it upon himself to speak occasionally to his fellow citizens. Corruption in the highest quarters roused his temper, ordinarily not quick to fire. Thus in spite of the promise made to himself not to divert his energies, he took time off to write a pamphlet during the presidential campaign of 1856, endorsing the candidacy of John Charles Frémont the Pathfinder against his Democratic opponents. A wide chasm lay between the stump-speaking Democrat of his youth to the "Black Republican" that he became, but he bridged it with his principles that knew no loyalty except to his own sense of right.

He wrote no inconsidered, rabble-rousing stump speech in "The Eighteenth Presidency!" He planned it carefully, weighing his words as scrupulously as for his poems. After all he was not merely the private citizen speaking, but the poet. "To editors of the independent press," he exhorted, "and to rich

214

persons. Circulate and reprint this Voice of mine for the workingmen's sake." That the sponsors he sought should have no difficulty with his handwriting, he pulled some proofs of the article himself.

Unfortunately neither editor nor rich man would touch "The Eighteenth Presidency!" with its dangerous outspokenness against the southern slaveholders and its communistic incitements to workingmen to assert their rights as citizens. "The President eats dirt and excrement for his daily meals, likes it, and tries to force it on the States," he fulminated. "The cushions of the Presidency are nothing but filth and blood. The pavements of Congress are also bloody . . . Now . . . the delegates of the politicians have nominated for the eighteenth term Buchanan of Pennsylvania and Fillmore of New York, separate tickets, but men both patterned to follow and match the seventeenth term, both disunionists, both old politicians, both sworn down to the theories of special parties, and of all others the theories that balk and reverse the main purposes of the founders of These States. . . . But another power has also arisen. A new race copiously appears, with resolute tread, soon to confront Presidents, congresses and parties, to look them sternly in the face and stand no nonsense, American young men, the offspring and proof of these States. . . ."

On them he founded his dream of the future perfect democracy, and to them he dedicated himself. "I am not afraid to say that among them I seek to initiate my name, Walt Whitman, and that I shall in future have much to say to them. I perceive that the best thoughts they have wait unspoken, impatient to be put in shape." From their ranks, the ranks of the workingmen, the mechanics, farmers, laborers, must come the man to redeem These States. "I would be much pleased to see some heroic, shrewd, fully-informed, healthy bodied, middle-aged, beard-faced American blacksmith or boatman come down from the West across the Alleghenies, and walk into the Presidency."

215

Better than he knew, the hope of the poet-prophet would be realized.

For the present he had, like Hamlet, to eat the air, promise-crammed; the proof sheets were laid away with others of his writings, to see the light long after his death. The dreamer, however, must make compromises to reality. The following summer, to help keep the pot boiling, he took the job of editor of the Brooklyn *Daily Times*. But bread-and-butter concerns must not overshadow his main purpose. To keep that object ever in view he admonished himself again in his private communing: "The Great Construction of the New Bible. Not to be diverted from the principal object—the main life—the Three Hundred and Sixty-Five.—It ought to be ready in 1859." It was then June, 1857.

Meanwhile the lover of life plunged with gusto into the business of living. People remarked him wherever he went, picturesquely colorful. The carpenter's clothes alternated with another of his costumes, the jacket of dark-blue cloth left open at the throat, the red handkerchief tied loosely round, the high cavalier boots into which he tucked his trousers, and the dashing broad-brimmed hat. His habits as editor remained the same. Up and down the streets he walked, back and forth along the avenues, as familiar with the corrupt Five Points where vice of all kinds pullulated as with the less exacting salons which were beginning to discover him. True to his pledge, he wrote of what he saw and felt. The prostitutes plying their trade between Houston and Fulton Streets on Broadway brought forth not an article of scorn on the unfortunates, some of them mere girls who "in encouraging circumstances, might make respectable and happy women," but a commonsense plea for state supervision of houses of prostitution which he was too much of a realist not to recognize as a necessary and too common evil under the contemporary social system. He became more outspoken against slavery and less critical of the champions of

Abolition. As in his pamphlet, he assailed the corruption of politics, cliques and classes and reaffirmed his faith in the goodness and might of the common people. All too human, he also settled a score with Fanny Fern at whose instigation, as he believed, he had been haled to court for the money he owed her husband. "We want a race of men and women turned out from our schools, not of pedants and bluestockings," he wrote on the subject of education. "One genuine woman is worth a dozen Fanny Ferns." Poor Fanny, who had been the first of her sex to defend him!

His pleasures had not changed. When the Academy of Music on Fourteenth Street opened its doors, he was there to comment on the architecture, the round, moonlike lights, the arched windows. He noted appreciatively that the acoustics were all that could be desired, though he deplored that the same care had not been given to the arrangement of seats; from half the house no view of the stage was possible. He attended the Opera as assiduously as ever, missing no performance in which the wonderful contralto, Marietta Alboni, sang. So deeply was he moved by her, especially by her rendering of the priestess' scene with her children in *Norma* that she supplanted his earlier admiration of the tenor Bettini, whose singing used to affect him to tears. He had put her without mentioning her name in *Leaves of Grass*, and was planning a suitable tribute to her in the next edition,—"To a Certain Cantatrice." Just as he employed the French he had so imperfectly picked up in New Orleans, to the exasperation of the college big-wigs, he loved to use words from the literature of music in his poems. "No dainty dolce affettuoso I . . . I hear bravuras of birds . . . I sing the endless finales of things; such be the recitative I bring to thee." These and other words became the unpardonable literary sin to the prim literati with their fixed poetic diction. To Walt they gave a naïve delight.

The wide circle of acquaintance he had among the stage

drivers had grown in the course of years to include almost two generations. In wet or cold weather he could be seen sitting on top of the bus. When the passenger pulled the check string fastened to the foot of the driver, and pushed up his fare through a round hole in front, Walt would take it and hand back the change as required. "Oh, I was famous for this," he reminisced when his bus-driving days were over. If one of his friends was ill Walt would take his place behind the horses so that the man would not lose his wages. He knew how to guide a bus through traffic, enjoying the sense of power it gave, as he had loved steering the Brooklyn ferryboats until, one night, while at the wheel, he nearly met with a bad accident. He left off piloting after that, but to make up for it, he constituted himself an unofficial patron of the stagers. He aided their needy families, attended funerals when, as it often happened, they met with sudden death; he raised subscriptions for unexpected illnesses, and helped to nurse the men back to health. At the New York Hospital to which bad accident cases were taken, he was well known by the surgeons whom he assisted in the dressing of wounds. He learned to steel himself against the sight of blood and horrible injuries, and knew how to allay pain with a heartening word. The doctors marveled at his strange power, and overlooked regulations for the comfort he brought the patients. Only half in jest they spoke of him among themselves as "the Saint." The Caresser of Life was serving his apprenticeship as a soother of suffering and death.

Whitman was doing more than that, however. In his experiences of devotion to his fellow man he was putting to practice his gospel of the creative function of the love of comrades. Privately, in the elaboration of the "Three Hundred and Sixty-Five," he was adding the calamus to *Leaves of Grass*. The idea came to him as a result of the demands of his own inclusive nature. With him friendship was a passion as strong, perhaps stronger, than love. It required the physical presence of the loved one; it gave everything and excluded no emotion from its expression. It was boundless in its scope toward the building of "the new city of friends" yet as intensely personal as a heartache. It knew violence, jealousy, the bitterness of betrayal and the transports of perfect communion. For him adhesiveness, as he called comradely love in the jargon of the phrenologist, was as universal a fact of nature as the instinct of the bird to fly and of man and woman to mate. Sex was perforce a part of it, as it must be in anyone of such a highly sensual yet mystical makeup. It was a case of where extremes not only met but formed an indissoluble unity. Always he had held sex to be the core of being; to deny it now in a context that premised the birth of a new spiritual order, was to deny God. That fire of passion which turned the material world into flame must not be withheld from the soul.

When he gave early form to his ideal of manly affection, therefore, he wrote, as in the 1856 version of the "Song of the Broad-Axe," with daring sexuality:

Their shapes arise, the shapes of full-sized men!
Men taciturn yet loving, used to the open air, and the manners of
    the open air,
Saying their ardor in native forms, saying the old response,
Take what I have then, (saying fain,) take the pay you approached
    for,
Take the white tears of my blood, if that is what you are after.

Later he omitted the passage, but not the conviction that in comradely attachment, as much as in the passion of men and women, the roots of universal love found nourishment. For while the physical union of lovers renewed the race, the love of comrades which for him had a completeness denied to the love between the sexes, gave promise of the era of the spirit that friends and lovers would alike inherit.

He chose the calamus plant, or sweet flag, for his symbol of manly affection, as he had chosen the humble, close-growing,

219

widespread grass to represent the multitudinous ranks of humanity. Often he had seen the calamus growing in close clinging tufts, blade against blade, each helping to hold up the others like equals bound together for common support. The roots, faintly tinged with red, breathed a delicate freshness that lingered after the grass had faded, as friendship remained even after death, in memory.

Here the frailest leaves of me and yet my strongest lasting,

he wrote.

Here I shade and hide my thoughts, I myself do not expose them,
And yet they expose me more than all my other poems.

On this suggestion a tissue of conjectures has been woven, in predominantly dark colors. Was Whitman a homosexual, and was his love of comrades another name for homosexuality? Treatises have been written for and against such an interpretation of the Calamus poems, few arriving at any acceptable conclusion. Whitman was an exceptional man. Everyone who knew him had stories to tell of the remarkable effect of his mere physical presence upon those who met him for the first time. An initial reading of his book came always as an experience. Men confided in him and women loved him.

Thoreau who went to seek him out in Brooklyn with Amos Bronson Alcott late in 1856, betrayed the disturbing impact of that meeting on his perfectly balanced intellect in the letter he sent to a friend. "It is as if the beasts spake," he said of Whitman's sexual poems, closing with the extraordinary contradiction, "We ought to rejoice greatly in him. He occasionally suggests something a little more than human . . . He is awfully good . . . He is a great fellow." The loquacious Alcott who for once in his life let others have the floor, summed him up as "the very god Pan." Thomas Cholmondeley, Thoreau's correspondent, found Whitman, "further ahead of me in yonder West than Buddha is behind me in the orient," yet deplored to see "the gentleman altogether left out."

Young and emotional disciples who knew him during the tragic years of the nation looked upon him as another Christ. Indeed, William Douglas O'Connor saw no irreverence in so portraying him in a story. John Burroughs, a serious young man of twenty-six when he met Whitman, confided to his diary the weird spell cast upon him by the man. "Notwithstanding the beauty and expressiveness of his eyes, I occasionally see something in them as he bends them upon me, that almost makes me draw back. I cannot explain it—whether it is more or less than human. It is as if the Earth looked at me—dumb, yearning, relentless, immodest, inhuman." To a friend he wrote: "I love him very much. The more I see and talk with him, the greater he becomes to me . . . Walt has all types of men in him, there is not one left out."

When Emerson who had hailed the portent finally saw him face to face he found his own blood, rarefied by six generations of Puritan ministers, coursing nervously before the hearty companion and his "noisy fire-engine society." The son of Transcendentalism had too disturbing an admixture of the common breed for the man of the study. Emerson, somewhat taken aback, disapproved of the workings of nature in this case, and frowned upon Whitman's unliterary choice of companionship. "He took me there and was like a boy over it, as if there had never been such a thing before." But how was Emerson to know that among the beer mugs and the fire-engine crew Whitman was celebrating the mystery of universal brotherhood? From Christ to rowdy: the paradox of Whitman was on its way.

Burroughs has left numerous records of how he felt immediately bound to Walt in a spontaneous burst of Calamus friendship. "He loves everything and everybody," he wrote. "I saw a soldier the other day stop in the street and kiss him. He kisses me as if I were a girl." Simply, without overtones, Burroughs reported what to the world might have appeared dubious behavior. Walt, as all his friends had to accept, saw no evil in giving physical proofs of his affection to members of his sex. The letters he wrote to his protégé Peter Doyle are lavish in kisses and embraces. Since love was to him a force as needful to life as air, and equally beyond good and evil, he bestowed it upon all things that breathe, making no distinctions where nature made none. There was nothing human that he could not worship with his body as in a mystic marriage. On that solemn and reverent fact his whole morality was founded.

That he knew the existence of such a sexual deviation as homosexuality at the time he was composing his Calamus poems is very doubtful. He could not have written so nakedly had not entire innocence guided his pen; nor would he have shown such hysterical shock, long afterward, when the persistent John Addington Symonds demanded an explicit answer to what he thought the homosexual implications of those poems. "I often say to myself about Calamus," a very puzzled old man mused, "—perhaps it means more or less than what I thought myself; perhaps I don't know what it all means—perhaps never did know. My first instinct about all that Symonds writes is violently reactionary—is all for no, no, no. Then the thought intervenes that maybe I do not know all my own meaning." Whatever doubt he had concerned the interpretation alone. For the fact itself the answer was emphatic—"No, no, no."

However, for the suspicious, Whitman left plenty of bait in the frankness of his expression. The man who had violated the rigorous taboos of his day by "yawping" the most private mysteries from the rooftops was not going to mute his song in the message he considered basic to his gospel. Let people make what they would of it in their limited day. The time of its just interpretation would come. Therefore he exposed himself in the poem:

222

The love of comrades

Earth, my likeness,
Though you look so impassive, ample and spheric there,
I now suspect that is not all;
I now suspect there is something fierce in you eligible to burst forth,
For an athlete is enamour'd of me, and I of him,
But toward him there is something fierce and terrible in me eligible
    to burst forth,
I dare not tell it in words, not even in these songs.

He had told enough to damn him with the literal-minded
who forgot that the poet, especially when he is also a prophet,
deals in the apocalyptic. In the poems treating of love between
the sexes which he was bringing together and enlarging in the
group "Enfans d'Adam"* he gave a portrait of himself as a
phallic god, a Priapus, sowing offspring everywhere. Yet the
women who knew him saw a reserved, mild, rather sentimental
man who carried in his pocket the photograph of his sweetheart.
There was no more of the homosexual about him than there
was of the libertine.

Closely examined, the facts reveal a highly sensitive, unusual
personality, keyed by nature to respond to every stimulus of
sensual and spiritual beauty, in him always inseparable. Male
and female traits mingled in him. Though full-bearded and
fond of showing "the scented herbage" of his breast, he had a
skin as fair and rosy as his mother's. The brawny body combined with masculine strength the indolent grace of a woman's.
He despised athletics, preferring to loiter at his leisure and
float—not swim—in the tides of life as well as of the sea. With
the courage of a man he had a woman's gentleness which made
him a perfect attendant at a sickbed. While writing without
shame of the body and its functions, he was so excessively
modest that he took more pains than a young girl to conceal
his nakedness, even before his own sex. Everything about him
points to an anomalous duality with all that it implies, but of
homosexuality there is none. The best denial is contained in

* Now "Children of Adam."

the brief poems included not in the Calamus group, but in "Enfans d'Adam":

I am he that aches with amorous love;
Does the earth gravitate? does not all matter, aching, attract all
    matter?
So the body of me to all I meet or know.

In that *all* lies the answer, and in the Whitmanian concept of the body as part of God. "I am not content now with a mere majority—" he wrote elsewhere in a poem. "I must have the love of all men and all women." Let him who can, interpret literally the boundlessness of such love.

During the time Walt had fallen out of the public gaze he had entered a circle that gave him at last a measure of the admiration his ego required. Charles Pfaff, a rotund, good-natured German Swiss with a fondness for conviviality and a respect for learning, had in the mid-'fifties opened a beercellar in the heart of the city—Broadway, near Bleecker. The service was unexampled. Handsome German girls dispensed the beer, waiters knew when to make themselves unobtrusive, and a potent brew of coffee arrived at one's call, steaming hot, to banish the lethargy of alcohol. As for the German pancakes, the quality of the liquor and the ripeness of the cheeses, a steady line of patrons vouched for their excellence. Every night the subterranean dining room resounded with the play of knife and fork against the counterpoint of the footsteps overhead. But it was not till Henry Clapp, recently returned from Paris, saw the possibilities of Pfaff's cellar, that it arrived at its true function as the meeting place of New York's Bohemia.

The word was new to America in its artistic connotation. To Henry Clapp, fresh from the Parisian Murgeritis that had been breaking out in all manner of cénacles since the appearance of *Scènes de la Vie de Bohème*, it was the open sesame to the kingdom of good companions. Collecting about him the literary men of his acquaintance, he formed New York's first Bohemia of which he became the acknowledged king. Pfaff, familiarly known as Charlie, expanded in the importance his cellar attained. People came from all parts of town to see the celebrities. Pfaff's was as much on the map as Niblo's Garden. Charlie glowed with warmth like the large-bellied bottles of Haut-Graves and Bonnes Sauternes, Malvoisie Royale, Beaune and Volnay, as the bon-mots flew across the tables, or some poet, impatient for an audience, read his latest over the glasses. French manners and the spirit of France sank their roots under the pavement of Broadway.

Solicitous for the comfort of his literary covey Charlie Pfaff gave them a perch of their own along a narrow table in a vaulted niche directly under the sidewalk, away from the community of the dining room. Here the poets might drink and talk till the small hours, spied upon but unmolested by the curious who came as much to steal a glimpse of the exalted as to enjoy Charlie's generous brews. George Arnold, John Swinton, Charles Stoddard, Ned Wilkins, the envious Willie Winter and the Byronic Fitz-James O'Brien often sat at the long table, putting up a front when occasionally brownstone respectability invaded their cave in the person of Thomas Bailey Aldrich or the Ohioan, W. D. Howells. But the observed of all observers and the darling of Charlie Pfaff was the bearded bard who came almost nightly to bask in good fellowship.

"Ah, there comes the unclean cub of the wilderness," Walt would be greeted banteringly by one of the party, quoting from an uncomplimentary article. Smiling in his slow, quiet way, and no doubt with a gesture of the perpendicular hand, he would then take his place among them. He felt at ease in the smoke-clouded atmosphere, though he never touched tobacco, and forgot his early "Franklin Evans" preachments in an occasional mug of beer, drunk slowly, like the cup of brotherhood. Sometimes after a visit at the New York Hospital, amidst its

225

fine old elms off Pearl Street nearby, he would bring his friends the doctors, and occasionally a visitor from the stronghold of Boston, to make him see for himself that though the Brahmins had no use for Walt Whitman, here he was not without appreciation.

Indeed, Henry Clapp seemed almost to have founded the *Saturday Press* for the purpose of forcing Whitman upon the balking public. There was a touch of the quixotic in the defense of the little, wiry, Voltairean, witty Clapp of the humorless, leonine Whitman, lumbering his slow way to immortality. But it was no fawning relationship on the part of Clapp. He had too independent a spirit, and a forked tongue of lightning, whose flashes carried over the country. Millions laughed when, in the next decade, at the award of an honorary LL.D. to General Grant by Union College, he commented, "Not that the General needed a degree but the college needed a Grant."

"Walt, you include everything," he once said to Whitman in mock-seriousness. "What have you got to say to the bed-bug?" It was coarse but perhaps justifiable criticism of the poet's indiscriminate tolerance. Walt answered with his goodnatured smile, knowing that such banter was nothing against the devoted logrolling of the editor of the *Saturday Press*.

The weekly of the Bohemians had been launched in 1858, a year after the Boston mandarins issued the stately *Atlantic Monthly*. As editor of the Brooklyn *Times* Walt had noticed rather superciliously the first copy, comparing the newborn *Monthly* not too favorably with the plump, adolescent *Harper's Magazine*, making its way to brisk growth with its cartoons, fashion-plates, jokes and British serials. But then, besides his "Master" Emerson's poem "Brahma" the *Atlantic Monthly* had contained the names of writers whom Walt looked upon not only as philistines but as enemies. The goaded lion might be forgiven his growl.

It was against the Boston school, the literary *bête noire* of

Clapp and his group that the *Saturday Press* was directed. Impudent, aggressive, with no regard for the long beard of tradition, Clapp's irreverent supporters tweaked it heartily with every issue. They wanted no learned stodginess, so they blasted it with their laughter. They tolerated no pomposity, however respectable its name. Lined up with their well-sharpened arrows, they aimed and hit the mark—and stuffed shirts deflated. Clapp's trenchant style, learned from the French *feuilletons* had the piquancy of novelty amidst the stereotype of the day. Moreover he was fearless, and he encouraged youth.

For a time it looked as if the *Saturday Press* might supplant the *Atlantic Monthly* as the writer's desired goal. Alas, like all things too intense, it burned itself out. But not before it had shouted the name of Whitman from the editorial mouthpiece. "We announce a great Philosopher," the *Press* heralded with a disturbingly familiar accent, "—perhaps a great Poet—in every way an original man. It is Walt Whitman." Even in Clapp's hand Walt had guided the laudatory pen with his Jovian disregard of literary ethics.

Those were happy times at Pfaff's

> where the drinkers and laughers meet to eat and carouse
> While on the walk immediately overhead pass the myriad feet of
> Broadway.

Sitting back in his chair Walt watched strange and well-known figures coming down the flight of steps from the street—business men, artists, actors whom he had admired on the stage and a sprinkling of women who, flouting convention, joined as the equals of the opposite sex in the comradeship of art. Daisy Sheppard, now forgotten, and Agnes Franz, counted themselves Bohemians, but the chosen queen whom the men adored and their wives dreaded was the brilliant, mysterious Ada Clare.

The Pfaffians worshiped her. Walt, looking upon her as the "new woman," gave her his benison and advice. Henry Clapp accepted her as a gifted Musette in his Bohemia. He also accepted her past, which included an affair with a celebrated pianist, a clandestine trip to Paris where she had drunk the waters of the Murgerian spring, and a little boy, her son, three or four years old. To the questions of her admirers who knew her only by her incandescent verses, Clapp would answer tersely, "She is young, pretty, unmarried, and has a boy." When pressed about the child he said he believed it was an immaculate affair.

Ada herself had no such reticence. As a self-styled love-philosopher, she was past master in that branch of learning, with no dearth of willing initiates. "Ada Clare," said a man who knew her, "is virtuous after the French fashion, namely, has but one lover at a time." She made no denial. On the contrary, she vaunted the example of liberation she was setting her sex, and scandalized the virtuous by introducing herself and her boy as *"Miss* Ada Clare and son." Approving, Walt nodded at her behavior. But even he had once to pull at the rein of Ada's high-stepping freedom, when she urged an inexperienced country lover to seduce the girl to whom he was engaged. "It will do you good. You will both learn something, and then you may come back to me," she said. Walt lectured her severely on her cynicism, which must have sounded strange from the ex-toller of sexual emancipation.

But Walt at that time had reason to brood on the consequences of his own brief flare of passionate love. Like the pianist in Ada Clare's life had he been in the life of the girl in New Orleans. In the summer of 1859, in the notebook that contained the fading tintype of a woman, he wrote with self-reproach: "It is now time to stir first for money enough to live and provide from M—" Shortly afterward the *Saturday Press* published a poem of the magic only he could weave, an ocean-sung dirge of love and separation, made unbearably poignant by the scent of lilac and the heartbroken song of the bird call-

ing its lost mate in the night. Lilac scent, stars, and mourning
bird—out of them the poet made beauty of his private sorrow.

O rising stars!
Perhaps the one I want so much will rise, will rise with some of you.

O throat! O trembling throat!
Sound clearer through the atmosphere!
Pierce the woods, the earth,
Somewhere listening to catch you must be the one I want.

Shake out carols!
Solitary here the night's carols!
Carols of lonesome love! death's carols!
Carols under that lagging, yellow, waning moon!
O under that moon where she droops almost down into the sea!
O reckless despairing carols.

But soft! sink low!
Soft! let me just murmur,
And do you wait a moment you husky-nois'd sea,
For somewhere I believe I heard my mate responding to me,
So faint, I must be still, be still to listen,
But not altogether still, for then she might not come immediately
    to me.

Hither my love!
Here I am! here!
With this just-sustain'd note I announce myself to you,
This gentle call is for you my love, for you. . . .*

Once again, out of the same heart-drawn elements, he was to
sing the nation's grief.

* From "A Word Out of the Sea," now "Out of the Cradle Endlessly Rocking."

Chapter XVIII: Walt amid the Brahmins

CONCORD, in the spring of 1860, was thrown out of its
philosophic calm by the news that Walt Whitman would
be coming to Boston to see the third edition of *Leaves
of Grass* through the press of Thayer and Eldridge. As that part
of America whence had issued the first commendatory note of
the poet, Concord must expect to entertain him. Emerson,
Thoreau and Alcott who had visited him in his home town,
thought it the civil thing to invite him to their houses, but the
women would not hear of it, from the mild Mrs. Emerson to
Thoreau's sister Sophia. The men had no alternative but to
make the best of an awkward situation. It remained for Emerson to do the tactful thing: he went himself to see Whitman.

"When people want to talk in Boston," said he with a hint
of guile, "they go to the Common. Let us go there." So to the
Common they went, and up and down the length of Beacon
Street between the elms, talking for nearly two hours of a sharp
though sunny noon. It might be more accurate to say that Emerson talked, as Whitman, firm in his view of the subject under
discussion, buttressed his forces against the Concord philosopher.

Emerson disapproved of the inclusion of the "Enfans
d'Adam" group in the new edition of *Leaves of Grass*. Not that
he was shocked by the poems—he was too much the universal
man not to accept sex as the motive force of existence—but he
had doubts of the wisdom of putting them into a book meant
for general acceptance. Golden tongued, magnetic, he drove
his points home, using intellect and emotion to make his
Transcendental son see what to him was so clear. Whitman
listened, almost overpowered by the strategy of logic mustered

against him—like an army corps in order, he thought it, artillery, cavalry, infantry. Every point that Emerson made struck him as unanswerable. But the more Emerson talked, the stronger grew Whitman's certainty, rising from the soul whose voice he always heeded, that he must disobey and follow his own road.

"What have you to say then to such things?" Emerson inquired in the end.

Whitman, pausing a moment, blurted his answer: "Only that while I can't answer them, I feel more settled than ever to adhere to my own theory . . . I feel, if possible, more strongly than ever that those pieces should be retained."

"Very well," said Emerson. "Then let us go to dinner."

And to dinner they went at the American House. What a sight for Beacon Street, that spring day, as the wise man of Concord, with intent, birdlike movements, tried in vain to swerve the slow-going Walt from his stubborn road.

Those were tense times in the nation and like a seismograph, New England, sensitively alert from the outset to the perilous question of slavery, gave warnings of the coming upheaval. Four years earlier, Charles Sumner, United States Senator from Massachusetts, had been assaulted on the very floor of Congress by the Southerner, Preston S. Brooks, for his speech in favor of admitting Kansas into the Union under a state constitution prohibiting slavery. The gray-haired man had been left on the point of death by his assailant, but after two years of a painful recovery, he had been re-elected to the Senate where he was now waging harder than ever the fight for a nation of free men.

Only a few months earlier, in the autumn of 1859 John Brown had been seized with his handful of followers at Harper's Ferry in a wild idealistic scheme to capture the arsenal, liberate the Negroes and destroy the curse of the nation. A terrible, bearded old man, passionate in his righteousness, John Brown fought his war by the might of his personality, unyielding as a stone, knowing no weakness in himself and making no allowance for it in others. His words set the imagination afire where they fell. Throughout the country, but most of all in New England, the conscience of the nation flamed at the example of the man. "Think of him!—of his rare qualities!—such a man as it takes ages to make, and ages to understand . . ." Thoreau flared up while John Brown was lying in prison awaiting death for treason. "A man such as the sun may not rise upon again in this benighted land. To whose making went the costliest material, the finest adamant; sent to be redeemer of those in captivity; and the only use to which you can put him is to hang him at the end of the rope."

To no purpose Thoreau and other men like him protested Brown's sentence. In vain Frank Sanborn and Theodore Parker plotted secretly to help him in prison. Brown had to die. Before his execution a number of pro-slavery preachers from the South offered to give him consolation and prayer. He sent them away with the words that the prayers of the upholders of slavery would be an abomination to God.

"Shall I give you a handkerchief," asked the sheriff when Brown stood on the drop with the noose round his neck. "Shall I give you a handkerchief and let you drop it as a signal?"

"No. *I am ready at any time,*" answered the unbroken old man. "But do not keep me needlessly waiting."

He seemed to have spoken for the North in the tragic difference that had been splitting the nation for so long. "I am ready at any time. Do not keep me needlessly waiting."

In March of 1860 the last of John Brown's men had been hanged. The body of the martyr lay moldering in the grave but his spirit was marching on in the ranks of free men who could not rest till the cause for which he died was avenged. Wherever Abolition had sympathizers—and they had grown to legion since the publication of *Uncle Tom's Cabin*—the incident at

232

THE WHITMAN OF *LEAVES OF GRASS*, 1855
Plate from photograph by Gabriel Harrison

"Sure as the most certain sure . . . plumb in the uprights, well entre-tied . . ."

—Whitman

Harper's Ferry had its aftermath in demonstrations and trials. Boston, at the time of Whitman's stay, was concentrated about the old Court House where Frank Sanborn, the schoolmaster of Concord, was undergoing trial for his participation in the John Brown raid.

In spite of himself Whitman was drawn into the turmoil. (In spite of himself only because, as always in his life, his book remained the chief concern.) At home, when he had read the news of John Brown's capture and imprisonment, he had been affected, but not enough, as he put it baldly, to impair his appetite. He had seen in the raid a menace to the Union, and while admiring the daring of John Brown, he reprehended its possible consequences. "If things go on at this rate," he wrote in a lecture note of this period, "an amazing prospect opens before us, the Union is threatened with a destiny horrible as it is altogether a novelty, something that never happened to any nation before—it is likely to be saved to death."

In Boston, however, the issues themselves outweighed consideration for the Union. From the time Garrison had spoken out for the Negro, Boston had heeded his words and carried them out in works. Here the Negro, as Walt saw with naive astonishment, was a person. No post that he could attain was closed to his race. He was accepted, a free man among the free. "I have seen one working at the case in a printing office, and no distinction made between him and the white compositors. Another I noticed, (and I never saw a blacker or woolier African) an employee in the State House, apparently a clerk or under-official of some kind." At the eating houses he saw Negroes coming in and taking seats wherever they found them. "And nobody minds it." Least of all, he observed with gratification, the mechanics and workingmen.

Still, a certain embarrassment at conditions that did not prevail at home came through his selfconsciously generous approval. "As for me, I am too much a citizen of the world to have the least compunction about it. The blacks here are certainly of a superior order—quite as good to have in contact with you as the average 'of our own color.' There is a black lawyer, named Anderson . . . practicing here in Boston, quite smart and just as big as the best of them. And in Worcester, they are now put on the jury list." At this rate it might not be long before equality reigned. But there were still the "three hundred and fifty thousand masters of slaves" who would not yield such valuable property without bloodshed.

The thing he saw and the people he met in Boston stirred his latent approval of the anti-slavery cause to action. Not long since, at the office of Thayer and Eldridge, he had met a hot-headed young Irishman who was just publishing an abolitionist novel, *Harrington*. He liked the young man, William Douglas O'Connor, and listened willingly to his inflammatory enthusiasm. His Concord friends, boiling with excitement at the Sanborn trial, no doubt communicated some of it to him. One April morning, therefore, when the grass was turning green on the Common and the elm buds glimmered russet in the sun, Walt made his way to the old Court House and found a seat near the entrance with a group of Frank Sanborn's friends who had arranged to rescue him from the Federal authorities if the trial went against him. Walt, in his conspicuous green jacket and open throat, was hardly the ideal conspirator, but he was prepared to use his strength with the others should the court not decide right.

This experience and the Boston idolatry of John Brown made Walt see the greatness that he had failed to acknowledge in his mother's Brooklyn kitchen; for his imagination with which he felt more than with his heart, was touched, and the poet kindled. By that process which made him participate in whatever he could poetically conceive, he paid his tribute to John Brown in the pregnant record of the "year of meteors, brooding year."

Walt amid the Brahmins

I would sing how an old man, tall, with white hair, mounted the
    scaffold in Virginia,
(I was at hand, silent I stood with teeth shut close, I watch'd,
I stood very near you old man when cool and indifferent, but trem-
    bling with age and your unheal'd wounds, you mounted the
    scaffold.)

That was his true response, for it was the poet who spoke.

All the while the new edition was taking shape, Thayer and
Eldridge, "a couple of young Yankees, so far very good specimens," giving him a free hand in the printing of the book.
For nearly three hours every day he would hang over the case
at Rand's printing establishment, seeing to it that everything
was done according to his direction. At first the foreman de-
murred at his unorthodox demands and told him with Boston
bluntness that he was crazy. But Walt would take no advice on
how to dress his child. When the job was done and the large
handsome volume was ready for the public, Walt had the satisfaction of making the foreman eat his words. "It's the freshest
and handsomest piece of typography that has ever passed
through my mill," he said. Whitman in a letter to Jeff found
it "first-rate" though he felt he still could have improved upon
it. "It is quite odd, of course." But fortunately Thayer and
Eldridge thought that whatever he did was right.

The young publishers, "go-ahead fellows," held high hopes
of the book they had had the courage to print with not a word
omitted that had given offense in the previous editions. Indeed, the very poems that had stirred up the critical tempest
had now been grouped together as much in defiance as in bold
self-assertion. "I believe in the procreant joyful love of men
and women," the poet seemed to say. "Take it, for it is holy."
And he elaborated on its holiness by dwelling on physiological
details, and by speaking out where other poets had been silent.

Of physiology from top to toe I sing . . .

he was to explain in a later inscription;

235

Of Life immense in passion, pulse and power,
Cheerful, for freest action form'd under the laws divine,
The Modern Man I sing.

Such had been his purpose from the initial prompting of the Spirit. Toward its accomplishment had he set out on a lifelong course of self-education (though he denied it) seeking from books, but more from life, the affirmations for his modern Bible. Countless manuscripts attest to the seriousness of his purpose, each labored scrawl a witness that he did nothing, thought no thought, which had not some bearing on the construction of his task. In his long view of his book he ignored the present, albeit he had experienced enough of the fate that pursues "beginners" to write for himself the cold comfort of

How there is something relentless in their fate at all times,
How all times mischoose the objects of their adulation and reward.

He knew that in his day, perhaps till long afterward, he would be misunderstood, therefore he let no compromise to the moment obstruct his course. That to him was clear, however many esoteric confessions, purposeful confusions, half-truths and mysteries he wove into the great design. Those who were ready for the message would see it revealed. Others would have to labor toward it as he himself had labored in his unproductive years, to his ripe manhood, when at last his soul plunged to his bare-stript heart. For them he wrote the furtive allegories that held the most daring secret of his faith; to them he dedicated his Calamus poems which had burst from the source of inspiration before the Adamic group. To them he gave himself body and soul in the transubstantiation of his book. There, too, the word of his doctrine was love.

Nor will the candidates for my love, (unless at most very few,) prove
victorious,
Nor will my poems do good only—they will do just as much evil,
perhaps more,

236

Walt amid the Brahmins

For all is useless without that which you may guess at many times
    and not hit—that which I hinted at,
Therefore release me, and depart on your way,—

until the time of complete understanding. For he was comrade
to Christ, and knew that "the same inexorable price must still
be paid for the same great purchase," in twisted meanings, reviling, sometimes martyrdom.

Walt was hardly a martyr, however, as he explored the streets
of Boston in the leisure at his disposal, testing the hardness of
the cobble and quaint kidney stone pavements. Sumner and
Franklin Streets peered out of half-shut blinds at the phenomenon. Milk Street, center of the clothiers, gasped at such sar-
torial vividness. Beacon Hill sniffed superior, while Washington
Street did everything at once. "I create an immense sensation . . ." Walt preened himself before Abby Price. "Everybody here is so like everybody else—and I am Walt Whitman!"
The exclamation was his own.

He met a great many people some of whom he liked, regret-
ting however the "cramper" under which Bostonians operated,
—"What will people say?" He saw to it that they realized he
had no such concern. He was Walt Whitman! He wished, nevertheless, that they had been a little more hospitable. When he
left Brooklyn he had some notion that he would be invited to
dine by his Concord friends. The antipathy of the Concord
women, however, put a "cramper" to that. He was forced to
take all his meals out. "Oh, the awful expense I have been
under here, Jeff," wailed the stranded bachelor, "living the
way I have, hiring a room and eating at restaurants—at seven
cents for a cup of coffee, and nineteen cents for a beefsteak—
and me so fond of coffee and beefsteak!" His mother should
have come to Boston and boarded him.

Money matters were becoming a source of secret worry to
Walt. Not for himself. Years since, while preparing his prose
manifesto for *Leaves of Grass*, he had taken account of the

poet's needs, and modest indeed they were—"a little sum laid aside for burial money—a few clapboards around and shingles overhead, and a lot of American soil owned—a few dollars to supply the year's plain clothing and food—and then away." The clapboards and shingles were, of course, to shelter his mother without whom he could never make plans. The thought of a home for her had been the spur of his economies in New Orleans and the anchor of his passionate unrest. It was the rock toward which he turned for solidity after the emotional tempest, in the despairing cry: "O how I long for the day when we can have our quiet little farm and be together again!" With his father gone, he wanted more than ever to give her a hearth of her own where she could take care of him and of Eddie, and of the other children as they needed her; for the solid unit of the family which Louisa had kept together was disintegrating through a sequence of tragic circumstances.

Eddie, of course, would never be other than he was. Science could do nothing for him. But Jesse, the firstborn, too, had been showing signs of dangerous mental derangement that broke out in fits of violence. Walt tried not to alarm the family by his fears, nor lose hold of himself by brooding, but he saw too clearly what the end must be for the unhappy man. "The great laws do not treasure chips, or stick for the odd cent," he universalized the private tragedy, adding later, when Jesse had to be confined in an asylum: "I know for my consolation of the great laws that emptied and broke my brother." But that reference to his broken brother had been made for his eyes alone.

With the exception of George and Jeff, the other children had not fared too well. George, however, had concerns of his own. He hoped to marry* some day, and being of a practical turn of mind, wished to put aside a little money on his own

* Some authorities state that George was married before the Civil War broke out. He did not marry, however, till 1871. Source—an unpublished letter of Jesse Whitman's correcting the error from an entry in the family Bible.

238

account. Jeff who had taken a wife, Mattie, on the ninety dollars a month he earned as an apprentice engineer in the city water works, had now also to provide for a baby, a daughter euphoniously named Mannahatta, "a word, liquid, sane, unruly, musical, self-sufficient," as Walt sang in his poem of that title.

Of Walt's sisters one hears little of the elder, Mary Elizabeth. The other, Hannah, married to Charles L. Heyde, a landscape artist, had gone to live with him in Burlington, Vermont. The marriage had been tempestuous from the first and a source of anxiety to Walt and Louisa who saw the proud, spirited girl forcing herself to make life tolerable with a selfish, vain, brutal man too often under the influence of alcohol. The fact that Heyde had had a good education did not improve matters, for he exercised his literacy only to prove his superiority to everyone else in the family, so far below him in the social scale, including Walt whose book he had hastened to characterize as "irregular, disorderly, indifferent or defiant—the lower animal instincts—no accountability or moral sense or principle." For the sake of his sister Walt put up with his difficult brother-in-law, appeasing the troubled waters with his calm advice and, what was of more importance, helping the family budget with gifts of money. On his way home from Boston he went on to Burlington, marking with perhaps a touch of sadness the peaceful rural landscape—the grazing horses, the grass-grown fields waiting to be mowed.

For the other brother, Andrew, Walt could do nothing, nor could any power on earth. He died a few years later of the tuberculosis that had racked him, leaving his wife Nancy and his small children with no means of support. The family helped the widow as much as their meager funds allowed. But Nancy's morale was broken in the struggle to keep body and soul together. She took what her world called the easiest way, and sent her children begging in the streets. Walt, with his tenderness for all outcasts, never forgot the unfortunate in his own family, and when others had long ceased to speak her name, mentioned her in his will.

On the publication of the new *Leaves of Grass*, however, Walt had no such sorrows to brood upon. Indeed, he had much to rejoice him when his Yankee publishers not only showed their confidence in the book by bringing out a substantial edition, but managed also to suscitate a lively interest in it. Their enterprise astounded him, it was so unlike the reserve of the other Bostonians with their stiff collars and their eternal proffering of "My respects." Thayer and Eldridge knew they had no respects to offer in *Leaves of Grass*, and therefore set out to play it up in tremendous puff advertisements which went beyond anything Ned Buntline or the *Ledger* had ever perpetrated in New York. For once Walt was embarrassed by publicity. On the pretext of making some corrections in the copy, he took the advertisements to his lodgings and threw them into the fire. He liked better the booklet of quotations from favorable reviews which was being distributed with copies of the *Leaves*. On the whole the Boston sojourn had been profitable, in spite of the high cost of coffee and beefsteak. On the score of prestige it might have been counted a triumph: the *Atlantic* which he had treated so cavalierly accepted a poem of his, "Bardic Symbols," published without his name in the April issue of 1860. Paumanok and himself were the themes, but humbled in the magnitude of nature before which self was as froth, sands, fragments, and the poet forced to be

Aware now, that, amid all the blab whose echoes recoil upon me, I
    have not once had the least idea who or what I am,
But that before all my insolent poems the real me still stands un-
    touched, untold, altogether unreached. . . .

At last Walt had publishers—and highly respectable publishers—for his book. No longer was it necessary for him to peddle copies to unwilling booksellers. He was a poet as worthy of a firm's investment as Longfellow. Who knows, he might even sell as well. What must Emerson think to be proved so timorous a prophet? Without the omission of a single line, of a word even, from the basic poems, the book was forging ahead like an army with banners in its assault on Puritanism. The critics began to write well of it. It was making friends among the people. The publishers continued pushing it with zeal, overlooking in the response of the public such sermons as that from the Boston *Post* which furnished no material for their complimentary booklet: "Grass is the gift of God for the healthy sustenance of his creatures, and its name ought not to be desecrated by being so improperly bestowed upon these foul and rank leaves of the poison plants of egotism, irreverence, and of lust run rampant and holding high revel in its shame! . . . Woe and shame for the Land of Liberty if its literature's stream is thus to flow from the filthy fountains of licentious corruption! . . . The most charitable conclusion at which we can arrive is that both Whitman's *Leaves* and Emerson's lauda- tion had a common origin in temporary insanity." Like an echo the London *Literary Gazette* and other upholders of the reign- ing codes took up the invective.

Unknown to him, however, Walt had been for some years the admired object of a select coterie of left wing artists and poets in London, the Pre-Raphaelites on whom he had de- scended in, of all mutations, the form of a Christmas box. Wil- liam Bell Scott, a saturnine painter-poet of the Pre-Raphaelite periphery had first come upon *Leaves of Grass* at a second-hand book stall among the volumes that had made their way across the ocean in a jobber's pack. He had taken the book home and read it, and bursting with the excitement of discovery, hastened to communicate it. Since it was Christmas time he sent the copy as a gift to William Michael Rossetti with the caution: "Oblit- erate . . . half a dozen lines and half a dozen words, ignore the author altogether and read as one does the books that express human life like the Bible." *Leaves of Grass* would then grow up in a wonderful manner, he said.

William Michael lost no time in sharing his treasure with his brother Dante Gabriel, the center of transmission. From then on everyone in the circle held the book, read it, memorized the electric lines. Many a night Dante Gabriel gave readings from it in the Chatham Place studio, his voice chanting the verses with the virtuosity of an opera singer, while the unstable little Swinburne shrieked his delight, his long thin hands fluttering at his sides, like the wings of his excitement. From the moment of discovery the interest of the group grew to a cult, as they kept pace with their prophet. In time the 1860 edition reached them. "Have you seen it?" they asked one another. "There is one new poem in it . . . about two birds on the sea-beach," Swinburne communicated breathlessly to the literary Lord Houghton, "which I really think is the most lovely and wonderful thing I have read for years and years. I could rhapsodize about it for ten more pages, for there is such beautiful skill and subtle power in every word of it—but I spare you."

In this edition of *Leaves of Grass* Whitman's poetry achieves its most powerful and perfect form. It contains all the germinal poems that make his book what it is. Challenging, virile, healthy in body and mind, in a voice reverberant over continents, he sings his chant of humanity, his laud of democracy, dilating to include the world. For he is himself the world. All of America is absorbed in him; the peoples of the earth, the different races, unite within him in the common blood of mankind. He is as boundless as the universe and as self-contained. But so also are all men under his dispensation. His comrades alone do not suffice him. Insatiable as he is generous, he must possess all humankind in his cosmic embrace. "I consider'd long and seriously of you before you were born," he speaks lovingly to you and to me and to those who will be here when you and I are gone.

With the 1860 edition the edifice was finished. Henceforth he could only add annexes. For the songs he wrote subsequently, when the Civil War had given him another kind of depth, thrilled in a different key. His youth had done its work. Later, although he strove to recapture the old ecstasy, he never attained the same grand climax. The new poems were to belong to a different order of greatness.

Chapter XIX: Drum-Taps

T HE curtain fell, the gaslights dimmed at the Academy of Music on Fourteenth Street, and the people poured out into the street on the night of April 13, 1861. Nothing unwonted disturbed the sense of satisfaction after a fine performance. Whitman, who loved the city at night, turned west toward Broadway and was making his way southward toward the Ferry when suddenly the sidewalks came alive with the rush of the newsboys tearing frantically from side to side, yelling their incoherent panic. Walt bought an extra and crossed over to Niblo's to read the news under the blazing lights. Others had gathered there before him, and as they read their faces clouded anxiously. Passersby who had not yet seen the papers joined the crowd with apprehension in their voices as they asked what was the matter. Someone read the telegram aloud to them: Fort Sumter and the flag had been fired upon by the Southern Secessionists at Charleston Harbor. Without a word the people looked at one another, their faces sternly set under the midnight lamps. Then slowly they disbanded. Alas, what did it mean?

Even before Lincoln's election on the 6th of November, five months earlier, the people had known they were entering upon bitter times as state after state in the South began to disregard constituted authority. The gravity of the situation was brought home to the Federal Government, however, only after the position of South Carolina, in assuming its right to the Government forts, pointed to what Washington might expect from other rebellious states. On the 20th of December South Carolina seceded. On the 22nd its convention elected three commissioners to go to Washington and treat for the delivery of all forts, magazines and fortifications within the state limits, to the state itself. The men never saw the President. The very day they were to have presented their claims, they learned that Major Robert Anderson, in command of Fort Moultrie, seeing that he could not defend it against the state forces preparing to capture it from the Government, had secretly transferred his position to the stronger and better equipped Fort Sumter. The state authorities protested loudly to Washington, but the Government refused to order Anderson back to Moultrie and certain destruction. Meanwhile, under General G. T. Beauregard, the Confederate forces began setting up batteries to destroy Fort Sumter. The first incident occurred when the steamer, "Star of the West," sent with provisions and re-enforcements for Anderson, was fired upon by the Confederate batteries before she could reach the fort. Anxiously President Buchanan received the alarming news, but thought it best to temporize. Only two more months and his term would be over.

The new President of the United States left no doubt of his position in his inaugural speech on March the 4th. "To the extent of my ability," he declared, "I shall take care . . . that the laws of the Union be faithfully executed in all the States . . . The power confided to me will be used to hold, occupy and possess the property and places belonging to the Government . . ." He would not use force unnecessarily, Lincoln added, but United States property must be protected.

Accordingly, early in April, he ordered a fleet of ships sent for the relief of Fort Sumter. Immediately General Beauregard demanded the surrender of the fort and when Major Anderson refused, threatened attack. On April 12, therefore, at four o'clock in the dawn, the Confederate batteries opened fire, continuing their bombardment until the following afternoon. Valiantly Anderson and his men returned shot for shot as long as the casemate guns remained serviceable. But they were no match for the enemy's powerful mortars. For two days the battle raged. On the second day the red-hot shot from Beauregard's guns set fire to the wooden barracks inside the fort, putting the magazine in serious peril. With incredible heroism, officers and men put the fire under control and continued fighting, but on the morning of the 14th, Sunday, with the walls of the fort crumbling under the merciless Confederate bombardment, the garrison surrendered. Within sight of the rescuing fleet, the national flag was lowered and the palmetto banner of South Carolina raised in its stead.

Not a man had been lost in Anderson's command, nor did Beauregard report any deaths, despite the violent engagement; but the spark had been set to the explosive nation. It was war, civil war, as Lincoln sadly foreboded on the threshold of his four tragic years. In the North feelings ran high, patriotism mingling with indignation at the insult to the national flag that had been torn down from its own ramparts. Now even those who had been inclined to blame the crisis on fanatical anti-slavery policies, and had justified the seceding states to the utmost of fairmindedness, upheld the President and the Union. The time for action in self-defense had come. The Union must be preserved.

"In your hands, my dissatisfied fellow-countrymen, and not in mine, is the momentous issue of civil war," Lincoln had said before the firing of a shot. "The Government will not assail you. You can have no conflict without being yourselves the aggressors. You have no oath registered in heaven to destroy the Government, while I have the most solemn one to preserve, protect and defend it." Like a friend, rather, like a father, Lincoln had addressed the Secessionists. They had answered with an act of violence. Facing a majority in Congress politically opposed to him, the President took the helm for the stormiest passage of the Ship of State.

Whitman who in his political thinking had come to see eye

246

to eye with Lincoln, had been struck by the awful calm before
the storm when the gangling, homely, black-garbed President-
elect had stopped at New York's Astor House on his way to
Washington. As usual the city had overflowed the streets to
catch a glimpse of the celebrity passing by. But here was no
glamorous figure, no Jenny Lind or bemedaled Kossuth, or
the boy Albert Edward, Prince of Wales, who had been sent
only six months earlier by his royal mother to cement good
feeling between America and Great Britain. Lincoln, with his
stove-pipe hat and dark-brown face, whose whimsical humor
lightened what might have been a tragic mask, looked no one's
ideal of a national hero.

From the top of a bus Whitman had watched the coaches
file by. Lincoln stepped out, paused for a moment on the sidewalk, and looked up at the hotel. "And then, after a relieving
stretch of arms and legs, turned round for over a minute to
slowly and good-humoredly scan the appearance of the vast and
silent crowds. There were no speeches—no compliments—no
welcome—as far as I could hear, not a word was said." Only a
grim, forbidding silence. But Lincoln did not let it affect him.
"He look'd with curiosity upon that immense sea of faces, and
the sea of faces return'd the look with similar curiosity. In both
there was a dash of comedy, almost farce, such as Shakespeare
puts in his blackest tragedies."

A black and epochal tragedy it was that broke out with the
first shot at Fort Sumter, a tragedy that spread over a continent,
that involved rich and poor, free men and slaves, a terrible
drama that ignored the unity of time in the changes of the
seasons, torturing with sun and snow, that swept in space over
a canvas of mountain chains and rivers now locked with ice,
now melting in the ooze of tropical heat. North and South, the
people rose up and armed, each to defend what he thought to
be right; in the village and the city, in the outpost of the West
and the harbor metropolis, men left their work and armed.

247

Among them marched George Whitman, enlisted as a private in the 51st New York Volunteers, the 13th Division. He was starting out as a "thirty days' man," each soldier in the division carrying a piece of rope tied to his musket-barrel, for the noose in which to bring home his captive Southern rebel!

For in spite of the wave of indignation that had swept the fighting Notherners from their homesteads, they could not believe South Carolina would soon be joined in secession by Virginia, Georgia and other states. "It'll blow over in sixty days," a national official predicted. Walt, too, was inclined to take the same optimistic view. A week before the battle of Bull Run he was writing to George, returning to Brooklyn on a short furlough: "We are all glad the 13th is coming home— mother especially . . . All of us here think the rebellion as good as broke—no matter if the war does continue for months yet."

But the months passed and the rebellion, far from breaking, stiffened its back. As the Northern troops met with discouragement and failure, the call for volunteers which had received such generous response in the beginning, fell on deaf ears. The Government had to resort to the draft. It would take a year, perhaps years, to break the rebellion, people now realized, and the prospect dismayed those who put self-interest above patriotism. A sinister evacuation began, to escape the draft. In the cities the passport offices could scarcely cope with the sudden urgency that called thousands of able-bodied men to Europe. For thousands of others all roads led to Canada—at least until the South had been put in its place. By the end of 1862 special laws had to be passed to keep at home men under sixty.

At the first call of patriotism Walt had joyfully welcomed the test to which the good ship Libertad would be put.

Welcome the storm—welcome the trial . . .
Why now I shall see what the old ship is made of,

THE LABORER PORTRAIT
From a photograph

"Since he must do everything consistently, he adopted a laborer's costume."

he exulted. He had seen how Manhattan, roused at dead of night at the news from the South, "incens'd struck with clinch'd hand the pavement." To the summons of the drum-taps he had beheld

The young men falling in and arming,
The mechanics arming, (the trowel, the jack-plane, the blacksmith's
    hammer, tost aside with precipitation,)
The lawyer leaving his office and arming, the judge leaving the court,
The driver deserting his wagon in the street, jumping down, throw-
    ing the reins abruptly down on the horses' backs . . .
Squads gather everywhere by common consent and arm,
The new recruits, even boys, the old men show them how to wear
    their accoutrements, they buckle the straps carefully,
Outdoors arming, indoors arming.

But Walt Whitman, forty-one and able-bodied, did not arm, either then or when the bleeding North sent out its cries of despair for every man who could shoulder a gun. Even when the four thousand dead and wounded of the first big engagement reddened the banks of Bull Run, proving that here was no rebellion but a war, Whitman did not join his brother George in the ranks of the Nationals. Yet like George he too was unmarried, and therefore free to fight. Jeff, of course, had to remain at his job to care for his wife and child. What reason had Walt for not taking arms? The man could perhaps have given no answer but that his conscience was against the taking of life. Walt had never been a fighter. His great strength was like the still prowess of a marble athlete, all in the form. Knowing his deficiencies Walt did well to avoid engaging in something for which he was unfit. The poet gave the best explanation of himself.

Arous'd and angry, I'd thought to beat the alarum, and urge relent-
    less war,
But soon my fingers fail'd me, my face droop'd and I resign'd myself,
To sit by the wounded and soothe them, and silently watch the
    dead. . . .

Unexpectedly the call had come, but it had been immediately understood and obeyed. One morning in the middle of December, 1862, after the disaster of the first Fredericksburg battle, Walt, scanning the military lists in the New York *Herald*, found his brother George's name among many others, and the information that the injured were being transported to the Washington hospitals from the battlefield. Walt had seen his mother's face—(How vividly was he to describe one such mother's face in "Come up from the fields father"!)—he had marked her hurried steps trembling at the ominous news. At an hour's notice he had packed his few things, put some money into his pocketbook, and taken the ferry from Manhattan to Jersey City where he bought his train ticket to Washington.

How was he to go about finding George—if he was still alive? Washington was a strange city to him. But he had a name in his pocketbook, William Douglas O'Connor's, with whom he had cemented a friendship when they had been in Boston together, looking after the printing of their books. *Harrington*, for all its righteous anger—and O'Connor could excite his Irish temper to superb polemic—had come too late to be effective in the Abolitionist fight. The Civil War had broken out, carrying in its destructive wave not only O'Connor's novel and *Leaves of Grass*, but the promising firm of Thayer and Eldridge. Both O'Connor, the unsuccessful author, and Charles W. Eldridge, the junior partner, had found themselves berths in Washington, O'Connor in the lighthouse division and Eldridge in the office of the paymaster.

When Walt arrived in Washington on a bleak December night, he could not have been more despondent and alone. In the jam of changing cars in Philadelphia, someone had picked his pocket, and here he was, without even the fare to take him to O'Connor's. Fortunately, on asking directions, he found that he could easily walk to 394 L Street, near Fourteenth, and there he announced himself, not too late for a hearty welcome. Nellie

O'Connor was won over at once by the poet of *Leaves of Grass* whose praises William had been singing since their first meeting. Whitman, she decided, would share their two-room apartment till he found his brother. A sweet, lovely woman, she was courageously sublimating in acts of kindness the grief over the death of her son, not many months since. She found comfort in her little girl, but the heartache of her loss remained.

O'Connor's small salary hardly sufficed to keep his household, but he managed to make Walt a small loan. It was too late to do anything about George that night. Early the following day Walt made the rounds of the hospitals. As the medical buildings filled, churches and private mansions were taken over. In government chambers whose frescoed walls and crystal chandeliers had shone on scenes of gaiety, men groaned on their narrow cots, too often their death bed. Trains of horse-drawn ambulances lumbered ceaselessly down the avenues with their freight of wounded and dying. At the wharves, with every boat from the battle fronts, the lading grounds made a bed of agony for wrecks of men, lying on army blankets, their heads, arms and legs bound with bloody rags, their glassy eyes pleading to the attendants who, as the numbers of the wounded increased, grew indifferent and callous. The soldiers made little outcry as they patiently waited their turn. But now and then a scream of pain pierced the air, and staring eyes shut tight when wounds broke open as the body was lifted to the stretcher. Often the men, sick with diarrhea, the curse of army life, had to remain where they lay, till a hospital could be found. On the outskirts of Washington medical barracks were being rapidly built. From the high places that commanded a sweep of the land, Walt could detect the low, white huddles of the camps and the outlines of convalescent tents edging the city, in whose center the great shell of the Capitol dome was rising from the heap of iron and glass.

For two days Walt haunted the hospitals. Hopefully he

scanned the lists posted at the doors, but nowhere could he find George's name. He was either dead or not badly enough wounded for hospital care. He must go to Fredericksburg. With the help of O'Connor he obtained a pass to Falmouth. On the 19th of December he found the encampment of the Fifty-First and his brother, who was astonished to see him there. George's wound had not been serious—only a gash in the cheek from a bit of shell. "You could stick a splint through into the mouth," Walt told his mother whom he knew strong enough to bear the detail, "but it has healed up without difficulty already."

Walt spent nine days in his brother's camp, lodging with five others in the tent of one of the captains. He had good news to send Louisa. As a result of his part in Fredericksburg, George had received his commission of captain. "When you write, address Capt. George W. Whitman." He had other information to impart, not so welcome to his mother: "I will stay here (in Washington) for the present, at any rate long enough to see if I can get any employment at anything." He had seen enough of anguish to know that his place was there.

Again O'Connor came to his aid. Remembering that Eldridge had a clerkship in the paymaster's office, he and Walt went to see him together. At the time Washington was overrun with office seekers. Lines of applicants surrounded the public buildings; officials in power had to develop an impenetrable incognito to avoid them. Walt was lucky, therefore, to receive a part-time job from the chief of Eldridge's department. For that matter, a part-time job was exactly what he wanted. It would provide for his needs and give him time to do his chosen work —for he knew now what his task would be in the adversity of the nation.

He was required to spend only a few hours a day in Major Hapgood's office, a pleasant room with a view of the Potomac and the green of the trees that knew no such thing as war in

252

nature's ordered seasons. The rest of the time was his to do with as he chose. He volunteered as hospital missionary.

Perhaps the idea had come to him from seeing the work done by the delegates of the Sanitary Commission in Washington and the United States Christian Commission, the first in providing hospital needs, and the other spiritual comfort to the wounded. It may be that for a time he served his apprenticeship as a delegate of the Christian Commission, in spite of his hatred of priests and formalism in religion. He makes no mention of any such affiliation in his meticulous record of the war years. In the Library of Congress, there is, however, among Whitman material, one of the form booklets furnished by the Christian Commission to its workers. Inside the cover appears in the poet's unmistakable hand, "Walt Whitman, Soldiers' Missionary to Hospital, Camp and Battlefield." Had he perhaps found the book and appropriated it to his use, adopting those printed suggestions that appeared good to him, and improving on others? It is more reasonable to suppose that Whitman served as an approved delegate. Surely he himself would not have taken the trouble to have his name stamped, with the Commission's, on the book.* However, if he did work under the direction of the organization, he did not do it for long. As in his poetry Whitman had to do in his own way whatever he undertook.

Certainly in this instance it was the best way. In New York, while ministering to the accident cases at the hospital on Pearl Street, he had become accustomed though not hardened to pain. Then on the banks of the Rappahannock, at his brother's camp, he had had his baptism of blood in caring for the wounded of Fredericksburg in the Lacy House, a handsome brick mansion that had been converted to an emergency hospital. Every cot was filled. On the floors, soldiers, writhing in

* For a complete account of Walt's connection with the Christian Commission see W. C. Barton's *Abraham Lincoln and Walt Whitman*, Indianapolis, 1928.

the agony of untended wounds, waited for relief when some bed should be vacated by death. Out in the yard, long straight forms lay motionless side by side under army blankets. In the fields fresh graves were waiting for them, to be marked, like the others already filled, with a name scrawled on a barrel stave. "One of the first things that met my eyes in camp," Walt wrote in his earliest letter home, "was a heap of feet, arms, legs . . . under a tree in front of . . . the Lacy House." Other and more woeful sights were to be his in the terrible, pitiful catharsis of the war.

In his country's agony the man Walt Whitman found himself, as he gave the unexpended largesse of his love in the service of his suffering fellows. Here was a vessel ample to receive it, deeper than the ocean and infinite as life, like suffering itself. Personal love had been all too limited. Perhaps he had been wiser than he knew when after his brief ecstasy he had wrenched himself from happiness, albeit to a nostalgic, lifelong regret. How could he have dammed his enormous love to mere domestic uses? The woman had understood, happy, it may be, in the knowledge that she had given what he had most desired, release for his pent-up creativeness, and freedom. In the final summation of the loves of his life Walt forgot his debt to the woman. But he spoke truly when he said that his love for his mother and for the wounded soldiers of the war had been the great loves of his life. In a complete psychological fusion, the two were at their height during the three years he devoted to the service.

Not a day passed but he was writing some part of the long letters he sent to Jeff, to Mattie whom he loved as dearly as a sister, and most frequently to his mother. He now had a room of his own in Washington, he told her, on Sixth Street, not far from Pennsylvania Avenue and the Capitol. He often saw the President come by. The room itself was perhaps too small, but it had a good view and it would make good winter quarters since it was under the roof. He liked the old lady who ran the house. "There is a little girl of four or five. I hear her sometimes calling *Grandma, Grandma,* just exactly like Hat; it made me think of you and Hat right away." During his absence he had become an uncle again, for Mannahatta, or Hat, had a baby sister. California,* Jeff called her, honoring the West as he had the East in the largeness of outlook he had acquired from Walt. The proud uncle rose to the new tribute. Guessing a little at the disappointment of the parents that the child was not a boy, he had soothed them: "I am sure from Jeff's description it is a noble babe—and as to its being a girl, it is all the better. I am not sure but the Whitman breed gives better women than men."

Nothing happened at home that failed to interest him. He must know every detail of their lives. When Louisa told him that Jeff's monthly salary had been cut to fifty dollars, a reduction of almost half, he went into an epic fury that had its ludicrous side in the letter he sent back. "It is a pretty time to cut a man's wages down, the mean old punkin heads . . . I think after Jeff has been with the Brooklyn water works from the beginning and so faithful and so really valuable, to put down to $50—the mean, low-lived old shoats!" He made his peace with the mean old shoats, however, after Jeff explained the reasons for the cut.

It was easy to see that the family was not having an easy time of it, although Jeff gave Walt small contributions for the wounded soldiers and took up collections among the engineers at the water works. Isaac Van Anden, too, sent in his offering through Jeff. Walt worried at the economies his mother was making, and rebelled when she stinted herself in food for the sake of the others. "Mother, you mustn't do so as long as you have a cent," he pleaded. "I hope you will, at least four or five times a week, have a steak of beef or mutton, or something

* California later became Jessie.

substantial for dinner." He was proud of her at the same time, and boasted, "The greatest patriot in the family is my old mother. She always wants to hear about the soldiers, and would give her last dime to any soldier that needed it." He encouraged her visits with Mattie to the wounded in New York. It did the boys good, he assured her, to see a woman, even an old woman, at their bedside. Knowing she would be glad to welcome any of his soldier boys on furlough, he freely gave them her address. "You just use them as you know how to without ceremony," he quieted her housewifely worries, "and if you happen to have pot luck and feel to ask them to take a bite, don't be afraid to do so."

Absolutely without pretense, he wrote to her, as he had always been in the habit of speaking, using the common words they had between themselves, the unvarnished colloquialisms, the ungrammatical but intimate misuse of the verb. With the simple, untaught woman, he was the son she knew—and never is he more endearing than when he has his heart-to-heart talks with her in their own uneducated tongue. "Mother, don't you miss *Walt* loafing around, and carting himself off to New York toward the latter part of every afternoon? . . . Well, mother, when the bundle came, I was so glad—and the coats, too, worn as they are, they come in very handy—and the cake, dear mother, I am almost like the boy that put it under his pillow and woke up in the night and eat some. I carried a good chunk to a young man wounded I think a good deal of, and it did him so much good—it is dry but all the better, as he eat it with tea and it relished. I eat a piece with him, and drinked some tea out of his cup, as I sat by the side of his cot."

She was no poor old gammer who had to be entertained with light talk, however. With a son at the front and her dearest risking his life in the malarial fever wards, among smallpox cases—with him the only one of the volunteers to tend the patients—and in the presence of wounds that made strong men faint, she had to show the stuff she was made of. Walt knew her strength and the depths of wisdom in her uncultivated mind, and therefore, in grave matters, spoke to her as to an equal. His letters form almost a history of those years of trial of great men in fearful times.

"Mr. Lincoln has done as good as a human man could do," he defended the careworn Captain when all others were against him. "I still think him a pretty big president. I realize here in Washington that it has been a big thing to have just kept the United States from being thrown down and having its throat cut; and now I have no doubt it will throw down Secession and cut its throat—and I have not had any doubt since Gettysburg." Again, "O how the conscripts and substitutes are deserting down in front and on their way there—you don't hear anything about it but it is incredible!" "There are getting to be *many black troops*," he observed after the Negroes had been found worthy to fight for their freedom. "There is one very good regiment here black as tar; they go around, have the regular uniform—they submit to no nonsense." Once he described one of the inglorious pageants of war. "Mother, while I have been writing this a very large number of Southern prisoners, I should think a thousand at least, has past up Pennsylvania Avenue, under a strong guard. I went out in the street, close to them. Poor fellows, many of them mere lads—it brought the tears; they seemed our flesh and blood too, some wounded, all miserable in clothing, all in dirt and tatters—many of them fine young men. Mother, I cannot tell you how I feel to see those prisoners marched."

And then the moral agony, the nightmare doubt that filled the sleepless nights of thinking men: "Mother, one's heart grows sick of war, after all, when you see what it really is; every once in a while I feel so horrified and disgusted—it seems to me like a great slaughter-house and the men mutually butchering each other—then I feel how impossible it appears,

257

again, to retire from this contest, until we have carried our points (it is cruel to be so tossed from pillar to post in one's judgment)."

In the White House, another, too, was torn between the cause for which the North was fighting and the terrible wages of the contest. In many ways Whitman, who had presaged his coming, experienced his agony. As the President's face grew rigid with the lines of suffering, Whitman's eyes reflected the scenes of sorrow through which he walked. They were the eyes of a man who had seen hell but who had visions of the spiritual good accruing from that pain.

> Allons! through struggles and wars!
> The goal that was named cannot be countermanded.

No, that goal, the preserving of the Union, could not be countermanded. But the flesh could have too much of suffering; the tortured spirit could be goaded to revolt.

"This war must stop!" Whitman cried out on his return from the hospital one day, to his friend O'Connor.

"But the issues are not settled yet! Slavery is not abolished!" the Abolitionist reminded him.

"I don't care for the niggers!" Whitman exploded. "I don't care for the niggers in comparison with all this suffering and the dismemberment of the Union. . . ."

It was the exasperation of anguish snapping the nerves too tightly drawn. But the very man who exclaimed he did not "care for the niggers" was one of the very few who ventured into the Negro camps and nursed the sick through operations and wounds crawling with corruption. He had developed a merciful coolness in the presence of appalling sights. Steadily, with firm hand, he washed and bandaged, but often when at home, or walking alone, he felt sick and trembled at the memory of what he had seen.

He kept remarkably healthy at first. As he went through the

258

wards the eyes of the sick men, some of them beardless boys, followed him about. Glazed pupils lighted with pleasure; hands stretched out feebly to touch his hand. "Walt!" came from all corners of the room. "Come here, Walt! This way, Walt!" For he carried many little luxuries for them in the haversack slung across his shoulders, and comfort in every fiber of that generous frame, overflowing with love. Whenever any of his boys had to face the surgeon's knife, it was Walt who would be called upon to hold the trembling hands.

In the hot Washington summer he would stuff pockets and haversack with oranges for fevered lips. Sometimes he would come with quarts of ice cream, or little jars of jellies which Mrs. O'Connor made. Books, newspapers, postage stamps and notepaper he distributed to those who needed them, and for others too sick to move, he would write letters home—to mothers, preparing them for the worst, to sweethearts whom the boys would never marry. Sometimes, when not required for serious duty, he would gather a group of convalescents about him, away from the others who needed quiet, and read to them, or recite an amusing poem, or play with them the game of "Twenty Questions" which never failed to entertain them. He stinted them nothing, his time, his love, and what little he earned. For the sake of his "darlings" he solicited contributions. Emerson sent him a little sum, and others in New England followed suit. From Brooklyn former newspaper friends sent him their bit. But most of his funds he obtained from war letters that he wrote for the New York *Times*, the *Eagle*, the *Union* or whatever other paper would publish them.

"Here is a characteristic scene in a ward," reads a communication to the *Times* of December 11, 1864. "It is Sunday afternoon . . . I am taking care of a critical case, now lying in a half lethargy. Near where I sit is a suffering Rebel from the Eighth Louisiana . . . He has been here a long time, badly wounded, and lately had his leg amputated. It is not doing very well. Right opposite me is a sick soldier boy laid down with his clothes on, sleeping, looking much wasted . . ." It is a formal report, written for the press. To his mother he gave the usual, direct, human accounts. "One soldier brought here about fifteen days ago, very low with typhoid fever . . . I have particularly stuck to, as I found him to be in what appeared a dying condition, from negligence and a horrible journey of about forty miles, bad roads and fast driving; and then after he got here, as he is a simple country boy, very shy and silent, and made no complaint, they neglected him . . . I called the doctor's attention to him, shook up the nurses, had him bathed in spirits, gave him lumps of ice, and ice to his head; he had a fearful bursting pain in his head, and his body was like fire . . . He did not want to die, and I had to lie to him without stint, for he thought I knew everything. . . ."

He tended them all, making no distinction between the soldiers of the North and of the South. They were all brothers to him who had a quenchless faith in brotherhood. "Was one side brave? The other was equally brave." The maimed, bleeding bodies made an equal claim upon the wound-dresser in their suffering. Even the debris of corpses piled high in the hospital yards gave him no sense of revulsion. For he knew

> The bullet could never kill what you really are, my friend,
> Nor the bayonet stab what you really are.

The "incredible god" that dwelt in each no weapon of war could destroy.

For himself he wanted nothing but the love of his comrades, the soldiers. That alone was reward for the squalor in which he lived, for the malarial fever he contracted in the wards, for the poisoned cut in his hand got while helping the surgeon to amputate a gangrened limb, for the awful days of watching his living arm inflamed and swollen, the veins under the skin like red snakes running up to the shoulder, for the gradual sapping of his energy which made him issue from the war a broken man, carrying invisible wounds graver than any he might have received had he fought at the front like his brother. But he had the love he wanted above all else, the final test of his Calamus poems.

"I believe no men ever loved each other as I and some of these poor wounded sick and dying men love each other," he told his mother. "In the hospitals," he wrote to Abby Price, "among the American young men, I could not describe to you what mutual attachments, and how passing deep and tender these boys. Some have died, but the love for them lives as long as I draw breath." That love endured. Almost the last words taken down from his lips years later, were an affirmation of his Calamus ideal: "I never weighed what I gave for what I got but I am satisfied with what I got. What did I get? Well—I got the boys, for one thing; the boys, thousands of them: they were, they are, they will be mine. I gave myself for them; myself: I got the boys. Then I got *Leaves of Grass*. But for this I might never have had . . . the consummated book."

For up to that time he had put only his joyous life-loving self into his poems, and the United States advancing toward the front ranks of the nations. He had sung his songs of America, and of himself the American, meeting the world, as he loved to say, on equal terms. Now they had to meet themselves and prove by the supremest test their own validity. The test of the body had been met. It was the turn of the spirit. From the moment he had stood under the Broadway lights at midnight reading of the shot fired at Fort Sumter, he had known that the heart of the Union was the target and that its life-blood would flow in the sacrifice of her sons. By that wound and the blood lost would America know herself alive, would know also that every drop was her own, and precious.

Before Walt had started out to look for his wounded brother, he had written a cluster of poems on America fighting which he had left behind. He thought of them again only after their martial tunes had been drowned by the groans of the dying, and then he wrote his mother to see that nothing happened to the "little MS book *Drum-Taps*." Meanwhile he had been adding to them, writing in the light of the bivouac fires, in the watches of the dying, sometimes in the streets, turning aside into some doorway, the tears streaming down his cheeks as he wrote. There were songs of vigils kept in the field at night, watching a brave boy die till, just as the dawn appeared,

My comrade I wrapt in his blanket, envelop'd well his form . . .
And there and then and bathed by the rising sun, my son in his
    grave, in his rude dug grave I deposited.

There were poems of self-probing, when he asked himself, "Must I change my triumphant songs? Must I indeed learn to chant the cold dirges of the baffled?" Would the test of America fail?

But as he gazed on the faces of the dead he knew that they too had been the builders of America, that their blood had cemented the cleavage of North and South, and that henceforth the nation would stand, made firm by a foundation more enduring than brass—the sacred blood of heroes, North and South. For each man looking down on the face of death had learned to say

My enemy is dead, a man divine as myself is dead.

Chapter XX: The good gray poet and Peter Doyle

I N APRIL, 1865, Walt was at home with his mother, both to recover his health and to see *Drum-Taps* printed. The previous summer his health had broken down. Headaches, spells of deathly faintness gave the warning signals, but he still walked through the scorching Washington streets from hospital to hospital, his haversack on his back and his aching head shielded by his hat and parasol—"quite a Japanee," as he jestingly said. But it needed more than a parasol to protect him against contact with disease of all kinds, as thousands of living corpses were brought to the hospital barracks after three years at the front. Finally the doctors forbade Walt's continuing in the wards and insisted on his taking a leave of absence. That autumn he sent in a substitute and returned for a few weeks to Brooklyn where he spent a large part of his time campaigning for the re-election of Lincoln.

Again in Washington, he made another attempt with the help of his friends to secure a more remunerative post than the one he held under Major Hapgood. This time, perhaps in recognition of his election support, he was appointed to a clerkship in the Indian Bureau of the Department of the Interior, at twelve-hundred a year, more money than he had ever earned in his life. Soon his salary was raised to sixteen hundred, giving him enough not only for the convalescent soldiers he continued visiting long after Lee surrendered to Grant at Appomattox Court House, but also for his mother and Eddie, and for Jesse now in an asylum.

Drum-Taps had not been so fortunate as the third edition

of *Leaves of Grass* in finding a publisher, even though it was of momentous timeliness and contained no word that could have given offense. The *Atlantic Monthly* which had accepted one of his poems in 1860 found no room for those he sent from *Drum-Taps*. Again Walt became his own publisher. The thin but moving little book was about to come out when Walt and his mother read the news that shocked the world. President Lincoln had been murdered.

With copies of *Drum-Taps* and a blue-covered working volume of *Leaves of Grass* in a drawer of his desk, Walt resumed his post at the Indian Office, and brooded on the death of the great good man whom he had often seen but never spoken to. He recalled Lincoln riding down Pennsylvania Avenue in his shabby barouche, his little son by his side and a crowd of civilians with huge yellow scarves over their shoulders following. He remembered another day, a year earlier, when Burnside's army had marched through Washington. For three hours he had waited for George's regiment, as rank after rank of soldiers passed by, sunburnt and sweaty, their equipment on their backs, their clothes worn and soiled but their muskets clean and bright as silver. On a low platform, not conspicuous from the rest, the President had stood with the General by his side, taking his hat off as the regiments marched past, saluting the black troops equally with the rest. Walt thought back also on the closing levee, the Saturday night of the second inaugural reception, when the grounds swarmed with people about the Capitol. Swept onward by the stream, Walt found himself pushed through the Blue Room, the great East Room, upholstered like a parlor, to the reception salon. A marine band was playing somewhere. Then Walt caught sight of Lincoln, black-suited, with white kid gloves and a claw-hammer coat, shaking hands with the interminable procession, "looking very disconsolate, and as if he would give anything to be somewhere else." On still another day, while calling on John Hay at the President's house, Walt had seen him, only a few feet away, talking with a man who appeared to be a dear friend. They had never spoken to each other, the President and the poet, but always they had nodded in greeting. Lincoln may, or may not have said, "Well, *he* looks like a *man*," on seeing Whitman come by in the street; there is no doubt that in their devotion to the Union and their faith in democracy they were kin.

And now the President, the Captain he had hailed at the helm of the ship Libertad was dead, killed by the assassin's bullet. Walt had read of the murder in the papers—how on the evening of April 14, Good Friday, Abraham Lincoln had gone with Mrs. Lincoln to Ford's Theatre. While sitting in the proscenium box, enjoying the performance of Laura Keene in an amusing comedy, he was shot from behind by John Wilkes Booth, who then leapt on the stage, limped to the wings and fled on his horse, tethered at the stage entrance. But none of the newspaper accounts equaled in vividness the eye-witness report of Walt's young friend, the horse-car conductor, Peter Doyle, who had been in the theater during the shooting.

The small house had been packed. From his seat in the second gallery Pete who, though only nineteen, had fought with the Confederate army throughout the war and had been recently paroled, watched the face of the President with more interest even than he did the play. "I heard the pistol shot," he recounted. "I had no idea what it was, what it meant—it was sort of muffled. I really knew nothing of what occurred until Mrs. Lincoln leaned out of the box and cried, 'The President is shot!' . . . I saw Booth on the cushion of the box, saw him jump over, saw him catch his foot which turned, saw him fall on the stage. He got up on his feet, cried out something which I could not hear from the hubbub and disappeared." Pete had been among the last to leave. As he was still lingering with a handful of others, one of the soldiers who had been scouring the theater for accomplices of the assassin, came into the gallery, and seeing him shouted, "Get out of here! We're going to burn this damn building down!" Meekly Pete answered, "If that is so, I'll get out." He had had enough of violence.

Even if Pete had heard Booth's theatrical *Sic semper tyrannis*, the plain, untutored son of an Irish blacksmith would not have understood a syllable. Nevertheless the account he gave of the doings of that night was to inspire Whitman to the writing of the famous lecture he delivered on many occasions in his old age.

They had met in the horse-car on which Pete worked as conductor. It was a stormy night. Whitman, who had just left Burroughs, stepped into the tram. The blanket he wore instead of an overcoat was thrown over his shoulders. His blue jacket, buttoned up against the rain, gave him the look of a sea-captain. "He was the only passenger," Pete retold the first meeting. "It was a lonely night so I thought I would go in and talk with him. Something in me made me do it, and something in him drew me that way. . . . He did not get out at the end of the trip— in fact went all the way back with me. . . . From that time on we were the biggest sort of friends." O'Connor, hard and sharp as a diamond, the thoughtful Burroughs, John Hay, Eldridge, the soldiers with whom Walt continued to correspond for many years—and now Pete Doyle who brought no qualities of intellect but only his youthful simplicity and an affectionate heart. With all men and all classes Whitman practiced his Calamus friendship and found it sound.

At his desk in the Indian Bureau Walt had ample time for his duties and enough to spare for the revision of *Leaves of Grass*. His friends were all very considerate. John T. Trowbridge who had procured him his recommendations kept a solicitous eye open for him. Judge William T. Otto, assistant to the Attorney-General, and J. Hubley Ashton, also in the same office, watched over him and put in a good word wherever they could with their chief, the Secretary of the Interior, John P. Usher. It was Judge Otto, who thought highly of the poet as well as of the wound-dresser, who had obtained him an increase hardly three months after his appointment. But at the very time Whitman had most reason to rejoice, the fates were weaving political trammels to enmesh him when Secretary of the Interior Usher resigned and Senator James Harlan succeeded in his stead.

An astute lawyer and politician, James Harlan was also a man of rigid principle who suffered no deviation from the line of the strict Methodism he had preached from the pulpit in Iowa City. A new broom, he believed in sweeping his department clean of superfluous clerks, especially since thousands of returned soldiers and soldiers' widows were clamoring to be put into clerical positions according to the recommendation of Congress. He looked about his department, made his notes, and on June 30, 1865, sent out a number of communications, one of them tersely reading: "The services of Walter Whitman, of New York, as a clerk in the Indian Office, will be dispensed with from and after this date."

The dismissal fell like a bombshell upon Whitman and his supporters. He enjoyed the atmosphere of the Indian Bureau, with its romantic visitors, the Red Men from the West who would come in their feathers and paint, and headpieces of empty buffalo skulls, and sit on the floor, awaiting their turn. He also appreciated the comfort of his office, far pleasanter than his dingy boarding-house room. Most of all he liked his clerkship, an even more delightful "sit" than his *Eagle* position had been. Now, suddenly, after only four months, it was being taken away from him. Judge Otto, O'Connor, and Ashton, among others, wished to know the reason why.

The day after Walt's dismissal, Ashton drove down to Harlan's office and arranged for an interview. Why had the new

Secretary of the Interior discharged Walt Whitman? Had he been found inattentive to his duties, or incompetent?

No, it was not that, Mr. Harlan answered.

"Then what is the reason?" asked Ashton.

"Whitman is the author of *Leaves of Grass*," came the astounding reply.

"Is *that* the reason?" Ashton hardly believed his ears.

"Yes, yes it is," affirmed Harlan who then launched into an explanation. He had been going through his department one evening after hours, when in Whitman's office he came upon a copy of *Leaves of Grass* in a blue cover. The pages, he noticed as he turned them, were full of marks and corrections. Puzzled and not a little shocked by some of the passages so marked, he took the book to his own office for closer examination. There he found matter so outrageous that he determined to dismiss the writer.

Ashton rose to the defense of the poet, explaining his purpose in writing *Leaves of Grass*, but Harlan would not be convinced. Whitman was a free lover if he could write such things, he insisted, and *Leaves of Grass* an indecent book which ought to be publicly burned. Again Ashton spoke up for Whitman, this time stressing the virtues of the man, his work among the wounded, his selflessness. After a while Harlan said, "You have changed my opinion of Mr. Whitman's personal character, but I shall adhere to my decision. It's no use, Mr. Ashton," he swept aside the advocate's remonstrance. "I will not have the man who wrote *Leaves of Grass* in this department if the President himself were to order his reinstatement. I would resign myself rather than put him back."

There was nothing more Ashton could do against such rectitude, so he hastened to the office of the Attorney General James Speed, to see whether he could not obtain another clerkship for Walt in the Treasury Department.

But now a redoubtable champion took up the cudgels on

learning from Ashton the reasons for Whitman's dismissal. There was nothing O'Connor loved better than a fight except Walt Whitman, and here was a chance for him to serve his friend while exercising his favorite sport. For a month he wrought himself up in a terrific war-dance, despite the fact that Walt had in the meantime secured another desk in the Treasury Department at an equally desirable salary. For two weeks more O'Connor turned over his library in search of literary instances, ancient and modern, to disprove that it was a crime to worship perfect candor, even as Whitman had worshiped, and to justify him by arguments so irrefutable that if *Leaves of Grass* and its author were condemned as indecent, so too must be the great works of the world, including the Bible. "I claim," he challenged in his polemic, "that to expel an author from a public office and subject him to public contumely, solely because he has published a book which no one can declare immoral without declaring all other great books immoral, is to affix a penalty to thought, and to obstruct the freedom of letters."

The sizzling pamphlet, soberly titled *The Good Gray Poet*, was issued by Bunce and Huntington of New York in January of 1866. Wendell Phillips found it the most brilliant piece of controversial literature of the nineteenth century. Sanborn, in an anonymous review in the Boston *Commonwealth*, twitted the hapless Secretary with the remark that considering the nature of some of President Lincoln's *bon-mots* one wondered how such a man as Harlan could have accepted office under him. Whitman's supporters aligned themselves behind O'Connor's manifesto and by repeating "The Good Gray Poet! The Good Gray Poet!" forced upon Whitman a designation that made a Blake Jehovah out of the American titan. Gray he was —he had begun to be gray before thirty—and good, though the Harlans of the world denied it, and a poet for those who had the insight to discover him under his many forms. But in 1866

269

he was still in spirit the obstinate revolutionary who would tone down for no power on earth the brave, youthful daring of his gospel poems. "I dare not do it. I dare not leave out or alter what is so genuine, so indispensable, so lofty, so pure." It was no good gray poet who had stolen the sacred fire from the gods. That he was still to become.

After the tumult of the war of words had subsided, Walt settled down to his work once more. He was happy in the new post which in the end amounted to a shifting of desks under a more sympathetic chief. He had a handsome office in the Treasury building, in one of a suite of seven rooms. The largest chamber contained a library of many volumes, mostly on law, but there were some five or six hundred miscellaneous works with which Walt lost no time in making himself acquainted. In the Attorney General's office, spacious and well appointed, he could look with pride on the paintings of patriots from Washington's time who had helped to make America, each in his way. Best of all he loved his room whose great south window framed the living painting of streams and hills, gardens and trees, and on the river the boats sailing. As he had a set of keys, and knew the doorkeepers of the building, mutilated veterans of the war, he could go to his office after hours and on Sundays. Indeed, it was more home to him than his room in the house of the chief of the Passport Bureau where he could neither work nor sleep, so thin were the partitions and so lusty was the snoring of his fellow lodgers. He could not, every night, make his protest by dropping a fifty-pound boulder in the room opposite the snorers, as he had once done, after tossing sleepless on his bed for hours. So he remained as late as he could at the desk in his office, working on a fit memorial to the martyr President, by the light of a splendid astral lamp, a luxury he had never before enjoyed.

He mingled in the life of Washington, not forgetting, however, the convalescent soldiers who, now that the war was over,

270

did not receive as much attention as before. Walt made his rounds several hours a day and all afternoon on Sundays, when he would arrive with navy plug, pipes and tobacco, and a huge cake, specially baked by a mulatto woman who kept a stand in the market. Sometimes Burroughs accompanied him with doughnuts and pies made by his wife Ursula, who had no love for poets and "scribblers" in general and for Whitman in particular. "Walt Whitman, poet and *person*," she would say, referring to the book Burroughs was busy writing on his dearest friend. Ursula's sarcastic stress spoke volumes for her feminine irritation, perhaps jealousy, of the man who cast such a spell on husbands, her own as well as Nellie O'Connor's. Nevertheless she sewed shirts for Walt, cutting them large enough for his big frame, and made her best griddle cakes for the Sunday breakfast to which he invariably came late, smiling and unapologetic. There was no reforming the poet and *person*.

But both Walt and Burroughs looked forward to those Sunday mornings when they would saunter out of the little redbrick house on Capitol Hill with its neat rows of potatoes and its cow in the back yard. Slowly, in after-breakfast pace, they would amble past the White House, when Walt would soon unearth a smooth round stone from its hole behind an old fencepost and toss it from hand to hand, while walking, as they tossed verses and thoughts back and forth in their conversation. On the way back Walt would put the stone back in its place till the next time.

With Pete Doyle, too, he would spend pleasant hours riding on the "Old 14" as far as Georgetown and back past the circle, the President's house, Willards', Capitol Gate, the Hill, sights as familiar to him as the landmarks of Broadway. In the evening, on Pete's leaving the car, they would often take long walks together, sometimes as far as Alexandria. Happily they plodded along the road, the blue-suited Treasury clerk and the horse-car conductor, comrades together. Walt was all tenderness to the boy. "Dear Pete, dear son, my darling boy, my young and loving brother," he addressed him, and the artless Pete reciprocated with the affection the older man craved. They talked of all sorts of things together, Walt with his arm about Pete's shoulders as the young face frowned up to him in the effort to understand.

"There is a pretty strong enmity toward me and *Leaves of Grass* among certain classes," Walt confided to him, trying to bridge the gap between them, "not only that it is a great mess of crazy talk and hard words all tangled up without sense or meaning—which, by the by, is I believe your judgment about it—" And Pete, too honest to pretend, did not contradict.

"I don't know what you are trying to get at," he would say, revealing in those candid words the lack of comprehension of the class which Walt loved and glorified, knowing that the time of awakening would come.

By dint of patient repetition Walt made him see his meaning. "All other peoples in the world have had their representatives in literature," Pete at last repeated the well conned lesson. "Here is a great big race with no representative. He would undertake to furnish that representative. It was also his object to get a real human being into his book. This had never been done before." So much Pete acquired, but no more.

Walt never seemed to tire on their excursions, which was not true of Pete after his day's work. As they trudged mile after mile, Walt singing snatches from the operas, reciting, or talking about the stars for the entertainment of his young friend, the boy, exhausted by the time they reached the ferry opposite Alexandria, would say to himself, "I'll draw the line here—I won't go a step further." But he could do nothing against the indefatigable Walt. Crossing the river they would walk back on the other side, to 7th Street where they parted.

"Dear son," Walt wrote him tenderly after one such jaunt, "I can almost see you drowsing and nodding since last Sunday,

272

going home late—especially as we waited there on 7th Street and I am telling you something deep about the heavenly bodies —and in the midst of it I look around and find you fast asleep, and your head on my shoulder like a chunk of wood—an awful compliment to my lecturing powers. . . ."

Without being aware of it Walt found in Pete not only an outlet for his adhesiveness, but also for his desire to wake a mind uncontaminated by prejudice. Could he impress his theories upon this representative of the powerful uneducated? He taught him arithmetic and gave him a geography book which he counseled him to look into often. He also bought him a pocket dictionary. "With fifteen minutes' writing every day," he encouraged Pete, "and correcting by the dictionary I would warrant you becoming a correct speller and real handsome writer in a year or less." (To Pete he spoke the same language he employed with his mother.)

Sometimes Pete asked him questions which delighted him by showing him that to a certain extent he was penetrating that virgin mind. "Is there a hereafter?" Pete inquired one day, wondering what would be the answer of a man who never went to church and "didn't seem to favor preachers at all." Walt thought a moment, then said, "There must be something— there can't be a locomotive unless there is somebody to run it." Another time he told Pete that if a person was the right kind of person—and Pete knew that Walt thought all persons the right kind—he couldn't be destroyed in the next world or this.

Once when Walt as usual gave money to a beggar, Pete who had his views on tramps asked, "Don't you think it's wrong?"

"No, it's never wrong, Pete," Walt answered.

"Wouldn't they drink it away?" Pete insisted.

Walt shook his head. "No, and if they did it wouldn't mat- ter. For it is better to give to a dozen who do not need what is given than to give to none at all and so miss the one who should be fed."

For years the two continued their simple relation based on the beauty of common humanity, untroubled by barriers of class or orthodoxy. "Yours for life, dear Pete, and death the same," Whitman closed one of his letters to him. And Pete was true. "I do not ever for a minute lose the old man," he said when he too had grown old. "When I am in trouble— in a crisis—I ask myself, 'What would Walt have done under the circumstances?' and whatever I decide Walt would have done that I do."

In 1866 Walt finished his poems on the death of Lincoln. As *Drum-Taps* had already appeared, and as the Civil War poems would not have been complete without a worthy memorial to the "dear commander," Whitman published a separate pamphlet containing the new productions and inserted it in the remaining copies of the book, thus making it the second edition. The little volume was well received, but it was the "Sequel to *Drum-Taps*," the four poems on the President's death, that established him in the hearts of the people more firmly than *Leaves of Grass* had as yet managed to do.

A throbbing rhythm like the rolling of death drums accompanied the solemn "Hush'd Be the Camps To-day" as the coffin of the martyr was laid in its vault. In contrast to it, the three rhymed verses of "O Captain! My Captain!" chanted their grief with the roused voice of the people, incredulous at first, then tragically convinced that their Captain lay fallen, cold and dead, on the deck of the racked ship, nearing port at last, the hard-fought victory won. In the simple ballad rhythm beat the heart of the folk. The poet's grieving they knew to be their own, and the poem became part of them. Years later when Harper and Brothers asked permission to print it in their *Fifth Reader* Walt, then an old man of seventy who had waited in vain for *Leaves of Grass* to root itself in the people of America as that poem had done, cried out in exasperation: "It's 'My Captain' again, always 'My Captain!' The school readers have got along as far as that! My God! When will they listen to me for whole and good?" It was the impatience of the mere man. As one of the band of "beginners" he should have remembered how people respond to them, yet know them not.

The triumph of his achievement, however, lies not in the popular "O Captain! My Captain!" but in the long threnody, "When Lilacs Last in the Dooryard Bloom'd." Strangely reminiscent, the dirge recaptures the mood of "A Word Out of the Sea." Now it is the nation with which the poet identifies himself, and the nation's sorrow, his own and the world's for ages to come, that he pours out in incomparable beauty. Like the themes of a symphony, the intimate motifs that never failed to strike fire from his imagination—the trinity of lilac blooming, the star dropping in the west and the hidden bird warbling a song—mingle and merge in sublimest music, as their emotional values attain breadth and depth at the "thought of him I love" now enfolded in death. They are intimate, familiar objects, these symbols, but in their commonness dwells the miracle, the miracle also of Whitman's use of them in a poem whose simplicity is the highest art. Lilac and star and bird twined with the chant of his soul. But now they twine also with the hearts of all who have heard the name of Lincoln, and bring with them the ultimate expression of the poet's belief in the beauty of death, so intimately known as a bringer of peace in the wards and battlefields. Ecstatic, the bird sings its carol to the dark visitant, and the soul of the poet, attuned to the souls of his comrades in the night, re-echoes:

Come lovely and soothing death,
Undulate round the world, serenely arriving, arriving,
In the day, in the night, to all, to each,
Sooner or later delicate death.

Prais'd be the fathomless universe,
For life and joy, and for objects and knowledge curious,
And for love, sweet love—but praise! praise! praise!
For the sure-enwinding arms of cool-enfolding death.

Dark mother always gliding near with soft feet,
Have none chanted for thee a chant of fullest welcome?
Then I chant it for thee, I glorify thee above all,
I bring thee a song that when thou must indeed come, come un-
    falteringly.

Approach, strong deliveress,
When it is so, when thou hast taken them I joyously sing the dead,
Lost in the loving floating ocean of thee,
Laved in the flood of thy bliss O death.

It is the final grand acceptance. Had Whitman written nothing but that threnody his name would endure forever.

Meanwhile, the country recovering from the wounds of war,
Whitman finished revising the copy of *Leaves of Grass* that had
so much offended Harlan, and in 1867 brought out the fourth
edition, including all the poems he had written to that time.
They were not yet the "Three-Hundred and Sixty-Five," but
the days were building in his poetic span. A certain recognition was coming to him, too, fostered by the devotion of his
small but active coterie. Burroughs, the year of the enlarged
Leaves of Grass, had in readiness the *Notes on Walt Whitman
as Poet and Person* that had so annoyed his wife. But although
the work bore his name, it was really the child of Whitman.
The book, whose modest size belied its contents, spoke only to
the few. The rest, rightly, remained satisfied to know Whitman by the genuine utterance of the war poems where the
great heart of the man spoke to all.

Soon after Burroughs' contribution to the master's personal
fame, O'Connor published in *Putnam's Magazine* a war story
called "The Carpenter." The resemblance of the Christ-like
hero to Whitman was patent to all, though not a few disap-

proved likening the author of an "obscene" book to the Carpenter of Nazareth, however woodenly-virtuous the wound-dresser was made to appear in his admirer's idealization. The Christ cult and the good gray poet's had begun, and O'Connor had started them both.

Mrs. Whitman in Brooklyn kept up with her son's growing fame. She read everything he sent her and let him know what she thought. She liked Burroughs' book, she declared, not knowing Walt's hand in it, but she preferred O'Connor's defense. Walt himself, however, quite understandably derived most pleasure from the spontaneous compliment paid him in the published memoirs of the refugee count, Adam de Gurowski, long a well-known figure in Washington. "The incarnation of a genuine original genius," wrote the count, "Walt alone in his heart and in his mind has a shrine for the nameless, the heroic people." The good man spoke and died. Grateful for the brief but welcome tribute, Walt joined with "all the radicals" who saw the old revolutionary to his grave.

The letters continued passing regularly back and forth between Walt and his mother. In 1867 Jeff, Mattie and the children went to live in St. Louis where Jeff had been called to fill a position in his branch of engineering. Louisa remained for a time alone with George and Eddie. Then George married. The patriotic old woman was proud of her soldier son who had fought through the four years of the war, who had wounds to show and tales to tell of prison life in the Confederate camps, and who had come back an officer. Still, her pride in him was nothing to what she felt for her favorite. She lived for his letters, but still more for the time all correspondence should cease and she and Walt would live under the same roof—their own —with Eddie. Impatiently she waited for the letters from Washington—tipping the postman for prompt delivery—and not because the money they contained was almost the sole income of an old woman and her helpless son. George and Jeff disapproved of her keeping house at all. But as she grew older and somewhat critical of others, she clung to her independence. Perhaps some day when Walt decided to settle down, he might build the house they had always talked about—and she sent him her plans for it.

In most of her letters, in the clear, firm hand Walt knew so well, she wrote him about his work, together with the doings of the scattered family. Unlike George who when he finally dipped into *Leaves of Grass* became convinced that it was "a funny book," Louisa had grown to have a real appreciation of what Walt was trying to do. His eyes filled with tears as he read her pathetic, illiterate letters, so full of pride, and yet so much concerned for this strange son who, albeit a poet, had never commanded the respect of a Mr. Longfellow or a Bryant.

"the book for mary came friday and the galaxy to day with the ballad of sir ball" she wrote him. "i had forgotten all about the piece till i see it and then i had to think where i had heard of it and then it came to my mind what piece it was it is signed w i hope nobody will think you wrote it walt" He had been in so much trouble on account of what he wrote. Again, "well walt" she informed him, "i have the whisper of heavenly death it lays here on the table by my side i have read it over many times . . . i felt as if i should preserve it for i liked it it was so solemn" Often, however, the cricket note of domestic worries sounded above her pride in him. "i dont know what i would do walt if it wasent for you to think of me it seems as if all other sons and daughters has their own to attend to which is perfectly natural George and loo and Jeff insists on my breaking up housekeeping and they dident only insist but almost commanded me i told them i should remain here this winter if i lived the none of them want edd Walter and they would soon get tired of paying his board and we aint much expense to any but you walter dear."

Finally she was obliged to live with George and his wife

278

who had established themselves in Camden, New Jersey. Eddie was sent out "to board." Regularly Walt sent his share toward the maintenance of his brother.

He was now fixed in Washington. His work gave no one cause for complaint and provided him not only with the means of discharging his numerous obligations, most of them self-imposed, but also with a place to go to for quiet and study. For he studied assiduously, much as he strove to keep secret his debt to the writers of the past in his claim of originality. The large homemade scrapbooks he kept throughout his life as the savings funds upon which to draw for his poetry, attest to the breadth of his interests. Geography, Eastern literature, Goethe and other German writers, Carlyle, Dante, Tasso, George Sand, the Greek dramatists, all had their place in his literary treasure house which he jealously guarded from even his closest friends. He must never cast doubt on his pristine genius; his independence from the past must not be impugned. There was indeed about him "the furtiveness of an old hen." And slyly also a little of the cuckoo. But he always hatched eagles.

Post-war Washington was a thrilling city. Walt loved to feel the pulse of the nation, as it were—and the pulse was there, under the Dome, surmounted by the Genius of Liberty—that same genius he had come upon during the war, lying on the Capitol grounds, dismembered like the Union. He was acquainted with many of the men who guided the destiny of the re-United States. There was Senator Garfield with his large manly voice who always greeted him with, "After all not to create only." And President Grant strolling out of the White House alone to pay his morning visits to a certain lady, his cigar in his mouth, his short legs energetically trudging the pavements. Pete Doyle often passed him in his tram and would beckon Grant inside, to Walt's amusement. But the President always shook his head. Later, on the way back, they would see him leaning on the sill of "the old lady's" window.

The two companions had their laugh together, but it was one-sided mirth for Walt who in the privacy of his solitude was writing frantic warnings to himself against the dangers of excessive amativeness. The writing alone with its dashes and capitals showed the perturbation of his spirit.

"Cheating, childish abandonment of myself, fancying what does not really exist in another, but is all the time in myself alone, utterly deluded & cheated by myself, and my own weakness—REMEMBER WHERE I AM MOST WEAK, and most lacking. Yet always preserve a kind spirit and demeanor to 16. BUT PURSUE HER NO MORE."*

Was he referring to the painful delusions of Hope, represented by the Fowler phrenological chart as a woman in the cranial section that bore the number 16, or was he admonishing himself against over-interpreting the demeanor of a flesh and blood temptress whom he must force himself to pursue no more?

The still more emphatic note that followed implied a fascination stronger than any that an ethereal, however tempting Hope, could have exerted.

"TO GIVE UP ABSOLUTELY *for good from this present hour* (all) this FEVERISH, FLUCTUATING, *useless, undignified pursuit* of 164—*too long* (much *too long*) persevered in —so humiliating—*It must come at last* & had better come now —(*It cannot possibly be a success.*) LET THERE FROM THIS HOUR BE NO FALTERING, or NO GETTING—at all henceforth, (NOT ONCE under any circumstances)—*avoid*

---

* Professor Edward Hungerford in his ingenious article "Walt Whitman and his chart of bumps" in *American Literature*, Volume II, pp. 350-384, interprets "16" to mean Hope which the phrenological charts represented as a woman. The article is convincing as far as it goes, but even Professor Hungerford admits that another quotation which immediately follows (see below) refers to no merely figurative woman.

seeing her, or meeting her, or any talk or explanations—or
ANY MEETING WHATEVER, FROM THIS HOUR
FORTH FOR LIFE. July 15, '70."

He could not have meant that he must no longer cheat himself with pursuing the hope that his work should eventually
succeed. He had had discouragements aplenty, it is true, but
even when he was writing down those frantic notes to himself
he was preparing the fifth edition of *Leaves of Grass* which he
brought out in 1871. If hope were the abstraction in question,
it would have taken more fanciful make-believe than Whitman, or any other man, was capable of to enable him to "always preserve a kind spirit and demeanor to 16" or to "avoid
seeing her, or meeting her, or any talk or explanations." It
would have involved an active participation that an abstraction
could never give. Again, if hope in his work were intended, he
who had faith in its inevitable triumph, reckoning in quad-
rillions of years, would not have written, "It cannot possibly
be a success." Neither would he have outlined for his improvement, soon after writing the last note, the sketch of "a superb
calm character"—such as he could not claim to be while in the
throes of passion—whose "emotions etc. are complete in himself irrespective of whether his love, friendship etc. are returned
or not. . . ."

The 16 or 164 whom he must pursue no more was a woman,
a married woman in Washington whose husband watched over
her in jealousy and suspicion. Nellie O'Connor made mention
of this love affair when she wrote an article for the *Atlantic
Monthly* on Whitman as she had known him in Washington.*
Thanks to Walt's confidences to her, she even furnished a description of this all too tangible abstraction as a pleasing person, quite fair, with brown hair and eyes, very womanly and

* See the *Atlantic Monthly* for June, 1907. She signed the article Ellen M.
Calder after her second marriage. The references to the woman, omitted in the
published article, may be found in Professor Emory Holloway's *Uncollected Poetry
and Prose of Walt Whitman.*

sweet and gentle. Walt had met her and loved her some five years earlier. It was of her he had written:

Out of the rolling ocean the crowd came a drop gently to me,
Whispering *I love you, before long I die,*
I have travel'd a long way merely to look on you to touch you,
For I could not die till I once look'd on you,
For I fear'd I might afterward lose you.

Now we have met, we have look'd, we are safe,
Return in peace to the ocean my love,
I too am part of that ocean my love, we are not so much separated,
Behold the great rondure, the cohesion of all, how perfect!
But as for me, for you, the irresistible sea is to separate us. . . .

Chapter XXI: The noblest woman friend

WHITMAN was still struggling against the amativeness of his nature, complicated by his numerous Calamus friendships, when in the middle of September, 1871, he received one of the most extraordinary letters that had ever come to him. Not long before, the postman had brought him a flattering invitation from the American Institute to read a poem at the opening of its annual exhibition. He had been staggered by the honor, but he had written his poem and delivered it on the 7th of September, with himself not the least attentive of his audience in the great barn-like edifice housing the industrial machinery most recently developed in These States.

> After all not to create only, or found only,
> But to bring perhaps from afar what is already founded,

he sang out to the thousands of listeners, throwing his voice to reach the fringe of workingmen for whom the poem was intended. It had not been one of his happiest efforts in spite of the democratic fervor with which he had goaded on his Pegasus. Too many catalogues, too much machinery stood in the way of its flight. The few hundred workmen listened with respect, especially when he mentioned "manual work for each and all, . . . the hammer and the saw, (rip, or cross cut)" but on the whole they went out unchanged through the same door from which they had come.

Walt, however, had enjoyed the sight of himself, another Lowell in the equivalent of the "Commemoration Ode" and he wrote to the Washington *Chronicle*, anonymously, this pleasant description: "His manner was at first sight coldly quiet, but you soon felt a magnetism and felt stirred. His great figure was clothed in gray, with white vest, no necktie, and his beard was unshorn as ever. His voice is magnificent, and is to be mentioned with Nature's oceans and the music of forests and hills." There was nothing small about Whitman.

The letter he held in his hand, like the one from the Institute, also contained an invitation but of such a nature that Whitman for once was confused and frightened. He had never read anything like it addressed to him, or for that matter, to anyone else. It was like something in a dream were it not that the envelope was real enough, with its stamp from England and the oddly familiar writing. The sender, he learned as he read, was a woman, a widow who had shared happiness with her husband—but, as she wrote, "To the last my soul dwelt apart and unmated, and his soul dwelt apart and unmated."

So much a poet might read with poise. One member of his public was inviting by her confession the consolation of an answer. But the letter did not stop there. "The time will come," it continued, "when man will understand that a woman's soul is as dear and needful to his, and as different from his as her body to his body. This is what happened to me when I had read for a few days, nay hours, in your books. It was the divine soul embracing mine. I never before dreamed what love meant: not what life meant. Never was alive before—no words but those of new birth can hint the meaning of what happened to me. In May, 1869, came the voice over the Atlantic—to me— O the voice of my mate; it must be so—my love rises up out of the depths of the grief and tramples upon despair, I can wait— any time, a lifetime, nay life times—I can suffer, I can dare, I can learn, grow, toil, but nothing in life or death can tear out of my heart the passionate belief that one day I shall hear that voice say to me, 'My mate.'"

Then Walt remembered the sender, Mrs. Anne Gilchrist, the Englishwoman whose article, "A Woman's Estimate of

284

Walt Whitman" had appeared in the *Boston Radical* in May, 1870, unsigned. It had all been strangely involved. In 1867, with Whitman's permission, William Michael Rossetti had edited *Leaves of Grass* for the British reader—with no alteration in the text, but with what Rossetti deemed subjects too daring for England omitted in their entirety. The book proved popular and brought Whitman many readers. One day in 1869, while visiting Ford Madox Brown, Anne Gilchrist found a copy of the Rossetti edition of Whitman and took it home with her.* The reading changed her whole existence. "It holds me entirely spellbound," she wrote to William Michael. Again and again she read the exhilarating poems, and because she must express to someone their effect upon her, she sent a long, frank letter to William Michael, minutely analyzing her emotions, at the same time defending the purity of Whitman's aim against the vociferous Philistines who, as in America, had arisen to attack the poet whom she now set up as her god. William Michael, who knew the ways of the literary world, invited her to expand her letter to an article in the service of her divinity, and sent it off to America.

Anne Gilchrist wielded a versatile pen. When her husband, Alexander Gilchrist died, leaving unfinished his *Life of William Blake*, Anne completed it and saw it successfully through the press. Before that she had published in learned periodicals articles on scientific subjects which men complimented by attributing to one of their own sex. She could play the pianoforte and she baked bread so tasty and digestible that Jane Welsh Carlyle, her next-door neighbor at Cheyne Row, came to take lessons of her. Anne's bread, it seemed, was the only food that would appease the lion gnawing at the dyspeptic Thomas's entrails. With all her neighborliness Anne managed also to bring up her four children whom she was nursing through scarlet

* For the place of Anne Gilchrist in the Pre-Raphaelite circle and for her relation with Whitman read the author's *Poor Splendid Wings*, Boston, 1933.

fever. It was then that her husband caught it and died, leaving her inconsolable.

Theirs had been a love match. At nineteen Anne had lost a dear brother with whom she had shared all her interests. But soon, as if in compensation, she met Alexander, who was studying for the bar. Like her he drank deep of the writings of the Transcendentalists and the poetry of Blake. He loved nature as she did, and he would sit dreamily listening whenever she played the pianoforte. He was her ideal of manhood. Starry-eyed with love, she found him, in her confidences to her friend Julia Newton, "altogether, both in intellect and heart, great, noble and beautiful." In February of 1851 they married and made their home at Guildford, enjoying together the things that made their life—daily writing and music and walks through the gracious countryside. At night they read aloud to each other. At Guildford their first son, Percy, was born. Then came Beatrice. In 1856, they moved to London where they took a little house next door to the Carlyles. There Herbert and Grace, their other children, were born.

Like the neighboring houses in that quiet, shaded street, theirs became a center of intense intellectual life. Alexander published his life of William Etty and then set to work on his Blake biography. He learned that Dante Gabriel Rossetti, that haunter of out-of-the-way bookstalls, possessed a precious Blake holograph. Alexander wrote to him. Generously Rossetti not only placed the manuscript in his hands but made him acquainted with his many friends, the dour W. B. Scott, Ford Madox Brown, Ruskin, the lovely pathetic Lizzie Siddal whom Gabriel adored but could not make up his errant heart to marry, William Morris, playfully called Topsy, and Ned Jones who had not yet become Edward Burne-Jones. Till 1861 the Gilchrists lived their happy, productive life—then had come tragedy.

With Alexander gone, Anne found it impossible to continue

in Cheyne Row. She was thirty-three years old, with four young children and a tiny income. But she had many beautiful things which she and Alexander had collected—pieces of fine carved furniture and blue china for which Dante Gabriel Rossetti and Whistler were setting the vogue, delicate knickknacks whose sole purpose was beauty, a painting of Reynolds', and Blake's wonderful "Elijah in the Fiery Chariot." All these treasures she gathered together and brought with her pianoforte to a little tile-roofed cottage, bowered in white clematis, on the summit of one of the Surrey hills. Gentle slopes circled the valley; a brook ran singing past the cottage. It was such a place as she and Alexander had had together in the early years of their marriage.

"Alec's spirit is with me ever," she wrote as she worked on the book left incomplete by death, "presides in my home, speaks to me in every sweet scene, broods over the peaceful valley . . ." But it did not quell the desire for life in her still young and ardent body. Here she took care of her children and wrote her articles, and here it was that she brought the fateful book which Ford Madox Brown had given her.

From that moment she lived under a spell. Whitman, rather, her conception of him as she saw him in his poetry, obsessed her day and night. She thought of him in her walks, she kept his book under her pillow in sleep. Here was a man at last who could satisfy her deep and desperate thirst for a complete life, engaging every fiber of her acutely awakened body, every thought of her mind. Like Blake whose mighty presence had brooded over her, here was one with the same, all-enfolding mysticism, his perceptions of things seen and unseen, his love of all beings. But better than Blake he was alive, accessible at a fortnight's voyage across the ocean.

Her health suffered from her concentration of desire. The year she published her "Estimate," she was so ill that thinking herself dying she called her children to her bedside and told

287

them of her love—as much of it as their immature minds could grasp. It must have been at about the time that Whitman, riding one day in the Brooklyn trams, met Helen Price and asked her whether she had read the article. The young woman answered that she had not, whereupon Whitman told her about it. On Helen's remarking that he must surely want to know the woman who had written it, "No," said he. "That does not much matter. I do not even know her name." Then after a pause he added, "But it was a great comfort to me."

Now that woman was writing: "O come, come, my darling, look into these eyes and see the long ardent aspiring soul in them. Easily, easily you will learn to love all the rest of me for the sake of that and take me to your breast forever."

Walt in his panic did not know what to answer; so he maintained a wise silence. His work needed him, the poems that gave him to all men and women. How could he surrender himself, even to a sister soul who had shown such understanding? Anne Gilchrist did not underestimate herself, any more than did Walt. She had been a Godiva, a greater than Godiva, "For she stripped the veil from woman's body for a good cause and I from a woman's soul for a great cause." Whitman was nothing if not grateful, but no earthly power ever availed to convince him that anyone could serve that great cause better than himself. High priest and god, he must himself prepare the incense for the altar, even though the world choked on its smoke.

An unofficial guiding laureate of the Union, he was now bringing out his work at frequent intervals in slim books and pamphlets. The fifth edition of *Leaves of Grass* (1871) with its brochure of "Passage to India" and other poems, was followed by the prose *Democratic Vistas*, a proud criticism, yet an affirmation of democracy, written partly in answer to *Shooting Niagara*, an indictment by Anne Gilchrist's erstwhile neighbor, Carlyle. Whitman, keen-eyed as the national eagle, saw the corruption in political circles after the war, and the spiritual blight that seemed to have penetrated the very soul of the people; but that, as he saw it, was but a temporary ill. Democracy could not die. Even the disastrous war so recently fought had been entered into by the will of the people, of their own choice, to attack the thing that threatened national unity. The most pacific beings on earth, the least disposed to regimental discipline, had sprung to arms—he had seen them do it—not for conquest, not to repel invasion, but for the "life, *the safety of the flag.*" Let Carlyle attack the theory of America! The people themselves would prove its eternal truth—the people, full of contradictions when viewed in the lump, but how grand when animated by that ideal! Democracy might seem lawlessness to the critical, and the right to vote but an insignificant thing. But how different to start out, an enfranchised man, an equal with the rest, obeying the laws of democracy!

"For," Whitman asserted, "democracy too is law—of the strictest, amplest kind." Then, in an intuitive flash, he illumined the heart of its greatness. "Topping democracy, this most alluring record, that it alone can bind, and ever seeks to bind, all nations, all men, of however various and distant lands, into a brotherhood, a family. . . . Not that half only, individualism, which isolates. There is another half, which is adhesiveness or love, that fuses, ties and aggregates, making the races comrades, and fraternizing all." This truth he wrote in *Democratic Vistas* and repeated in the poems of his maturity. The poet of America had attained his true dimensions. Beginning with the belief that the American stock had roots of its own in a new order of humanity, separate from any other race and possessed of special virtues, he realized at last that there is no new humanity, no newborn generation, but that all races and all men are offshoots of the tree of life, its roots

289

deep and wide, binding the world. The kelson here as in creation is love, under its broader name, democracy.

His post-war writings showed this new growth. What he had
lost in the audacious spontaneity that made the 1860 *Leaves
of Grass* the challenging book it is, his most individual, he
gained in world vision. It was no longer America alone, man
alone, but the whole world, and all humanity. "Passage to
India! Passage O soul to India!" he exclaimed in the poem
inspired by the opening of the Suez Canal and the trans-conti-
nental railway in America. "Passage to more than India!" concluded the erstwhile singer of "Pioneers! O Pioneers!" pointing not merely to the conquest of the West, but of the universe
of the spirit, whose ways are open to all, whose discoveries en-
compass space and time. And again the message:

> Passage to India!
> Lo, soul, seest thou not God's purpose from the first?
> The earth to be spann'd, connected by network,
> The races, neighbors, to marry and be given in marriage,
> The oceans to be cross'd, the distant brought near,
> The lands to be welded together.

Here as in the magnificent "Proud Music of the Storm," he
struck the great organ sounds, to be heard but once or twice
again in grandest diapason—and then an end.

For his work's sake, if for no other reason (that there were
others his diary notes showed) he could not respond to Anne
Gilchrist. Long ago, a young man in the fullness of his powers,
he had put away the greatest happiness that all men know;
he could not take it now.

For more than a month he heard no further from Anne Gilchrist and assumed that she had reconsidered her rashness when,
again, another ardent missive fell into his hands. "Try me for
this life, my darling—" she pleaded. "See if I cannot so live,
so grow, so learn, so love, that when I die you will say, 'This
woman has grown to be a very part of me. . . . It is I and she

290

together in a new, divine, perfect union that form the one complete identity.' "

He knew now that he must answer. The woman whose sole criticism of his poems had been that he violated the strong instinct of silence we have about some things, had herself broken that silence. In his reply, knowing that the flower of her love had sprung from the most vital part of her, he must be careful lest he strike at her very life. Yet he had to give a specific answer to her unequivocal offer: "I am yet young enough to bear thee children, my darling, if God would bless me." He wrote his letter in November, 1871. How long it took him, the cautious one, to pen his reply, no one knows. He could not have written with greater tact or delicacy—and subtlety— rejecting the gift by putting it on quite another plane from hers.

He had been waiting for the right mood in which to answer her, he said, and also for his work to let up. "I wished to give to it a day, a sort of Sabbath or holy day apart to itself. . . . I must at least show without further delay, that I am not insensible to your love. I too send you my love. And do you feel no disappointment because I now write but briefly. My book is my best letter, my response, my truest explanation of all. In it I have put my body and spirit. You understand this better and fuller and clearer than any one else. And I too fully and clearly understand the loving and womanly letter it has evoked. Enough that there surely exists between us so beautiful and delicate a relation, accepted by both of us with joy."

The markedly stilted style showed him treading gingerly on the edge of meaning. One word too little or too much and he was lost, that noble, generous and misguided woman with him.

But Anne did not choose to understand the "truest explanation of all" to be found in his book. It had for her now a deeper and more personal significance than she had seen when she wrote her "Estimate." She answered him on that point:

"Do you know, dear friend, what it means for a woman, what it means for me to understand these poems?—It means . . . that henceforth she cannot choose but live and die striving to be worthy to share this divine man's life. . . ."

Whitman had met his match in perseverance. Against her love-inspired guile he had only his caution—God grant that it might serve him in this instance! He was not in love with Anne, and therein lay all the difference. Unlike her, he could not be infatuated with an ideal and pursue it with passion, at any rate not if that ideal had as its embodiment a human being. He preferred *Leaves of Grass*, his bride, his children, his obsession. For its sake he answered Anne briefly, then not at all.

It took more than silence to keep Anne from sending her flaming coveys across the ocean. She too was obsessed by *Leaves of Grass*—in the person of Walt Whitman. "O I could not live if I did not believe that sooner or later you will not be able to help stretching out your arms toward me. . . ." she cried out month after month, then year after year, interpreting his very reticences as favorable signs. "I can wait long, wait patiently, know well, realize more dearly indeed that this wingless, clouded, half-developed soul of me has a long, long initiate to live through before it can meet and answer yours on equal terms. . . . But that is what I will live and die hoping and striving for."

Meanwhile other communications came from England, showing that many besides Anne Gilchrist had felt the power of *Leaves of Grass*. Swinburne, during the disaster of the Commune in Paris addressed a poem "To Walt Whitman in America" for a song overseas to them, in the twilight of terror. Sympathy with the revolutionists gave unwonted grandeur to his music, but he must call for inspiration upon that

> strong-winged soul with prophetic
> Lips hot from the blood-beats of song

which had roused him with the chants of liberty, long ago, when he had scarcely tried his own voice. Swinburne's poem meant a victory for Whitman. The old world was turning to the new.

Still another wrote to him in 1872, John Addington Symonds, a young poet and scholar who was seeking through the Calamus poems a way out of the maze in which his Greek studies had lost him. What did the songs of the sacred love of comrades really mean? Was Whitman offering an exalted comradeship for the virile friendship the Greeks extolled? "Are then the free men of your land really so pure and loving and noble and generous and sincere?" he asked. "Shall I ever be permitted to question you and learn from you? What the love of man for man in the past has been I think I know. What it is here now, I know also—alas! What you say it can and shall be I dimly discern in your poems. But this hardly satisfies me —so desirous am I of learning what you have to teach."

Taken aback by such ticklish questions Whitman resorted to the old dodge of offering his book as its own explanation. Symonds was not to be so cavalierly dismissed, any more than was Anne Gilchrist. He continued posing his questions, and when no satisfactory answer was forthcoming proffered an explanation of his own in a poem, "Love and Death: A Symphony," dedicated to the man who had called it forth.

Wide as the Atlantic stretched the distance between Calamus and the Symonds poem of the two lovers, Cratinus and Aristodemus,

> noble valiant fair
> Of equal youth and honor . . .
> Vast was the love between them—deep and wide . . .
> Sevenfold had it been proved and purified
> By yearnings, and by achings, and by tears.

If Whitman made anything of the honeyed verses with their invocations to Phoibos Apollon and their classical signposts, if he read through the lengthy effusions to the double suicide of these too, too sensitive youths, he could only have come to the conclusion that here surely was *not* his meaning. Cautiously, very cautiously, he put off his embarrassing questioner, feeding him promises for sixteen years, and then only to raise the most impenetrable mystery of his life. In a marginal note to a critic who found "the comrade's kiss, the arm around the neck" of Calamus friendship non-existent in men, and the evangel poems "simply disgusting" Symonds might have read Walt's true answer—"Yes, 'disgusting' to fops and artificial scholars and prim gentlemen of the clubs, but sane, heroic, full-blooded natural men will find in it the deepest God-implanted voice of their hearts." There was no perversity in the love of comrades.

In America, however, the very scholars he despised had become aware of Walt Whitman, the nation's voice. At least so he thought with immense satisfaction on receiving a request to read one of his poems at the commencement exercises of Dartmouth College. Had he investigated behind the scenes he would have learned that the invitation had come as a prank on the part of the radical students who thought that by enticing so unorthodox a lion they would shake out of their righteousness the dour Congregationalists of the faculty. The United Literary Societies had therefore acted together, and Walt Whitman found himself, in June of 1872, on the platform which none other than Emerson had held on a momentous occasion, many years before. He had a long new poem in his hand, clearly printed for his eyes that moistened easily with emotion, and in the voice he had so largely described, began intoning,

> As a strong bird on pinions free,
> Joyous, the amplest spaces heavenward cleaving,
> Such be the thought I'd think to-day of thee America,
> Such be the recitative I'd bring to-day for thee.

Politely the students listened to the enumeration of what the poet would or would not bring; with grateful recognition the faculty nodded at the names of Maine, Illinois, Texas, Tennessee and other places on the map; patiently all heard the exhortation to the Ship of Democracy to "Sail, sail thy best" and the cataloguing of the Union's virtues. Then, when Whitman came to "The Future only holds thee and can hold," they broke into relieved applause. It was no red-letter day commencement, and Walt knew that the poem he had read could not be counted as one of his best. The eagle was tiring in its flight; the source of strength was sapped.

Physically, too, he was failing. The beard of which he was so proud had turned nearly white, like his hair. The thick, peaked brows looked like eaves laden with snow. He weighed two hundred and ten pounds, but the too heavy body had no energy. The dizzy spells that used to make the solid earth swim about him recurred with greater frequency. Nevertheless he did his work at the Treasury office and in his spare hours, by the light benevolently provided by the Government, read and worked on *Leaves of Grass*. Neither wind nor weather could keep him at home.

The night of the 23rd of January, 1873, was one of the stormiest of that winter. Rain and sleet came down with stinging force in the icy darkness. Nevertheless Walt, lured by the thought of the comfortable fire he could have in his office, braved the storm and went to the Treasury building. He did not feel like writing, so when the fire was cheerfully blazing, he took up Bulwer's *What Will He Do With It?* and settled down to a cozy hour or two. As he read, the letters blurred before his eyes. A feeling of uneasiness made him put the book aside several times; but he took it up again and forced himself to read. Thus the hours passed, until, quite late, he got up to go to his lodging, farther down the street. He was not conscious of anything unusual, and was surprised when one of the friendly guards asked him what ailed him. "You look quite ill," he said, and offered to accompany him home.

"No, I can go well enough," Walt declined.

The man insisted, and when Walt again refused, walked down the Treasury steps with him and stood at the door, lighting him with his lantern until he saw him disappear into his lodging-house.

With difficulty Walt climbed the steps to his room where he undressed and went to bed. Suddenly toward three or four o'clock, he awoke and found that he could not move his left side. He was in no pain; he did not even feel particularly uneasy, but his arm and leg remained inert. Somehow he fell asleep again and slept until morning. When he tried to get up, he realized with horror that he could not move. He did not call for help. Quietly he lay there until, several hours later, some friends came in who immediately sent for a doctor. It was as they feared. Walt had had a paralytic stroke. The years at the hospitals with their drain upon his strength and emotions had finally taken their toll.

Pete Doyle it was who nursed him, taking turns with another of Walt's humble friends. They made him as comfortable as they could, and followed the instructions of Dr. W. B. Drinkard who applied the new-fangled electricity to restore life to the deadened limbs. O'Connor, the champion of Walt's reputation, was not there. A difference of opinion on the old Abolitionist question had estranged them. Nor was John Burroughs at his bedside. Only a few weeks before Walt's stroke, Burroughs had been sent to another post in Middletown, New York, as bank examiner for the state. But Ursula made up for his absence. When she heard that the "poet and person" was lying helpless in a lodging-house room, she went to nurse him and when, about a month later, he was able to leave the house, she took him out driving. He enjoyed it like a child. But he confessed his fears of his true condition. It had not been only

THE BUTTERFLY PORTRAIT
From the "Birthday Edition" of *Leaves of Grass*, 1889

*"The natural man sat for the photographer with a butterfly anchored
by a perceptible string to his forefinger . . ."*

a stroke of the muscles, but also of the brain. Forgetting the old prejudice, Ursula comforted him and kept her husband informed of his progress. Burroughs was grateful for her kindness to his dearest friend. "Love me, love Walt," he said.

Although he could scarcely hold his pen, Walt wrote to his mother, not to alarm her at the sight of a strange handwriting. He told her the truth about his condition, but he also made her believe he had improved more than the circumstances warranted.

The poor old woman had almost more sorrows than she could bear. Jesse died in 1870. Then, while she was recovering from the shock of Walt's stroke, she received word from St. Louis that Mattie, Jeff's wife, had died of tuberculosis. Nevertheless she wrote hopefully to Walt, and Walt introduced what lightness he could into his letters. "The sun shines out bright and cheerful this morning—and in my east window I have a fine healthy rose bush—I see it has got two roses in bloom. . . . I feel I shall get as well as usual yet, dearest mother—and then I shall surely get—hire or buy or build a little place here, room enough to live in for you and Ed and me. . . ."

The dream, one of the most modest and unselfish anyone ever dreamed, was never to be realized. Hardly two months later, when he was barely able to drag himself about with the help of a stick, he was called to Camden, to his mother's bedside. He reached her three days before the end. If Mattie's death had afflicted him, it was now as if part of himself had died. "It is the greatest cloud of my life," he wrote to Pete.

The day of the funeral George's cottage received all those who had come to take a last look at the good, simple woman who had been the greatest inspiration of a poet, next to America, the mother of his soul. In the front parlor they were all gathered, waiting for the services. From the inner room where Louisa lay in her coffin, a dull thud came intermittently, a beat that made the floor vibrate. Someone looked in through the half-open door and saw Walt, sitting alone by his mother's corpse, his hands clasped on his cane, his body bent over. From time to time he would lift the cane and bring it down heavily. He had been there, beating out his hopeless sorrow all through the night.

After Louisa was buried Walt put away the things that had been hers. On an envelope he wrote "Mother's last lines" and in it enclosed her pathetic leavetaking: "farewell my beloved sons farewell i have lived beyond all comfort in this world dont mourn for me my beloved sons and daughters farewell my dear beloved Walter." His name had been the last word she wrote. Her final thought had been for him.

One unwritten charge she left him Walt fulfilled on re-writing the will he had prudently made out after his stroke. "What little I have to leave," he wrote to Pete, "I have left mainly to my lame brother Ed, poor man—Pete," he added, "I have left you $200 and my gold watch—(but it will be much better for us to spend the money together, and I have no doubt we shall do so). . . ."

But the good times, the long walks were over. "The mute inglorious Whitman"—Burroughs' name for Pete—was henceforth to share only in imaginary rambles with his friend. Walt could go nowhere now without the big black stick that Pete had given him. When he valiantly returned to Washington, a few weeks after his mother's death, to resume his work in the Treasury building, his friends saw too clearly that here also, all was ended. Eldridge who watched him go about painfully, a mere physical wreck of his former self, doubted that Walt would ever recover, and was apprehensive of another attack. His mental powers, he wrote to Burroughs, seemed as vigorous as ever, but he could scarcely walk a block without having to rest. The doctor, however, hoped to restore him to a condition of comparative health and that, to the broken

man, was his sheet anchor. Alas, it brought him perforce to
harbor. For a year the Government held his post open under
a substitute, but finally Walt had to accept his formal discharge.
George built a new house on Stevens Street, with a room in
it for his brother. There Walt went to live.

Mrs. Gilchrist, alarmed by the news of Walt's stroke, yearned
more than ever to be with him. Her love and imagination both
told her what he must be enduring, what questions be passing
through his mind. Every night, when she went to bed, she
turned her face to the westward sky, the home of his "great
glowing heart of Love." She could not bear life without the
hope that some day she would be with him, sick, broken
though he was. "Perhaps if my hand were in yours, dear Walt,
you would get along faster," she comforted. "Dearer and sweeter
that lot than even to have been your bride in the full flush of
strength and glory of your youth."

The years slipped by, youth became a memory, and still
Anne gazed hypnotized on the dream that became the fixed
star of her life. With the regularity of the changing seasons,
the coming of night and day, her letters continued their westward course, receiving in reply a post card, a newspaper with
some account of Whitman's health and a note in his handwriting. When even this became too burdensome, he struck
upon a code of his own: a word underscored on the address
meant improving health; none, that he was no better. When
his poem, "The Prayer of Columbus" came out in *Harper's
Magazine*, he saw to it that she received a copy. He hoped
perhaps that she would read his own tragedy in the prayer of
that "batter'd, wreck'd old man . . . sicken'd and nigh to
death . . . venting a heavy heart." For in the words he put
into the mouth of Columbus, it was his own balked spiritual
adventure he told with noble fortitude, as he looked on the
past and the future and beheld on the distant waves greater
ships, and heard on the air anthems in new tongues saluting

him. He sang from the depths of despair, but his spirit remained undaunted, in the ineffable light that had shown him his way—

> Light rare untellable, lighting the very light,
> Beyond all signs, descriptions, languages:
> For that O God, be it my latest word, here on my knees,
> Old, poor and paralyzed, I thank Thee.

It was indeed his latest word, and a sublime one, as a swan song should be. In the long twilight of his remaining years he was to sing many lesser songs; but the mighty voice was feeble, the music but an echo.

For seven years the English Héloïse sent her passionate missives to an unresponsive Abélard. Her children were now grown. Percy the eldest was about to marry. Herbert was nearly twenty. Her old mother, whom she had always cared for, had died. There was nothing to keep her in England. One January day in 1876 Whitman, on opening one of her letters, read trepidantly the news that she had bought tickets for herself and her three younger children, and was sailing for America on the 30th of August. "Oh may I be full of sweet comfort for my Beloved's soul and body through life, through and after death," she reinforced her announcement in another letter.

Such a state of affairs required immediate attention. He could send no post card now. "My dearest friend," he wrote her. *"I do not approve of your American trans-settlement. I see so many things here you have no idea of—the social and almost every other kind of crudeness, meagreness, here (at least in appearance)."* What pangs it must have cost him to write those words on his beloved America! With what alacrity he took them back with his qualifying parenthesis! But he must prevent the foolhardy enterprise at any cost, even if he had to lie. And he lied desperately. *"If I should get well enough to voyage we will talk about it yet in London."*

He knew, and she knew, that he meant not a word of what

he said. But Anne knew also that unless she saw him, the spiritual quest that gave purpose to her life would be balked no less than his. With her carved furniture and her pianoforte, with her three children and Blake's "Elijah in the Fiery Chariot" to lead the way, she embarked on the high adventure.

When Whitman set eyes on her in the autumn of 1876 she was a woman of forty-eight, with not a silver thread in the dark hair framing wing-like a plain face lighted by intense, intelligent eyes. Her voice charmed him and her conversation delighted. "You did not have to abate the wing of your thought downward at all," he said in tribute. On Anne's part, her expectations, at least of the outward man, were not disappointed. Whitman, she wrote to William Michael Rossetti, fully realized the ideal she had formed from his poems. But it was too late for the love she would have given. Before the beautiful but shipwrecked actuality there could be no thought of bearing any sweet comfort but such as could be found in the sunset glow of their lives. And so they spent one year of it together in close communion of spirit. Every day Whitman would take the ferry across to Philadelphia where Mrs. Gilchrist had rented a house, and there he would pass quiet hours with her, the children who adored him, and the friends they gathered about them. Edward Carpenter who visited them spoke of "a kind of prophet's chamber" which Mrs. Gilchrist kept always in readiness for her "Darling" who gradually became, with a lessening of passion but a growth of friendship, "Dear Walt," and "Dear Friend." "My noblest woman friend," he called her.

The year over, Mrs. Gilchrist left Philadelphia for pilgrimages to Concord and Boston. Then she spent some time in New York. At the end of three years, she thought back on England, on her son Percy and his wife—and on a little ten months' grandchild. Perhaps her place was there. Walt, whose health had bettered, no longer needed her. She sailed back in June, 1879. The letters she wrote him came farther and farther apart.

In them she spoke most often of her grandchild. Instead of the postcards and newspapers he used to send her, Walt now forwarded her little maps on which he traced in blue ink his recent itinerary across the Rocky Mountains.

Each had returned to his own.

Chapter XXII: So long!

THE twilight lingered, long but not unproductive. *Leaves of Grass* kept growing. In 1876 Whitman who knew a friendly printer in Camden, brought out the sixth edition in two volumes, the second, *Two Rivulets,* containing his war memoranda and *Democratic Vistas,* together with the occasional pieces he had written. Unlike the volume of 1871, the new ones sold well in America, but even better in England where the Rossetti edition had opened the door to acceptance. Fearful, however, lest the new issue would suffer the fate of the previous ones, Whitman early in the year engineered the printing of an article in the well-known voice of Jacob, deploring his lack of recognition in America. The London *Athenaeum* took it up from the *West Jersey Press,* and soon with the help of the gadfly, Robert Buchanan, who, perhaps conscience-stricken that he had wounded one poet to the death* desired to make amends by helping another, roused all literary England to a realization of Whitman's neglect. For a few weeks an acrimonious controversy engaged England and America on the true state of the case; then it quieted down with Whitman a few hundred dollar the richer through the subscriptions that began coming in. It pleased him to see on the list from England the names of Lord Houghton, Edward Dowden, Tennyson, Ruskin and George Saintsbury, besides his faithful Pre-Raphaelites.

In 1879 he found another source of income and the accomplishment of a long-cherished dream when he delivered for the first time his Lincoln lecture on the anniversary of the

---

* In his savage attack on D. G. Rossetti, "The Fleshly School of Poetry" in the *Contemporary Review* for October, 1871.

President's assassination. Every year for the rest of his life, he was to read the lecture, in Philadelphia, in Boston, the occasion often becoming a demonstration of the loyalty of his friends who found it a tactful way of helping the aging poet without injuring his pride. Andrew Carnegie at one such reading, paid $350 for a box, sending in with his check the note, "When the *Pall Mall Magazine* raised a subscription for Mr. Whitman I felt triumphant democracy disgraced. Whitman is the great poet of America so far."

What Mr. Carnegie knew America had not yet discovered when James R. Osgood and Company of Boston published, at their own solicitation, the seventh and most unified edition of *Leaves of Grass* in 1881-2. Whitman had read with some suspicion Mr. Osgood's letter inviting him to have his book brought out commercially. He would agree, Whitman answered, provided he would not be required to make any excisions or expurgations. Perhaps he remembered with a touch of nostalgia the long, long walk under the elms of the Common when he had defended even against Emerson his right to make poetry as he pleased. The offer of a twenty-five cent royalty for every copy sold, however, had a silvery ring to the poet who in his fear of insecurity was beginning to suffer from a touch of the mania of owning things. He sent in the manuscript he had been planning to re-issue himself at Camden. After a few minor revisions not affecting the spirit of the *Leaves*, the book was sent to the printers. Whitman as usual, promptly followed, standing over the cases and correcting the proofs with the same tender care with which he had assisted at the birth of his cub in 1855. During the two months he spent in Boston he had plenty of time to muse under those same elms. But now he was an old man, leaning on his stick, dragging his leg painfully in a sideward direction as he limped along.

But greater changes had come over the men he had known.

304

Thoreau, long since, had suffered the final mutation. Over his grave, when Emerson delivered the brief funeral eulogy, he, Whitman, had been alluded to, though not mentioned by name, as among the three who had most affected the departed. The others had been John Brown and an Indian guide Thoreau had met in the Maine woods.

A change, too, had come over Emerson which had fallen on the once brilliant mind, rather than on the body, still hale. In the hours Whitman spent with him he marked the fresh color of the face, wearing its old expression of sweetness, the clear, penetrating glance of the eyes. But the light behind them had clouded. Frank Sanborn he found the same, though aged. Did Sanborn ever repeat to him a certain unfavorable comment made to him by the Master, that *Leaves of Grass* read like "a mixture of the *Bhagavad-Gita* and the New York *Herald*"? But then, Whitman would have known that Emerson had seen most clearly in 1855.

The new edition started off with éclat. In a few months two thousand copies had been sold. Interest in it continued in brisk sales when, on the 1st of March, 1882, Oliver Stevens, the Boston District Attorney, at the instigation of the Society for the Suppression of Vice, wrote the publisher an official letter saying that he intended to institute suit against *Leaves of Grass* under the statutes governing obscene literature. Mr. Stevens also forwarded a list of objectionable passages, and mentioned particularly "A Woman Waits for Me," "To a Common Prostitute" and "The Dalliance of the Eagles" a poem Whitman had written from a description furnished by John Burroughs.

Letters passed back and forth between Osgood and Stevens, and the matter was brought before the author by the publisher who tentatively sent him the list of objections. Whitman bristled. "The list, whole and several, is rejected by me," he answered defiantly, "and will not be thought of under any circumstances." Even when Mr. Stevens declared his willingness to be satisfied if the poet agreed merely to the omission of "To a Common Prostitute" and "A Woman Waits for Me"—no more than the compromises conceded to William Michael Rossetti—Whitman stood his ground. Was he now to forsake principle for the fleshpot? Was his struggle of a quarter of a century to yield in ignoble appeasement? Must he grant to a District Attorney what he had denied to an Emerson? Never!

In the face of such resistance Osgood had no choice but to turn over the plates to Whitman instead of royalties, and again the poet opened his arms to his inconvenient offspring. Promptly he printed a small edition to dispose of himself in Camden. Rees Welsh and Company of Philadelphia, however, to whose business David McKay succeeded, offered to take the the risks of prosecution, and toward the end of September *Leaves of Grass* reappeared in the dignity of a book with a publisher. The first printing of three thousand copies sold in one day, breaking a record. The District Attorney with his censorship had accomplished what all of Whitman's maneuvering had failed to do.

Distinguished visitors from abroad were now as anxious to behold America's poet as they were to hear the roar of Niagara. Both pertained equally to the New World. Before sickness had brought Whitman to Camden, Lord Houghton had visited him, as much for his own satisfaction as to justify his protégé Swinburne's enthusiasm. He had not been disappointed despite the foreboding of the Boston literati that he could find no point of contact with a New York rough. Whitman, indeed, was no flower of book-bred culture—no more hot-house grown than the potatoes of his dinner which he shared with his lordly guest. Back in London, Lord Houghton complimented Swinburne on his discernment. But alas for human consistency! Just when Whitman was enjoying a taste of fame at home, Swinburne turned against him. True, Swinburne had long ceased to be the poet of "raptures and roses." Theodore Watts had seen to that when he took the red-haired demon from the vices of London and carried him off bodily to Putney for purposes of reform.

Like all things in which Swinburne over-indulged, reform went to his head. Everything he had once admired turned to gall, and in it he dipped his pen when, at the instigation of Watts, he wrote an article on Whitman's art for the *Fortnightly*. What a transformation was there! No longer "sweet-smelling of pine leaves and grasses," the muse of the titan he had been among the first to acclaim became a "drunken apple-woman indecently sprawling in the slush and garbage of the gutter amid the rotten refuse of her overturned fruit stall!" But then, Swinburne had other songs to sing in his newly assumed role of the poet of innocence. The jingle of the infant's bells which was now his music made but a feeble sound against the torrent. John Burroughs, when Swinburne's article was called to his attention, heaved a sigh of relief; he had half suspected something wrong in Walt to rouse the ardor of such an admirer. Walt, on his part, contented himself with the exclamation which added another name to the many Swinburne had been called: "Ain't he the damndest simulacrum!"

Edward Carpenter followed Lord Houghton, and later had come the first of the group of disciples to cluster about the good gray poet. Dr. Richard Maurice Bucke, an alienist, was the head of an insane asylum in London, Canada. For years he had been a reader of *Leaves of Grass*, in which he thought he discerned the manifestations of "cosmic consciousness," a force that according to him would eventually bring about a higher stage of evolution. At first Whitman's poems had puzzled him. But as he read and let their meaning seep through his subconscious, he believed that here, in the poet, he saw the signs by which one must know the precursor. It was largely to verify this belief that in 1877 he found himself in Camden. On making inquiries about the prophet, it did not astonish him to discover how little known was Whitman in his own home. That was as it should be. The Camden directory, however, set him on the right track with its listing of "Whitman, Walt, Poet, 431 Stevens Street."

While waiting for him in the sitting room of Colonel George's house, Dr. Bucke realized that money contributed little to its simple comfort. Soon Walt came tramping heavily down the stairs, leaning on the banisters and taking each step slowly, like a child. A child's limpid eyes peered out at the stranger from the shagginess of an old man. He looked like a study in gray and white, his locks mingling with his beard and its silken hairs flowing over the open shirt to the gray, loose-fitting clothes. Dr. Bucke succumbed to the "influence" at once. When he left, with the invitation to call again, he could think of nothing striking in the conversation, no memorable word or phrase to set down as the pronouncement of the oracle. Nevertheless he was convinced that Whitman was "either actually a god or in some sense clearly and entirely praeter-human."

The exaggeration of a mystic, no doubt. Dr. Bucke would have been the last to deny it. From that day forward the two became fast friends. They met often, and in 1880 Whitman was Dr. Bucke's guest in Canada for four months. Down the St. Lawrence and on the Great Lakes they sailed together, and explored the Saguenay. Dr. Bucke had complete faith that Whitman was "the man." Gradually he too adopted the gray, loose-fitting clothes and the wide-awake hat. He let his beard grow long, and thanked time for every white hair that made his likeness nearer to his god's. He saw even some compensation in the accident that had lamed him when crossing the Sierra Nevadas as a youth. The limp of his artificial foot gave him Whitman's gait. The identification reached its height when, after Walt's encounter with the Boston censor, Dr. Bucke had the privilege of writing the poet's biography—really a collaboration, even though, as in Burrough's case, only one name appeared on the title page.

Still the foreign visitors continued coming, none more resplendent than the large, long-haired youth who appeared one day from the city of Brotherly Love across the Delaware. Oscar Wilde had come all the way across the Atlantic to preach in America his gospel of art for art's sake. He was, however, Speranza's son, and therefore a nursling at the breast of revolution. His brand of heresy had little in common with Walt's. Still, the spirit that jolted the Philistine out of inertia was in him as in the American bard, and both, in the end, believed "All beauty comes from beautiful blood and a beautiful brain." In the Camden parlor, and then in Walt's den upstairs, they had a few pleasant hours together, drinking sister-in-law Lou Whitman's elderberry wine, and then milk punch which Walt mixed with an expert hand. When Wilde left, with the old man's "God bless you" ringing down the street after him, he was partly consoled for the hostility Philadelphia had shown him at his lecture the previous night, and heartened for the rest of the tour on that year of aestheticism, 1882.*

George Whitman and his wife had not grown attached to Camden during the years they had been living there, and decided to move to Burlington, New Jersey. The house had unhappy associations. Walter, their only son, had died there. Always the sitting room reminded them of the tiny white coffin with its little corpse looking so pitiful under the profusion of tuberoses and geranium leaves, and of the grief-stricken Walt in a great chair nearby, surrounded by children. First the grandmother, then the grandchild. In vain had Walt written so bravely of death; the actuality, striking home, was not easy to bear. "You don't understand this, my dear, do you?" they heard him ask a little girl peering tiptoe over the side of the coffin.

* For details on the interview between Whitman and Wilde see the author's *Oscar Wilde and the Yellow 'Nineties.*

"No, sir," whispered the child. "Neither do I," said Walt, turning away.

Invalided though he was, Walt would not accompany his family on its removal. Instead he bought himself a little house at 328 Mickle Street* in Camden with the money he had been laying by, and the help of his friend George W. Childs. In many ways the compact cottage or shack, as he called it, answered the description of his dream house in "the poet's needs." Time and again he had passed it on his way to the ferries. His friends, when they saw it, hardly visualized it as the habitation of a poet. Thomas Donaldson thought it a coop at best. But the son of the Brooklyn farmer saw that it had been built true and to the line. The paneled door and the simple carving above it had grace and solidity. The marble carriage stone at the curb in front of the three wooden steps of the entrance would be a convenience to the more prosperous visitors who came to see him. Best of all, there was a large, spreading tree in front of it, and in the backyard bloomed a clump of lilacs, the flowers that meant childhood, home, poetry and everything that had power to stir the emotions and wake imagination. For the sake of the tree and the lilacs he could shut his ears to the clanging trains, ignore the smells of the guano factory, the noisy housewives with their passion for stirring up the water of the gutters with their brooms, and even the nasal Sabbath singing of the frightfully zealous choir in the neighboring church.

To his little house Walt transported his few belongings. Over the mantel hung the portrait of his father, keen-eyed, sullen; beside it, separated by an old clock, the picture of his mother with the peaked brows and the florid coloring he had inherited. Besides a bed, a few packing boxes, three or four ordinary wooden chairs and great heaps of the various editions of *Leaves of Grass*, he had little else. For a time he retained as housekeepers an elderly workman and his wife who had a dis-

* Now No. 330.

concerting way of shouting the arrival of visitors according to the conveyance that brought them—"Walt, here's some carriage folk come to see you!" But they soon left him, taking their furniture, and Walt remained alone in a house that would have been bare save for his books and the mounds of newspapers, clippings and manuscripts which rose higher and higher as he found it increasingly difficult to throw away the least scrap of writing or print.

Somewhere by the wayside he had picked up a plaster bust of Elias Hicks which he kept in a corner on the floor, its reverend bald pate protected against the dust by a nightcap of newspapers. In another corner stood, for no conceivable aesthetic reason, a statuette of Grover Cleveland, squat and graceless. Later Walt added to the collection a seated figure of himself, also under a protective covering of newsprint which, when incautiously lifted one day by William Sloane Kennedy revealed a nest of brown ants housed comfortably in the clay Walt's lap. Alone, the poor invalid looked after his needs, as he had done during the war in Washington, eating off a packing case for a table and warming his milk over a coal oil lamp. He had no money but what his infrequent lectures and *Leaves of Grass* brought in—and interest in it had died down after the Philadelphia flare. The prose *Specimen Days and Collect*, containing some of his best writing, sold no better than his poetry. Donaldson, who was pained by Walt's way of living, offered him rent-free a house and twenty city lots in Philadelphia, with a flower garden and comfort to enjoy as long as he lived, but Walt preferred his own untidy nest—and independence.

In 1885, however, his luck changed for the better. First of all, Mrs. Mary Davis, a sailor's widow who had often taken pity on the lonely old man peddling his books from a knapsack on his back, came to live with him as his housekeeper. The arrangement was a simple one. She brought her furniture and her canary; he provided the house.

Ever since she could remember, Mary Davis had tended the sick and the helpless. Walt Whitman remained her charge to the end of his days. Perhaps he took her many services a little too much for granted; it may even be that he was not considerate of her side of the financial burden, as posthumous wrangles indicated. At any rate the arrangement lasted for seven years to their mutual satisfaction and with, on Mrs. Davis's part, a sense of service done faithfully and well. Of course the neighbors talked, and posted their children outside the Mickle Street house to report on the comings and goings of its tenants. But by this time Walt had grown deaf to wagging tongues, and Mary Davis was too busy to care. She knew only that Mr. Whitman was a great man and that by keeping him comfortable she had some small share in that greatness.

He became her big spoiled child though he was so many years older than her trim, comely self. Whenever she heard the thumping of his stick on the floor of his bedroom above, she knew that he was up and ready for his breakfast. But she could sooner have controlled the wind blowing through the trees, than the capricious habits of Mr. Whitman. She soon grew used to his irregularity and ran the house accordingly. She knew, for example, that not a scrap of paper was to be thrown away, that the dust-rag must never disturb the accumulation of time on the mounting heaps of print. If a guest, or guests, came while Walt was at table, they must never be told to go but be made to partake of the chowder or potatoes, or the succulent oysters which an admiring fish dealer provided gratis for the poet's table. Whenever Whitman went out on days when his lameness was worse than usual, she walked with him arm in arm; she soon learned to support his weight. She was inordinately proud of his personal appearance. The man whom the venerable Dr. Horace Furness of Philadelphia stopped in the street to greet with an awed, "You are too beautiful for words," must always be made to look his best. So she saw to it that his

WHITMAN'S HOUSE IN CAMDEN
Photograph by Arnold Genthe. Courtesy Haddon Craftsmen

"The son of the Brooklyn framer saw that it had been built true and to the line."

gray clothes were always spotless, and when she sewed his white linen shirt she trimmed them with an edging of lace at the collar and cuffs that gave him the look of half god, half infant. The house assumed a gentle though untidy domesticity. Together with the canary, a cat joined the family circle and then a spotted dog that used to sit at Walt's feet and stare into his face by the hour.

One morning, as Walt was about to start out on his slow, painful walk, he found a sprightly horse and buggy drawn up by the carriage stone. Mrs. Davis, standing beside him, had a bright look on her face, and so had a number of his friends who by a strange coincidence had all dropped in at the same hour. With tears in his eyes, he learned that the phaeton was his, the gift of more admirers than he thought he had. Mrs. Davis had suggested the plan of a buggy to Donaldson, and Donaldson had carried it out by getting up a subscription among personal friends and literary men. The list read like a page from the American Parnassus. Oliver Wendell Holmes had contributed ten dollars, with Mark Twain, Talcott Williams, Richard Watson Gilder, Whittier, and many others. The Quaker Whittier who had thrown the 1855 *Leaves of Grass* into the fire, sent in a mild recommendation with his contribution —"that a kind, sober-paced roadster would be more serviceable to him (Whitman) than the untamed, rough-jolting Pegasus he had been accustomed to ride—without check or snaffle."

How little did the good Quaker know Whitman! No more patient with his earthly sober-paced roadster than with the Olympian, Walt soon exchanged his horse for a vivacious pony which he urged on, unrestrained, his white beard blown backward in the wind, his cheeks glowing, like an aged but untamed Apollo. Then one day the Philadelphia *News* carried some doleful verses in Whitmanian numbers, lamenting the disappearance of Walt's harness and horse-blanket. What thief had absconded with the property of the good gray poet?

313

I anger, I madden, I hump my amiability,
O the enormity, the enormous enormity of his badness!
My harness, who hath deftly extracted it?—
My sad, unbridled steed.
Slow police, slumbering locust men, I damn thee!
Poor traceless charger,
Uncollared horse, uncollared thief! . . .

The lost property came back, and Frank, the pony, sped again through the streets of Camden, bearing the smiling poet. It was a token of affection that he could be parodied, and so good-naturedly.

Time brought increase of illness, but also increase of friends and a modest degree of prosperity. Walt had a bank account, furnished to a small degree by the American and English editions of his work, by the proceeds of his Lincoln lecture, the contributions of admirers, and benefits arranged by the faithful. In 1887, through Kennedy, Boston, which Walt had always suspected of unfriendliness, sent him a subscription of eight hundred dollars. The money had been raised so that he might build himself a cottage at Timber Creek, near his friends the Staffords, where he had taken sun baths when he thought he could still be cured, and written the most charming nature sections of *Specimen Days*. But he was too old and too feeble even for such a change. He put away the money for another use. Toward the same object, as yet unrevealed to anyone, he also saved the proceeds of Robert Ingersoll's benefit lecture, "Liberty in Literature." How good they were all to him, Donaldson, Kennedy, J. H. Johnston, the Staffords, the Quaker Pearsall Smith of Germantown, Richard Watson Gilder, and the countless friends of "the old man" here and in England! With regret he thought of those who had died—Anne Gilchrist, the loyal O'Connor, and others, many others. It was time for him, too, to think of death. Young Horace Traubel with his pen and pencil taking down every word he said, was a constant reminder of mortality.

314

So long!

Traubel had come to Whitman as a boy in his teens when, after school, he would haunt the doorstep of George Whitman's house for a sight of the grand-looking old man who had a hale greeting for friend or stranger. Whitman encouraged the youngster. He liked his alert mind and his fondness for books, rather, his fondness for hearing him, Walt, talk about books. A warm relation established itself between the two. Walt was helpless; Horace, with his small, slight body, fleet and nimble. He made nothing of numerous trips to the printers with batches of copy under his arm. His fine, clear, grayish-blue eyes lighted up with intelligence and worship whenever Walt spoke to him, as he did freely, about his poems, and as he grew older, Horace had no hesitation about venturing his opinions. Amused yet fond, Whitman began to depend upon him.

Before Mrs. Davis had come to Mickle Street, Horace who was then employed in a bank in Philadelphia, used to help tidy up the place and make Walt his supper. And always it was talk, talk, talk, Horace asking his Boswellian questions and Walt, a less ponderous Dr. Johnson, answering with an eye on the impression he was making on his disciple, but more on the posterity whose reporter he knew the youth to be. Often, in the evening, when Walt would sit under the tree in front of the house, enjoying the cool of the evening with his friends, Horace would be there, observing the way the old man tapped with his foot against the trunk till he wore a hole in it, remembering every word, catching each turn of phrase which he later put down to the very accent, save for a generous interspersing of his own favorite *hells* and *damns*. He had a mission to fulfill— to portray Whitman not only as he appeared to be, but as he *was*, for Traubel, keen as a ferret, knew all the burrows in which Walt concealed his true self.

Odd scenes would be enacted between the two, Horace sharp and quick, Whitman a Jove cornered by his relentless Mercury.

"You told Emerson that they readily sold," he tackled Whit-

315

man on the subject of the first *Leaves*, one day in 1889. "Do you say to me now that they readily sold?"

"No, I do not," answered Walt.

"Well, why did you say it to Emerson?"

"At the time I thought the books were selling. A lot of them were consigned right and left. But there were no sales. They came back." He could afford to tell the truth now, so many years later.

Laughing, Horace remarked, "I was wondering whether you were not bluffing Emerson."

"You mean bragging?" asked Walt, adding after a moment, "maybe there was something of that sort in it."

"I can't forget, either," Horace insisted, "that in the same letter you call Emerson Master. Now you repudiate the word. What did you mean by it then?"

"They were salad days. I had undeveloped angles at that time." Walt evaded the difficult question. "I don't imagine I was guiltless. Someone had to speak for me. No one would. I spoke for myself."

Other, more intimate matters, Horace strove to get at, like John Addington Symonds, and Dr. Bucke. In some respects he got closer to them than the other two, but the canny Whitman in the end kept his secret by pretending to divulge it. The last years of his life became a fantastic game of hide-and-seek in the haze of conjecture between him and his "explainers." Why did he never marry? What was the meaning of the Calamus poems? Were the two questions somehow linked, and did they have a bearing on the "secret" of *Leaves of Grass*?

Most obdurate of all, John Addington Symonds demanded a definite answer. He might as well have asked of the Delphic oracle to speak without double meaning. "Symonds has a few doubts yet to be quieted," said Whitman in 1888 after his English explainer had managed to wreathe with thicker clouds the Jovian head. "Not doubts about me, doubts rather of himself . . . What does Calamus mean? What do the poems come to in the round-up?"

Whatever they meant, he knew the Calamus poems did not mean what Symonds intimated. In the *Contemporary Review* for September, 1887, Symonds had written an ambiguous defense of Whitman. The whole matter struck Walt as ludicrous, especially in the obvious striving of the Englishman to make the American giant fit into the mold of his preconceptions. But Symonds did not give up his search for what he thought the truth, and finally posed questions so direct that Walt, shocked by their unmistakable inferences of homosexuality, answered with a letter whose exaggerations showed the extremity of his panic.

"My life, young manhood, mid-age, times South etc., have been jolly bodily," he wrote on the 9th of July, 1890, with suspicious boastfulness, "and doubtless open to criticism. Though unmarried I have had six children—two are dead—one living Southern grandchild, fine boy, writes to me occasionally—circumstances (connected with their fortune and benefit) have separated me from intimate relations." A jolly bodily life, and *six* illegitimate children! That should put a stop to Symonds's impertinent questioning.

If ever a good round half-dozen children were summoned from the Hall of the Unborn, Whitman's assuredly were. Even to him, after he had written down the number, it seemed so implausible that he immediately, with a stroke of the pen, killed off two. *Four* children and one Southern grandchild had a slightly more convincing sound. Let the curious seek them out for themselves. He was sure no one would ever find them—sure because they never existed except as figments of an old man's boastful fancy.

Once the long-bow was shot, his questioners gave him no peace. But he was a match for them all. "Why did you never marry?" one asked him pointblank.

317

With the most solemn face in the world Walt gave him a string of preposterous nonsense: "The whole thing, my friend, like the Nibelungen or somebody's cat, has an immensely long, long tail to it. And the not being married, and the not, and the not, and the not, and the this and the this, and the this, have a great many explications. At the first view it may not be so creditable to the fellow. But go on, explicate still more, and still more, and still more behind all that—and after a while you see why it must be so in the nature of things."

Wise men would have desisted before such seeming ingenuousness, and come to the conclusion that perhaps the mystery of it all was that there was no mystery. Not so the zealous truth-seekers. At the least opening they plunged into the well, to find truth in but another of its favorite shapes, swimming contented behind its murky screen.

On the 23rd of December, 1891, when Whitman, as everyone thought, lay dying, Dr. Bucke questioned him anew. Men were known to tell the truth in the immediacy of death.

"Do you not want to say something to me about the Southern matter?" he asked, referring to Walt's will.

"My children?" asked Whitman.

"Yes."

"Well, I guess not," said Walt.

"Harned thinks someone ought to know the main facts in case of any trouble arising hereafter," Dr. Bucke insisted.

"In money matters, do you mean?"

"Yes."

"Oh, there will be no trouble of that kind," Walt assured him, going on to say that they were people of good family who "would of themselves never come forward to claim connection." They never did, because they never were. Nevertheless, perhaps because the unborn have no ghosts that can be laid, Walt's illegitimate brood continues to plague his biographers.

When Walt made out his final will, although he mentioned

318

relatives near and far, he wrote no word of any child or grand-child. Among the tokens bequeathed to friends, he left his gold watch to Traubel and his silver watch to Harry Stafford. Surely, had there been a living Southern grandchild, one of those watches might have gone to him without affront to the sensibilities of the "good family." No doubt Walt was telling his own case when a few months before he died, on being asked again about his complex "secret" he told of how as a youth he had seen a five-act drama. "The leading character was a prodigiously quaint old fellow who lugged a secret around with him. It was in a pack on his back, and some who expected to be his heirs watched this secret with eagerness. One day the old fellow died, and lo! the pack contained no secret. . . ."

The real answer was to be found, more than anywhere else, in *Leaves of Grass.* For the building of its legend he made for himself a glamorous figure, posed, romanticized, mystified. The new Adam let his beard grow; the natural man sat for the photographer with a butterfly anchored by a perceptible string to his forefinger in a season of the year when he had to wear a woolen sweater and butterflies had long done with flitting. He adopted his various costumes, of the dandy, the carpenter, the man of the open road and finally the good gray poet, retaining, however, his two personalities, that of the poet, first of all, sterling as the truest metal, and that of the poet's press agent who concocted the myths to capture the popular imagination. But the popular imagination would not be captured except toward the end, and then only because it had allowed itself to listen to the voice of the poet. As a press agent he remained as bad as the poet was great. Even he did not wholly realize his greatness; he made too much noise in his unsureness. At one of the final birthday dinners Gilder's comment in praise of Whitman's free verse, "The form in which the thought is expressed satisfies me," brought from the beaming old man the exclamation, "You don't mean that!" The seal of such authority on what to many still remained a "barbaric yawp" gave him confidence in his immortality.

To the end he constructed his monument of words. In 1888 he collected his later poems under the title of *Sands at Seventy*. His miscellaneous prose he brought together in *November Boughs*. The titles themselves sounded a valedictory. "Any day the slender thread may be cut—any day," he said. But he went on writing. There is a reminiscence of him turning in his hand with the absorption of a mystic a strange rosary, a new poem composed on scrawled odd pieces of paper, strung on white thread, each scrap containing a more perfect form of his thought, some more pleasing phrase of the "tune" which he always heard before he began writing. But he knew it would soon be time to say good-by to his Fancy—"dear mate, dear love."

Harrison Morris who had seen the poet at work, went to visit him again in 1890. Whitman was just about to go out in the carriage with Traubel and Warry Fritzinger, his companion, nurse and coachman. Walt invited Morris to go along with them. "Where shall we go?" Walt asked him.

As Morris had nothing to suggest Walt inquired, "You have not seen the tomb?"

"No," said the astonished Morris, whereupon Walt called out to the driver with the delight of a boy, "Same place, Warry!"

After driving a short distance through Camden they reached a deep dell near the entrance of Harleigh Cemetery. There, built into the hillside stood a rough, druidical hut constructed of grayish stone, an immense slab forming the lintel and a triangular companion piece the primitive pediment. The door gaped open as if waiting for its tenant. On the pediment, in large square letters, was carved the name, WALT WHITMAN. Laurel and fern already softened the ruggedness of the spot. Tall trees shaded it. Opposite, the sky was caught in the shimmering of living water.

So long!

"I have picked out a bit of hill, with a southern exposure," he had said with a twinkle to Donaldson after he had found his final resting place. "I like to be with the trees . . . Yes, I think I have selected a comfortable grave."

The building of his mausoleum cost much more than the "little sum laid aside for burial money." Indeed, he put into it thousands of dollars saved secretly for the purpose. But Walt who wanted to make sure of everything, must know before he died that he had the monument he deserved. Aware that the years would pass before posterity thought of raising a stone worthy of his fame, he raised it himself. With deep, black lines of emphasis had he underscored in his copy of the *Rubaiyat* the editorial comment, "Omar's epicurean audacity of thought and speech caused him to be regarded askance in his own time and country." Instead of Omar's name he saw his own.

Yet he had done much for his time and country by the time he said "So long!" to the living on March 26, 1892. Others might have excelled in heroism the Quaker who would not hold a gun against his brothers, but he dedicated what was more than his life, his proud health, to the service of his country. Still others towered above him in intellectual attainments, but he brought into literature the blood and brawn of the common people, their tolerance and open-mindedness, their diversity, their immensity, their faith in the democratic ideal, with liberty to experiment, to change, to blunder even, but always to see both sides in the freedom of discussion, and to build, stone on stone, a mansion for all humanity. Best of all, he brought to each man faith in the god within, and always the words of his true poems, the poems of the Answerer, that give more than poems, for

They give you to form for yourselves poems, religions, politics, war,
    peace, behavior, histories, essays, daily life, and every thing else,
They balance ranks, colors, races, creeds and the sexes . . .
They prepare for death, yet they are not the finish, but rather the
    outset.

Bibliography

ADIMARI, RALPH, "Unknown Whitman," *Saturday Review of Literature.* August 18, 1934.

AMERICAN ART ASSOCIATION, *Catalogue of Manuscripts, autograph letters, etc. of Walt Whitman.* New York, 1936.

American Phrenological Journal, October, 1855.

ARVIN, NEWTON, *Whitman.* New York, 1938.

BAILEY, JOHN, *Walt Whitman.* New York, 1926.

BARRUS, CLARA, *Life and Letters of John Burroughs.* 2 vols. Boston, 1925.

————, *Whitman and Burroughs, Comrades.* Boston and New York, 1931.

BARTON, WILLIAM E., *Abraham Lincoln and Walt Whitman.* Indianapolis, 1928.

BAXTER, SYLVESTER, "Walt Whitman in Boston," *New England Magazine.* August, 1892.

BAZALGETTE, LÉON, *Le poème évangile de Walt Whitman.* Paris, 1921.

————, *Walt Whitman, l'homme et son oeuvre.* Paris, 1908.

BENÉT, S. V., "Ode to Walt Whitman," *Saturday Review of Literature.* Vol. 12.

BENTZON, TH. "Un poète americain: Walt Whitman," *Revue des Deux Mondes.* June, 1872.

BINNS, HENRY B., *A Life of Walt Whitman.* London, 1905.

BLACK, GEORGE, "Walt Whitman," *New England Magazine.* August, 1892.

BLODGETT, HAROLD, *Walt Whitman in England.* Ithaca and London, 1934.

BORN, HELENA, *Whitman's Ideal Democracy.* Boston, 1902.

BOYD, ERNEST, *Literary Blasphemies,* New York, 1927.

BRADFORD, G., *Biography of the Human Heart.* Boston and New York 1932.

BRADLEY, S., "Mr. Walt Whitman," *Bookman.* March, 1933.

————, "Walt Whitman on Timber Creek," *American Literature.* Vol. 5.

322

Bibliography

BRADSHER, EARL L., "Walt Whitman and a Modern Problem," *Sewanee Review*. Vol. 22.

BRINTON, DANIEL G. and HORACE TRAUBEL, "A Visit to West Hills," *Walt Whitman Fellowship Papers*. Philadelphia, December, 1894.

BROOKS, VAN WYCK, *The Flowering of New England*. New York, 1936.

———, *New England, Indian Summer*. New York, 1940.

BUCHANAN, ROBERT, "Walt Whitman," *The Broadway*. November, 1867.

BUCKE, R. M., Ed., *Calamus*. (Letters of Walt Whitman to Peter Doyle.) Boston, 1897.

———, *Cosmic Consciousness*. Philadelphia, 1901.

———, "Memories of Walt Whitman," *Walt Whitman Fellowship Papers*. Philadelphia, September, 1894.

———, *Walt Whitman*. Philadelphia, 1883.

BURROUGHS, JOHN, *Notes on Walt Whitman as Poet and Person*. New York, 1867.

———, *Whitman, a Study*. Boston and New York, 1896.

CALDER, ELLEN M., "Personal Recollection of Walt Whitman," *Atlantic Monthly*. June, 1907.

CANBY, H. S., *American Estimates*. New York, 1929.

———, *Classic Americans*. New York, 1931.

CARPENTER, EDWARD, *Days with Walt Whitman*. London and New York, 1906.

CARPENTER, GEORGE R., *Walt Whitman*. New York, 1909.

CATEL, JEAN, Ed., *The Eighteenth Presidency!* Paris, 1928.

———, *Walt Whitman: La naissance du poète*. Paris, 1929.

CESTRE, CHARLES, "Walt Whitman, l'inadapté," *Revue anglo-américaine*. Année 7.

———, "Walt Whitman, le poète," *Revue anglo-américaine*. Année 8.

CHAPMAN, JOHN J., *Emerson, and Other Essays*. 1898.

CLARKE, WILLIAM, *Walt Whitman*. London, 1892.

CLIVE, ARTHUR, "Walt Whitman, the Poet of Joy," *Gentleman's Magazine*. December, 1875.

CONWAY, MONCURE D., *Autobiography, Memories and Experiences*. 2 vols. Boston, 1904.

———, *Thomas Carlyle*. New York, 1881.

COOKE, ALICE L., "Whitman's Background in the Industrial Movements of His Time," *Texas University Studies in English.* No. 15. 1935.

DARROW, CLARENCE, *Persian Pearl.* 1899.

DART, W. K., "Walt Whitman in New Orleans," *Publications of the Louisiana Historical Society.* Vol. 7.

DE SELINCOURT, BASIL, *Walt Whitman; a Critical Study.* London, 1914.

DONALDSON, THOMAS C., *Walt Whitman, the Man.* New York, 1896.

DONOSO, ARMANDO, "Walt Whitman," *Cuba Contemporánea.* Vol. 7. Havana, 1915.

DOWDEN, EDWARD, *The Poetry of Democracy.* London, 1899.

ECKERT, ROBERT P., "Friendly, Fragrant Fanny Ferns," *Colophon.* Part 18.

ELLIOT, CHARLES N., Ed., *Walt Whitman as Man, Poet and Friend.* Boston, 1915.

ELLIS, HAVELOCK, *The New Spirit.* London, 1892. Boston, 1929.

EMERSON, R. W., *Journals.* 10 vols. Boston and New York, 1909.

ERSKINE, JOHN, *Walt Whitman.* Dijon, 1919.

FOERSTER, N., *American Criticism.* Boston, 1928.

FRANK, WALDO, *The New America.* London, 1922.

FULLER, MARGARET, *Papers on Literature and Art.* New York, 1846.

FURNESS, CLIFTON J., Ed., *Walt Whitman's Workshop.* Cambridge, 1928.

GAMBERALE, LUIGI, "La vita e le opere di Walt Whitman," *Rivista d'Italia.* Vol. 1, Rome, 1903.

GILCHRIST, ALEXANDER, *Life of William Blake.* London, 1863.

GILCHRIST, ANNE, "A Woman's Estimate of Walt Whitman," *Boston Radical.* May, 1870.

GILCHRIST, GRACE, "Chats with Walt Whitman," *Temple Bar.* February, 1898.

————, "Walt Whitman as I Remember Him," London *Bookman.* July, 1927.

GILCHRIST, HERBERT, *Anne Gilchrist, Her Life and Writings.* London, 1887.

GLICKSBERG, CHARLES I., *Walt Whitman and the Civil War.* University of Pennsylvania. Philadelphia, 1933.

GOSSE, EDMUND, "A Note on Walt Whitman," *Littell's Living Age.* May 26, 1894.

————, *Leaves and Fruit.* New York, 1927.

GOULD, ELIZABETH P., *Anne Gilchrist and Walt Whitman.* Philadelphia, 1900.

HALSEY, JOHN J., "Walt Whitman," *Dial*. January, 1892.

HAMSUN, KNUT, "Walt Whitman," *Die Gesellschafft*. Vol. 1, Dresden, 1900.

HARNED, THOMAS B., Ed., *The Letters of Anne Gilchrist and Walt Whitman*. Garden City, 1918.

HARRIS, FRANK, *Contemporary Portraits*. Third Series. New York, 1922.

HARTE, W. B., "Walt Whitman's Democracy," *New England Magazine*. August, 1892.

HARTMANN, SADAKICHI, *Conversations with Walt Whitman*. New York, 1895.

HAYES, WILL, *Walt Whitman, the Prophet of the New Era*. London, 1921.

HERCOURT, JEAN, *Primauté de Walt Whitman*. Geneva, 1939.

HERVEY, JOHN L., "Growth of the Whitman Legend," *Dial*. June 24, 1915.

HIER, FREDERICK P., "The End of a Literary Mystery," *American Mercury*. Vol. 1, 1924.

HINTZ, HOWARD W., *The Quaker Influence in American Literature*. New York, 1940.

HOLLOWAY, EMORY, "Notes from a Whitman Student's Scrapbook," *American Scholar*. May, 1933.

———, "Some New Whitman Letters," *American Mercury*. Vol. 16.

———, "Whitman's Embryonic Verse," *Southwest Review*. Vol. 10.

———, *Whitman, an Interpretation in Narrative*. New York and London, 1926.

HOLLOWAY, EMORY, Ed., *Uncollected Poetry and Prose of Walt Whitman*. 2 vols. Garden City, 1921. Also New York, Peter Smith, 1932.

HOLLOWAY, EMORY, Ed., and RALPH ADIMARI, *New York Dissected*. New York, 1936.

HOLLOWAY, EMORY, Ed., and VERNOLIAN SCHWARTZ, *I Sit and Look Out*. Columbia University Press, 1932.

HUNEKER, JAMES, *Ivory, Apes and Peacocks*. New York, 1915.

HUNGERFORD, EDWARD, "Walt Whitman and His Chart of Bumps," *American Literature*. Vol. 2.

INDEX TO EARLY AMERICAN PERIODICAL LITERATURE, No. 3 *Walt Whitman, 1819–1892*. Pamphlet Distributing Company, New York, 1941.

INGERSOLL, ROBERT, *Liberty in Literature*. New York, 1890.

IRWIN, MABEL M., *Whitman, the Poet-Liberator of Woman.* Privately printed. New York, 1905.

JACOBY, JOHN E., *Le mysticisme dans la pensée americaine.* Paris, 1931.

JAMES, HENRY, "Walt Whitman; a Review of Drum-Taps," *Nation.* November 16, 1865.

———, *Views and Reviews.* Boston, 1908.

JANNACCONE, P., *La poesia di Walt Whitman e l'evoluzione delle forme ritmiche.* Turin, 1898.

JOHNSON, MAURICE O., *Walt Whitman as a Critic of Literature.* University of Nebraska, Lincoln, 1938.

JOHNSTON, ALMA CALDER, "Personal Memories of Walt Whitman," *Bookman.* Vol. 46.

JOHNSTON, J., *Diary Notes of a Visit to Walt Whitman in 1890.* Manchester, 1898.

JOHNSTON, J., and W. WALLACE, *Visits to Walt Whitman in 1890-1891.* London, 1918.

JOSEPHSON, M., *Portrait of the Artist as an American.* New York, 1930.

KELLER, ELIZABETH L., *Walt Whitman in Mickle Street.* New York, 1921.

KENNEDY, WILLIAM S., *The Fight of a Book for the World.* Stonycroft Press, 1926.

———, *Reminiscences of Walt Whitman.* Paisley and London, 1896.

———, Ed., *Walt Whitman's Diary in Canada.* Boston, 1904.

KNORTZ, KARL, *Walt Whitman, der Dichter der Demokratie.* Leipzig, 1899.

LAFOURCADE, GEORGES, "Swinburne and Walt Whitman," *Modern Language Review.* January, 1927.

LEGLER, HENRY E., *Walt Whitman, Yesterday and Today.* Chicago. 1916.

LONG, HANIEL, *Walt Whitman and the Springs of Courage.* Santa Fe, 1938.

LOWELL, AMY, *Poetry and Poets.* Boston, 1930.

LUCAS, F. L., *Authors Dead and Living.* New York, 1926.

MABBOTT, T. O., Ed., *The Half-Breed and Other Stories, by Walt Whitman.* Columbia University Press, 1927.

———, "Walt Whitman's *Franklin Evans,*" *Notes and Queries.* December 12, 1925.

MABBOTT, T. O., Ed., and ROLLO G. SILVER, *A Child's Reminiscence.* University of Washington Book Store, 1930.

Bibliography

MACY, JOHN, *The Critical Game*. New York, 1922.

――――, *The Spirit of American Literature*. New York, 1913.

MASTERS, EDGAR L., *Whitman*. New York, 1937.

MATTHIESSEN, F. O., *The American Renaissance*. New York, 1941.

MAYNARD, L., "Walt Whitman's Comradeship," *Walt Whitman Fellowship Papers*. Philadelphia. May 31, 1897.

MAYNARD, MILA TUPPER, *Walt Whitman, the Poet of the Wider Selfhood*. Chicago, 1903.

MERRILL, STUART, "La Question Walt Whitman," *Mercure de France*. Vol. 106.

MONAHAN, M., *Nemesis*. New York, 1926.

MONROE, HARRIET, *Poets and Their Art*. New York, 1926.

MONROE, W. S., "Whitman and the Professors," *American Mercury*. March, 1933.

MOORE, JOHN B., "The Master of Whitman," *Studies in Philology*. Vol. 23.

MORLEY, CHRISTOPHER, *Essays*. New York, 1928.

――――, *Plum Pudding*. New York, 1931.

――――, *Forty-four Essays*. New York, 1925.

――――, "Walt. A One-Act Portrait," *Bookman*. Vol. 59.

MORRIS, HARRISON SMITH, *Walt Whitman*. Cambridge, 1929.

MYERS, H. L. and OTHERS, *Walt Whitman: Five Articles. American Literature*. Vol. 6.

NEUMANN, H., "Walt Whitman," *American Scholar*. Vol. 2.

NEWTON, ALFRED E., *Magnificent Farce*. Boston, 1921.

O'CONNOR, WILLIAM D., *The Good Gray Poet*. New York, 1866.

――――, *Three Tales*. Boston and New York, 1892. (Preface by Walt Whitman.)

O'HIGGINS, HARVEY J., *Alias Walt Whitman*. Newark, 1930.

PAPINI, GIOVANNI, *24 Cervelli*. Milan, 1918.

PATTEE, FRED LEWIS, *The Feminine Fifties*. New York, 1940.

PERRY, BLISS, *Walt Whitman*. Boston and New York, 1906.

PHELPS, WILLIAM LYON, *The Poetry of Walt Whitman*. New York, 1924.

PLATT, ISAAC HULL, *Walt Whitman*. Boston, 1907.

POUND, LOUISE, "Walt Whitman and Italian Music," *American Mercury*. September, 1925.

――――, "Walt Whitman and the Classics," *Southwest Review*. January, 1925.

327

POUND, LOUISE, "Walt Whitman and the French Language," *American Speech*, May, 1926.

PRICE, HELEN, "Reminiscences of Walt Whitman," *New York Evening Post.* May 31, 1919.

RASCOE, BURTON, *Titans of Literature.* New York, 1932.

RIDLEY, HILDA, "Walt Whitman and Anne Gilchrist," *Dalhousie Review.* Halifax. Vol. 2.

RIVERS, W. C., *Walt Whitman's Anomaly.* London, 1913.

RODGERS, CLEVELAND, "Walt Whitman, the Poet of Democracy," *Mentor.* September, 1923.

RODGERS, CLEVELAND and JOHN BLACK, *The Gathering of the Forces.* 2 vols. New York and London, 1920.

ROGERS, CAMERON, *The Magnificent Idler.* Garden City, 1926.

ROSSETTI, W. M., *Letters of William Michael Rossetti concerning Whitman, Blake and Shelley to Anne Gilchrist, etc.* (Edited by Clarence Gohdes and Paull Franklin Baum.) Durham, N. C., 1934.

SALTER, WILLIAM M., *The Questionable Side of Walt Whitman.* Philadelphia, 1899.

SANBORN, F. B., *The Life of Henry David Thoreau.* Boston, 1917.

SANTAYANA, GEORGE, *Interpretations of Poetry and Religion.* New York, 1900.

SARRAZIN, GABRIEL, *La renaissance de la poésie anglaise.* Paris, 1889.

SAWYER, ROLAND D., *Walt Whitman the Prophet-Poet.* Boston, 1913.

SCHINZ, ALBERT, "Walt Whitman a World's Poet?" *Lippincott's Monthly Magazine.* October, 1913.

SCOVEL, JAMES M., "Walt Whitman as I Knew Him," *National Magazine.* May, 1904.

SELWYN, GEORGE, "Walt Whitman in Camden," *Critic.* February 28, 1885.

SHEPHARD, ESTHER, *Walt Whitman's Pose.* New York, 1938.

SHERMAN, STUART P., *Emotional Discovery of America and Other Essays.* New York, 1932.

SILVER, ROLLO G., Ed., "Thirty-one Letters of Walt Whitman," *American Literature.* Vol. 8.

SKINNER, CHARLES M., "Walt Whitman as Editor," *Atlantic Monthly.* November, 1903.

SMITH, LOGAN PEARSALL, *Unforgotten Years.* Boston, 1939.

SPIER, LEONARD, "Walt Whitman," *International Literature*. Moscow, 1935. No. 9.

STEDMAN, EDMUND C., "Walt Whitman," *Scribner's Magazine*. November, 1880.

STEVENSON, R. L., *Men and Books*. New York, 1902.

———, "The Gospel According to Walt Whitman," *New Quarterly Magazine*. October, 1878.

STRACHEY, J. ST. LOE, *American Soundings*. New York, 1926.

SWINBURNE, A. C., "Whitmania," *Fortnightly Review*. August, 1887.

SYMONDS, JOHN A., "A Note on Whitmania," *Fortnightly Review*. September 1, 1887.

———, *Walt Whitman, a Study*. London, 1893.

THAYER, W. R., "Personal Recollections of Walt Whitman," *Scribner's*. June, 1919.

THOMSON, JAMES, *Walt Whitman the Man and the Poet*. London, 1910.

TRAUBEL, HORACE L., Ed., *At the Graveside of Walt Whitman*. Philadelphia, 1892.

———, "Conversations with Walt Whitman," *Arena*. January, 1896.

———, Ed., *Conservator*.

———, Ed., *Good-bye and Hail, Walt Whitman*. Philadelphia, 1892.

———, "Talks with Whitman," *American Magazine*. July, 1907.

———, "Walt Whitman on Himself," *American Mercury*. October, 1924.

———, "Whitman on His Contemporaries," *American Mercury*. July, 1924.

———, *With Walt Whitman in Camden*. Vol. 1, Boston, 1906; Vol. 2, New York, 1908; Vol. 3, New York, 1914.

TRAUBEL, HORACE L. and R. M. BUCKE and T. B. HARNED, *In re Walt Whitman*. Philadelphia, 1893.

TRIGGS, OSCAR L., *Browning and Whitman*. University of Chicago. 1893.

TRIMBLE, W. H., *Walt Whitman and Leaves of Grass*. London, 1905.

TROWBRIDGE, JOHN T., *My Own Story*. Boston, 1903.

———, "Reminiscences of Walt Whitman," *Atlantic Monthly*. Vol. 89.

VAN DOREN, MARK, *Henry David Thoreau*. Boston, 1916.

———, "Walt Whitman, Stranger," *American Mercury*. July, 1935.

Walling, William English, *Whitman and Traubel*. New York, 1916.

Walt Whitman Fellowship Papers, Philadelphia, 1894-1899.

"Walt Whitman Looks at Boston," *New England Quarterly*. Number 1.

Waterman, W. R., *Frances Wright*. Columbia University Press, 1924.

Watts, Theodore, "Walt Whitman, an Obituary," *Athenaeum*. April 2, 1892.

Whitman, Walt, *Leaves of Grass*. Brooklyn, 1855.

———, *Leaves of Grass*. Brooklyn, 1856. (Printed by Fowler and Wells.)

———, *Leaves of Grass*. Boston, 1860.

———, *Drum-Taps*. New York, 1865.

———, *Leaves of Grass*. New York, 1867.

———, *Leaves of Grass*. Washington, 1871.

———, *Democratic Vistas*. Washington, 1871.

———, *Passage to India*. Washington, 1871.

———, *After All, Not to Create Only*. Boston, 1871.

———, *As a Strong Bird on Pinions Free*. Washington, 1872.

———, *Leaves of Grass* and *Two Rivulets*. Camden, 1876.

———, *Leaves of Grass*. Boston, 1881.

———, *Specimen Days and Collect*. Philadelphia, 1882-3.

———, *Leaves of Grass*. Philadelphia, 1884.

———, *November Boughs*. Philadelphia, 1888.

———, *Complete Poems and Prose*. Camden, 1888.

———, *Leaves of Grass* with *Sands at Seventy* and *A Backward Glance O'er Travel'd Roads*. Camden, 1889.

———, *Good-Bye My Fancy*. Philadelphia, 1891.

———, *Leaves of Grass*. Philadelphia, 1891-2.

———, *Prose Works Complete*. Philadelphia, 1892, 1894, 1897.

———, *Complete Writings*. 10 vols. New York, 1902.

———, *Criticism*, an Essay. Carteret Book Club, 1913.

———, "Isle of la Belle Rivière," *Cincinnati Post*. April 10, 1892.

———, *The Wound Dresser* (Whitman's letters to his Mother), Boston, 1898.

———, "Walt Whitman at Home," *Critic* Pamphlet No. 2. New York, 1898.

———, *Leaves of Grass*. (Inclusive edition, edited by Emory Holloway.) Garden City, 1924.

Bibliography

WHITMAN, WALT, *Pictures*. (An unpublished poem, with an introduction and notes by Emory Holloway.) New York, London, 1927.

WILLIAMS, FRANCIS H., "Walt Whitman as Deliverer," *Walt Whitman Fellowship Papers*. Philadelphia, August, 1894.

WILSON, FORREST, *Crusader in Crinoline*. Philadelphia, 1941.

WINWAR, FRANCES, *Oscar Wilde and the Yellow 'Nineties*. New York, 1940.

——, *Poor Splendid Wings*. Boston, 1933.

WOOD, CLEMENT, *Poets of America*. New York, 1925.

WOOLCOTT, ALEXANDER, "Walt Whitman, Dramatic Critic," *Bookman*. March, 1921.

WYATT, EDITH, "Answerer, Walt Whitman," *North American Review*. May, 1919.

——, "Whitman and Anne Gilchrist," *North American Review*, September, 1919.

ZUNDER, T. A., "Whitman and Nathaniel Hawthorne," *Modern Language Notes*. May, 1932.

——, "Whitman Interviews Barnum," *Modern Language Notes*. January, 1933.

Index

INDEX

INDEX

letter to Whitman, 209; recommends *Leaves of Grass* to Carlyle, 209; 210, 212, 221, 230-1, 241, 304, 305, 306, 315-16

Emerson, Mrs. R. W., 230

"Enfans d'Adam," 223, 224, 230

"English and an American Poet, An," 204

Etty, William, 286

Evening Post, 150, 164, 170, 180

Everett, Edward, 37

Expunging Resolution, 58

Fanny Fern, 99, 183-5; reviews *Leaves of Grass,* 202-3; 206, 217

Fern Leaves, 183-4

Few Days in Athens, A, 82

Fichte, J. C., 47

Fillmore, Millard, 172

"Fleshly School of Poetry, The," 303, f.

Follen, Charles, 47

Forrest, Edwin, 159

Fortnightly, 307

Fortunes of Nigel, 28

"Fourth of July Ode," 93-5

Fowler, Lorenzo Niles, 48, 154, 156, 186, 187, 197, 204, 206, 213, 280

Fowler, Orson Squire, 48, 154, 186, 187, 197, 204, 206, 213, 280

Fox, George, 179

Fox, Kate, 163-5

Fox, Margaret, 163-5

Francis, Dr., 164

Franklin Evans, 73-80, 83, 99, 112, 132

Franz, Agnes, 227

Freeborn, Mr., 94, 95

Free Enquirer, 27, 82

Freeman, Brooklyn, 147-8, 150, 151, 166

Freeman, Philadelphia, 37

Frémont, John Charles, his expedition, 66; presidential campaign, 214

Fries, Jacob Friedrich, expelled from Jena, 2-3

Fritzinger, Warren, 320

Fugitive Slave Law, 171

Fuller, Margaret, and Abolition, 38; and Transcendentalism, 47-8; launches the *Dial,* 63; 69, 84, 88, 149; her death, 173; 174, 205, 206

Fulton, explosion of, 19-20

Furman, Judge, 23

Furness, Dr. Horace, 312

Garfield, President James, 279

Garrison, William Lloyd, 34-6, 37, 233

George IV, 2

Gilchrist, Alexander, 285, 286, 287

Gilchrist, Anne, writes to Whitman, 284; affected by *Leaves of Grass,* 285; her children, 286; falls in love with Whitman, 287-292; 299; determines to come to America, 300; description of, 301; meets Whitman 301; death, 314

Gilchrist, Beatrice, 286

Gilchrist, Grace, 286

Gilchrist, Herbert, 286, 300

Gilchrist, Percy, 286, 300, 301

Gildemeister, 175

Gilder, R. W., 313, 314, 319

Gladding, James, 107

Globe, The, 150

Godey's Lady's Book, 214

Goethe, J. W. von, 46; his *Autobiography,* 148; 279

Good Gray Poet, The, 269

Graham's Magazine, 63

Grant, U. S., 226, 263, 279-80

Greeley, Horace, 88, 90, 149, 165, 181

Greenwood, Grace, 183

Grey, Earl, 162

Grimké, Angelina, 39

Grimké, Sarah, 39

Griswold, Rufus Wilmot, 88, 164

Guinea Trade, 34-5

Gurowski, Adam de, 277

Halleck, Fitz-Greene, 88

Hapgood, Major, 252, 263

Harlan, James, dismisses Whitman, 267; 268, 269, 276

Harned, Thomas, 318

Harpers, 148, 154, 274

Harper's Magazine, 226, 299

Harrington, 234, 250

Harrison, Gabriel, 95

Harrison, William Henry, 58; elected president, 59; death of, 60

Hartshorne, William, 33

335

INDEX

INDEX

339